LEAVING LITTLE ITALY

SUNY series in Italian/American Culture
Fred L. Gardaphe, editor

LEAVING
LITTLE
ITALY

Essaying Italian American Culture

Fred L. Gardaphe

State University of New York Press

Published by
State University of New York Press, Albany

For information, address State University of New York Press,
90 State Street, Suite 700, Albany, NY 12207

Production by Marilyn P. Semerad
Marketing by Anne M. Valentine

Library of Congress Cataloging-in-Publication Data

Gardaphe, Fred L.
    Leaving little Italy : essaying Italian American culture / Fred L. Gardaphe.
        p. cm. — (SUNY series in Italian/American culture)
    Includes bibliographical references (p.) and index.
    ISBN 0-7914-5917-9 (alk. paper) — ISBN 0-7914-5918-7 (pbk. : alk. paper)
     1. American literature—Italian American authors—History and criticism. 2. Italian
Americans—Intellectual life. 3. Italian Americans—Civilization. 4. Italian Americans in
literature. I. Title. II. Series

PS153.I8G38 2003
810.9'851—dc21   2002044771

10 9 8 7 6 5 4 3 2 1

*This book is dedicated to
the people, past and present, of Melrose Park, Illinois,
and the Little Italy I left there.*

Contents

Acknowledgments

Many of these chapters began as reviews, lectures, talks, or articles over the years since 1995, when I finished my first book. I am grateful to everyone who gave me the opportunities to test these ideas in speech and writing.

Chapter one, "The Southern Answer," was first presented in Djelal Kadir's comparative literature graduate seminar, "Rethinking America" during the fall 2001 semester. Portions of chapters two and three will appear in a collection of essays on post–World War II American culture, edited by Josephine Hendin and published by Blackwell.

Chapter four originally appeared in *Radical Revisions*, edited by Bill Mullen and Sherry Linkon. Chapter five began as papers presented at the Working Class Studies conference at Youngstown State University and at the Modern Language Association. Chapter six began as papers presented at conferences of the American Italian Historical Association and as an encyclopedia article for *The Italian American Experience: An Encyclopedia*, edited by Salvatore LaGumina and others.

Chapter seven brings together two articles: one on Frank Lentricchia, which originally appeared in the journal *Differentia* in a double issue devoted to Italian American culture, and the other on Sandra Gilbert, which first appeared in the *Romance Languages Annual* of Purdue University. Chapter eight was written first as a talk I presented in 1997 at Dartmouth College, to which Graziella Parati invited me; it was later revised for another talk in 2002 at Catholic University, to which Stefania Lucamante invited me. A version of chapter eight appeared in *LIT: Literature Interpretation Theory* volume 13.3. Chapter nine comes first from a talk I presented at Kate Kane's Colloquium on Food and Culture at DePaul University, and later from a talk at Union College to which Edvige Giunta invited me; versions were also presented as talks through the Illinois Humanities Council's Roads Scholars program. As for this volume's conclusion, versions were presented at Hunter College in 2000 and the 2001 Italian Cultural Studies Conference at Florida Atlantic University. I would like to thank Priscilla Ross and James Peltz of SUNY Press, and to freelance copyeditor Therese Myers, for their guidance and help in preparing the manuscript for publication. Marianna and Susan Gardaphe made the index possible and the work enjoyable.

Mille grazie to Anthony Julian Tamburri and John Paul Russo for reading the original manuscript critically. Their suggestions helped me to transcend my often-parochial perspectives and to present a better book. Others who have helped along the way are Mary Jo Bona, my colleague at Stony Brook, Josephine Gattuso Hendin, and Robert Viscusi. Susan, Rico and Mori provided me with the love I needed to get this work done; to them I owe my greatest debt.

Cover photo: Renato Rotolo.

Introduction

This book is my attempt to further our thinking about Italian American culture by looking at it through the concepts of class, race, gender, ethnicity, and lifestyle. I do this by making connections between what I have come to call Italian American studies and the larger field of American studies. My earlier work, represented by books such as *Italian American Ways*, *Italian Signs, American Streets*, and *Dagoes Read: Tradition and the Italian American Writer*, resulted from my search for what it was we could call Italian American narrative literature. I tried to map its evolution through key narrative texts. This book is quite different in that it represents my attempt to fix just what it is about what is called Italian American into what we call America. This means I look at what assimilation is and at what it means to stretch Italian American identity to show that when we study Italian American culture we are really practicing American studies. This justification comes not just out of my own curiosity, but out of a response I have had to provide to the State University of New York (SUNY) system when we were asked for explanations on how our Italian American studies courses would fulfill the American history requirements for its current Distributed Education designation.

Some of my earlier writing referred to Italian American culture as being orphaned by its parents: Italian and American cultures. That was then. Now, this orphan is beginning to be claimed, especially when a resulting product can earn profits, as in new television programs and new anthologies. With the arrival of HBO series *The Sopranos*, as much an Italian American icon of the twenty-first century as *The Godfather* saga was for the twentieth, the time has come for some serious understanding of Italian American presence before it dissipates into the thin air of historical amnesia and the clouds of pop culture imagery.

Josephine Gattuso Hendin's recent article in *American Literary History*, "The New World of Italian American Studies," signaled the arrival of Italian American studies in mainstream American studies venues. The acceptance of a permanent discussion group in Italian American culture by the Modern Language Association (MLA) after a three-year trial period, preceded by two outright proposal rejections, signifies that Italian American studies has been allowed a place in the arena, but can it garner enough attention to justify its existence as a legitimate field of study? This book will help us make sense of what America has done to the culture created by its citizens of Italian descent and to understand varying notions of selfhood, sexuality, masculinity, femininity, food preparation, and consumption.

Leaving Little Italy is the result of my attempts to understand the history of America's Italians, to see where they came from, what they created, and where it is all going. The goal is for us all to realize what this culture has been, is, and will be saying about American culture as it keeps reinventing itself. Since 1998 I have directed the Italian American studies program at SUNY–Stony Brook and have been involved in creating and maintaining courses for our minor in Italian American studies and our new major in American studies. As part of this work I have begun to search for a way of historicizing this project. What follows is a brief look at some of the earlier work done in the name of Italian American studies.

The Origins of Italian American Studies

It is less permissible today to imagine oneself as writing within a tradition when one writes literary criticism. This is not to say however, that every critic is now a revolutionist destroying the canon in order to replace it with his own. A better image is that of a wanderer, going from place to place for his material, but remaining a man essentially between homes.
—Edward Said, *Beginnings: Intention and Method*

Italian American studies probably began the moment the first Italian immigrant wondered to himself or herself, "What the hell am I doing here?" Until recently knowing the date and time of that precise moment never mattered. Because Italian American studies was not taken seriously enough, even by some of its practitioners, to warrant historization, the moment of its birth has never been a concern. Its parents, both American studies and Italian studies, had abandoned the child at birth, so it does not even know its own birthday. And this would remain true as long as Italians were the objects of, and not the agents of, studies in the academy.

The study of Italians in the United States has long been a function of social scientists, primarily the anthropologists, historians, and sociologists. Robert Forester's *The Italian Emigration of Our Times*, published first in 1919 by Harvard University, is one of the first major English-language studies of why people left Italy in large numbers between 1876–1909, and the phrase *Italian American* never appear in this more than 500-page study. Turn-of-the-century magazines are filled with articles decrying the coming of the

Italians or arguing for their acceptance as Americans. These range from accounts of crime and work accidents, in articles titled, "What Shall We Do with the Dago" (*Popular Science Monthly,* December 1890, February 1891; Moquin 259) and "Italians Can Be Americanized" (*North American Review,* 1896; Moquin 264). In many of these early studies, the authors used descriptions of their eating habits to demonstrate their strangeness, as in this April 1897 *Arena* magazine article by Frederick O. Bushee of South End House, a Boston settlement house in the manner of Jane Addams's Hull House:

> The dinner of the ordinary Italian is made up largely of macaroni, French or Italian bread, and usually some meat and potato. That form of flour preparation known as spaghetti is the most frequently used. This is boiled whole and served as a first course. The Italian experiences no difficulty in eating this slippery food, for he merely sucks it into his mouth from his fork in a very unconventional if not elegant manner. (Moquin 52)

If the tone of this seemingly innocuous article is not offensive enough out of context, then a brief look at the conclusion shows that Bushee's purpose is to argue for the relocation of Italians from the city to rural areas into "agricultural colonies composed of Italian peasants" (58). Not surprisingly, then, the authors of these early studies and accounts did not foresee the Americanization of the Italian and thus, the phrase *Italian American* would not, no, could not be used.

I began a search for the first usage of the hyphenated "Italian-American" and found what I will propose as its unofficial earliest usage in an article Viola Roseboro wrote for the January 1888 *Cosmopolitan.* Her "The Italians of New York" is based on "an unusually careful examination of the lower place in Little Italy, as Mulberry Street, particularly the part known as 'The Bend'" (Moquin 301). Roseboro cannot ignore what she calls the Italian's "defects": "There is no doubt," she writes, "that they do a great deal of slashing and cutting of each other" (Moquin 301); she also posits the possible transformation of the Italian living in New York into the Italian American: "The Italian-American," she writes toward the end of her article, "is to be a considered part of our population" (Moquin 302).

At what point then does the phrase *Italian American* begin to be used regularly to refer to Americans of Italian decent? At what point can the shift from the study of Italians to Italian American studies be identified, tagged, and used as a point of departure for those wishing to enter the field of Italian American studies? Although that precise moment may never be documented, this book gives you a sense of the moments that have been documented and that contribute to what I call the origins of Italian American studies.

Importantly, we must search for, if not find, the origins of Italian American studies because we are now in the business of developing curricula, planning conferences, and creating a great deal of published information in the field. Where does, for example, a survey course in Italian American studies begin? With Columbus? With the Italian contribution to the American Revolution? With the mass immigration of the 1800s? Why the fuss with beginnings? Edward Said once saw the word *beginnings* as reflective of something active and secular and the word *origins* as passive and religious or mythic. Unlike Said, I use the word *origins* for the beginning of Italian American studies because we do not have eyewitnesses to or certificates of its birth, its beginnings must always remain mythic. Said had trouble drawing intention out of origins, as he wrote: "The beginning, then, is the first step in the intentional production of meaning" (*Beginnings* 5); I see *origins* as a more useful term precisely because it defies intentions. We should find as many stories of the origins of Italian American studies as there are practitioners in the field because only through a multiplicity of perspectives will we ever be able to achieve a sense of inclusion that defies the exclusion of anything but lies and false scholarship, although even those have their place in the field. Besides, what is important is not when Italian American studies began, but when it began to be taken seriously.

Italian American studies begins in earnest in this country when the scholar, trained in the United States begins applying a disciplinary focus to the phenomenon of Americans of Italian descent living in the United States. However, Italian American studies becomes recognized as a field of study only when the very subjects of earlier studies turn the interpretative gaze back on the scientists and begin studying them and when these encounters become the material for writing about their own experiences. Italian American studies becomes legitimized as a serious field of study when institutions begin developing programs of study.

Without scholarly societies or formal programs inside institutions dedicated to the study of Italian American culture, American intellectuals of Italian descent who were intent on defining and developing Italian American studies had to do so independently, and more often than not their work was considered adjunct to their "real work." At least two generations of Italian American scholars could hardly teach a course dedicated to the study of Italian Americans, let alone vie for a professorship in Italian American studies.

Although many Italian American newspapers were published in which appeared creative and critical work by Italian American writers, so much of it was in Italian and mattered only to its readers and certainly not to those who were studying Italian in the universities at the time. The recent works of Francesco Durante (*Italoamericana,* 2001) and Martino Marazzi (*I misteri di Little Italy,* 2001) capture this well, but not until the children of Italian immigrants came of age in the 1930s would an articulate voice of Italian

Americana be heard in the mainstream media. I want to pause here and point to some key moments that could be sites of the origins of Italian American studies.

One of the earliest acts of indigenous Italian American study in the field of literary criticism was the late Jerre Mangione's 1935 *New Republic* review of Garibaldi Lapolla's *The Grand Gennaro*. Mangione introduces the rarity of meeting Italian Americans in American literature and credits Lapolla for "creating Italo-Americans who are vivid and alive and probably a novelty to the average person who, not knowing them intimately, is likely to draw his conclusions about them from the gangster movies" (313). A few years later, Mangione reviewed Pietro di Donato's *Christ in Concrete* in the *New Republic*, and although he praised the beginning writer's rendition of the Italian American life, he did not succumb to what I call Paesan Patting, or blind boosterism; he did not hesitate to point out the novels roughness and its "minor deficiencies" ("Little Italy" 111).

During the same time period, Leonard Covello, the New York schoolteacher who helped shape the social consciousness of progressives such as Vito Marcantonio, completed the first study of the Italian American schoolchild. His work led to major school reforms in New York City and established the concept of community education. He told his story with the help of novelist Guido D'Agostino in *The Heart Is the Teacher*.

Giuseppe Prezzolini, a member of the executive council that directed the Institute of Italian Culture in the United States, founded in 1923, and director of the Casa Italiana of Columbia University in 1930, although denounced as a proponent of fascism, often published commentaries on Italian American writers and encouraged Olga Peragallo to produce a survey of Italian American literary activities. Olga Peragallo's *Italian-American Authors and Their Contribution to American Literature* was edited by her mother and published posthumously in 1949. Prezzolini wrote the preface to this first attempt to historicize American authors of Italian descent. This primal text paved the way for the next major step in the development of Italian American literary history by an indigenous intellectual.

During the 1960s, Italian American intellectuals begin producing books based on studies of their own culture. Two that characterize best Italian American studies during this period are Richard Gambino's *Blood of My Blood*, and Patrick Gallo's *Ethnic Alienation: The Italian-Americans*. Only now are these books being read seriously and critiqued properly. For years Gambino attempted to develop Italian American studies through a minor at Queens College in New York. However, his efforts never were realized on a grand enough scale to claim anything more than start.

A more thorough attempt to organize Italian American literature was Rose Basile Green's 1962 dissertation at the University of Pennsylvania:

"The Evolution of Italian-American Fiction as a Document of the Interaction of Two Cultures." Published in 1974 as *The Italian-American Novel: A Document of the Interaction of Two Cultures*, Green's study was the first major attempt to identify and examine critically the contribution that American writers of Italian descent have made to American culture. Her work reflects an early stage of cultural examination, one that invites readers and critics to consider the fiction of Italian American writers through an essentially universal sociological paradigm related to understanding the process of Americanization through the experience of immigration. Green's scholarship enabled the formation of new dimensions of critical examination of the Italian American contribution to American literature. Like Giovanni Schiavo, Green's work is more catalogue than criticism, and although flawed in a variety of ways, it reflects the need of early scholars to simply get it in writing. To chart the presence of Italian Americans in the sea of American culture.

One key stage in the risorgimento of Italian American studies occurred in 1967 with the founding of the American Italian Historical Association, which although not dedicated to literary studies (its founding members were primarily historians and sociologists), did welcome and encourage literary analysis and dedicated its second conference to the Italian American novel. Through that association, some of Italian Americana's best literary criticism has come to be known.

Although early intellectuals such as Green were well acquainted with what had happened in Italian American culture, few knew enough about the literature—and American studies—to speculate what was coming. Several contemporary critics of Italian American narrative have produced exciting and vital alternatives to Green's methodology by turning to the future. Critics such as Helen Barolini, Robert Viscusi, Frank Lentricchia, Mary Jo Bona, Anthony Tamburri, Justin Vitiello, Louise Napolitano, Franco Mulas, Edvige Giunta, Paolo Valesio, Luigi Fontanella, and Simone Cinotto represent the development of an indigenous criticism and are those whom Viscusi refers to as interpreters "of the minority culture to which [they belong] to by birth" ("Literature Considering" 278).

Viscusi, whose work on Italian American literature paved the way for subsequent critics, contributed tremendously to the construction of a foundation on which an Italian American discourse can be built. In many of his articles he offers a culture-specific approach that educates the reader about Italian culture and the context it creates for interpreting Italian American narrative. Viscusi was the first critic bold enough to challenge the nostalgia that permeated Italian American studies through his complex essays, the result of rigorous thought and an incredible sense of humor. However, even the power of Viscusi was not enough to generate the force necessary to birth Italian American studies. It would take a lawsuit to create a distinguished professorship in Italian American studies, and I will not mention the first chair in Italian American studies, which has now gone to an Italianist. When the John D. Calandra Institute for Italian American Studies filed a lawsuit and was awarded permanent standing in the City University of New York (CUNY) through Queens College, it was also awarded a position for a distinguished chair. Dr. Philip Cannistraro, when he assumed that position after a national search, became the first distinguished professor in Italian American studies.

The critical writing and the editing of scholars such as Anthony Tamburri, Mary Jo Bona, and Edvige Giunta, combined with their teaching, has probably done more to create a sense of development of Italian American studies than the work of any other scholars and teachers. Their work treats Italian American literature as a colonized body of writing that gains its identity through its interaction between Italian and American cultures. In light of the exciting work being done today, more and more of the previously submerged American scholars, critics, and writers of Italian descent are surfacing to contribute to the journals *Italian Americana, VIA: Voices in Italian Americana, Differentia, Italian American Review*, and other ethnic-specific publications dedicated to Italian Americana.

One thing about the body of work that I have just mentioned is that most of what has been developed thus far in the field of Italian American studies has been accomplished by individuals rather than academic institutions. And so, although the efforts have been valiant, this field has little hope of thriving unless individual intellectuals come together to identify tasks, share existing resources, and codevelop new resources.

The future of Italian American literary studies needs a new sense of cooperation among scholars of Italian and American cultures. For years, we wanderers in the field have been wondering when what we do would be taken seriously, and it is beginning. Besides CUNY, SUNY has established a professorship in Italian American studies and has hired two professors since 1998. John Carroll University (Cleveland, Ohio) has hired a director for its new program in Italian American studies, California State University at Long Beach recently hired a distinguished professor in Italian studies who is responsible for Italian American studies. In the 2001–2002 school year New York University launched a rotating chair in Italian American studies that was endowed by the Tiro al Segno Organization of New York. Dr. Josephine Gattuso Hendin of the English department served as the first chair. The most recent institution to launch a campaign to create an endowed chair is Montclair State University (New Jersey). At last, the homelessness of scholars of Italian American studies is being addressed. However the greater needs include archival centers so that the papers of our writers, our intellectuals, can be used by a new generation of scholars. Right now, most of these papers are in basements gathering dust and mildew when they should be garnering attention.

From these archives scholars need to create critical editions of works that have too long been out of print. We need to take advantage of new developments in technology to create electronic databases, to create multimedia programs that introduce and document the careers of our writers. And for this all to be developed and used, we need a presence in academic programs that can encourage and direct graduate students.

In terms of publications, we currently have several interesting islands, which is better than previously when intellectuals were floating in the mainstream or in ponds; but the future needs to see a greater sense of interaction between and among publications. We need a good, ongoing bibliography project to identify, locate, and annotate relevant primary and secondary publications. We need monographs on all of our major writers—the two studies of Pietro di Donato and Stephen Cooper's biography of John Fante represent the greatest critical depth we have achieved, but we are standing deep in the shallow end; we need studies of all of our writers; we need to reprint deserving books that are out of print. Although we have activists and politicians, too few have turned attention to their own culture. Although we have a few journals, none are quarterly; we also lack a publishing center, and whereas a press would be nice, a more feasible alternative would be to create a publishing and editorial network that could be used as a clearinghouse to recommend books to publishers, and if possible, with a subvention. Yes, this all takes money, but before we can achieve the necessary financial support, we need to connect the streets to the academe by uniting the efforts such organizations as the National Italian American Foundation, the Order of Sons of Italy in America and UNICO to the needs of the intellectual community. Intellectuals must create products that they need, and they need to be able to see that creating these products can further their agenda. In conjunction with a greater development of intracultural studies, we need to establish a strong Italian American presence in the field of intercultural studies. This requires a greater awareness of the history and evolution of the cultural studies of other groups comprising the United States, an example of which I present herein.

This book examines the intersections between the individual personality and the communities that have helped shape that artist's identity. I examine the points of intersection to see what they say about becoming and being Americans. Part I is a historical survey of major cultural developments in Italian American literary studies, which I have divided into three chapters. Chapter one, "The Southern Answer: Making Little Italys," explores the development of the Italian American intellectual in the context of early mass Italian immigration to the United States and in light of Antonio Gramsci's important essay, *The Southern Question*, as translated by Pasquale Verdicchio. Chapter two, "Inventing Italian America," is a survey of the developments that combine to create a sense of Italian American culture during and after

World War II. Subsequent generations strengthen or destroy the work during this period in which the myths of Italian America are created. Chapter three, "Mythologies of Italian America: From Little Italys to Suburbs," continues the chronological survey of the writing Italian Americans produced into the twenty-first century.

Part II comprises seven chapters that examine examples introduced in that historical survey. Chapter four situates three major Italian American writers in American cultural history of the 1930s. Chapter five, "The Consequences of Class in Italian American Culture," is the first of the more conceptually based chapters and deals with the role that class plays in the creation and criticism of Italian American literature. Chapter six, "Variations of Italian American Women's Autobiography," answers a question that was posed to me in the early 1980s by Mirron Alexandroff, the late president of Columbia College in Chicago who wanted to know why he had not heard of any Italian American female writers. This chapter explores the writings of Helen Barolini, Diane diPrima, Louise DeSalvo, and Maria Laurino to understand how each has approached the task of writing about her life. Chapter seven, "Critism as Autobiography," explores how literary criticism can be read as autobiography using the works of Frank Lentricchia, Sandra Mortola Gilbert, and Camille Paglia.

Chapter eight, "We Weren't always White: Race and Ethnicity in Italian American Literature," considers the work of Italian American writers who have been ignored by the development of whiteness studies. Chapter nine, "Linguini and Lust: Notes on Food and Sex in Italian American Culture," examines the ways Italian American writers and filmmakers use food and sex in their work and how that use differs from other ethnic American artists. The book concludes with "Leaving Little Italy: Legacies Real and Imagined," a piece that notes how geographical space becomes transformed from external to internal significance and how paradigms of study shift as Little Italys real and imagined are abandoned for new developments and the greener grass of cultural suburbs.

Part I

A Historical Survey

Chapter 1

The Southern Answer
Making Little Italys

Intellectuals develop slowly, much more slowly than any other social group, by their very nature and historical function. They represent the whole of the cultural tradition of a people, seeking to summarize and synthesize all of its history. This is especially true of the old type of intellectual, of the intellectual born of the peasantry. To think it possible that such intellectuals could, en masse, break with the entire past and situate itself wholly on the terrain of a new ideology is absurd. . . . It is certainly important for the proletariat that one or more intellectuals, individually, adhere to its program and its doctrine, become enmeshed with the proletariat and become and feel an integral part of it.
—Antonio Gramsci, *The Southern Question*

Given the proletarian character and general illiteracy of the Italian immigration, it was not to be expected that the "Little Italies," would nourish intellectual pursuits. Educated persons were regarded with mistrust.
—Rudolph J. Vecoli, "The Coming of Age of the Italian Americans: 1945–1974"

In 1927, shortly after the United States had severely restricted immigration from southern European countries, Antonio Gramsci published *The Southern Question* in which he attempted to explain the failure of southern Italy to generate a revolutionary force. But years before Gramsci's article the southern Italians were answering the southern question in their own direct way by leaving the impossible socioeconomic situation that a unified Italy had produced for them. One of the effects of this emigration would be the development in the United States of intellectuals who, under different circumstances, might have become provocative instruments of a southern Italian-led revolution.

Gramsci saw the relationship of northern and southern Italy as a one of the dominant over the dominated, one in which the culture of the north created an hegemony over the culture of the south. Cultural critic Pasquale Verdicchio in *Bound by Distance: Rethinking Nationalism through the Italian Diaspora*, discusses the role Italian nationalism plays in the identities and

3

cultural productions of the descendants of the Italian Diaspora and uses
Gramsci's article to examine reproductions of Italian culture outside of Italy.
With Verdicchio's help, we can see how emigration from Italy was one of the
ways the southern question was answered.

Gramsci posited that the intellectuals in Southern Italy played a mediating
role between the peasants and those who owned the land on which the peasants
worked. For Gramsci, the intellectuals (local lawyers, doctors, and clergy),
comprised a rural middle class whose role was to centralize and dominate both
political and ideological trends. The role that intellectuals played in this process
of mediation between the lower and upper classes, according to Gramsci, easily
allowed the capitalist and industrial forces of northern Italy to become dominant in the country during Italy's unification period (1860–1870) at the expense
of the southern peasants. Unification, supposed to make Italy a modern European nation, began about 1780, lasted until 1870, and was directed primarily
by the minds and the monies of those who lived in the northern regions of the
country. Verdicchio reminds us that northern Italian culture represented Italy
long before the *risorgimento*. Dante saw Florence as "the new Rome that would
again unify Italy" (*Bound* 33); Florentine culture soon became the benchmark
for national culture. The goal of the risorgimento was the integration and stan-
dardization of institutions so that the resulting Italy, under a newly appointed
king, could become a genuine nation-state. True integration was never achieved,
and northern culture soon assumed a hegemony that exists to this very day. As
the Italian state economy was capitalized and industrialized, the north exploited
the south, some would even say colonized it. This colonization would have an
impact on the creation of the Italian American intellectual.

As we will see, the work of immigrant Italian American intellectuals was
largely focused on working-class issues and reflected the alienation that Jack
Goody and Ian Watt refer to in their essay "The Consequences of Literacy":

> From the standpoint of the individual intellectual, of the literate special-
> ist, the vista of endless choices and discoveries offered by so extensive
> a past can be a source of great stimulation and interest; but when we
> consider the social effects of such an orientation, it becomes apparent
> that the situation fosters the alienation that has characterized so many
> writers and philosophers of the West since the last century. (21)

Just as the immigrant was, for the most part, alienated from the mainstream economy—forced as most new immigrants are to take the work given
to them or to make work for themselves—the second generation, the children
of immigrants, became social immigrants searching for acceptance in the
larger society, something that would be easier for them once they lost the alien
trappings of *Italianità* and mastered the means of obtaining power in U.S.

society. Not until the third generation, then, can we see any mass movement into the cultural mainstream. The irony here is that to be successful culturally, they would have to accept or return to what their parents had to reject.

An observation by Margaret Mead, recounted in that Goody and Watt essay, sheds light on the effects that an American education might have had on heightening the alienation the Italian American experienced: "Primitive education," she writes, "was a process by which continuity was maintained between parents and children. . . . Modern education includes a heavy emphasis upon the function of education to create discontinuities—to turn the child . . . of the illiterate into the literate" (336). This experience in U.S. schools created division and difference; in essence the child became the teacher to the parent, the guide, the translator, and this became a notion that challenged the traditional structure of the Italian concept of family. *Italianità* became an obstacle to the entrance into American mainstream culture. Leonard Covello, who with the help of novelist Guido D'Agostino wrote his memoirs entitled *The Heart Is the Teacher*, recalls his experience in the American school:

> During this period [1900s], the Italian language was completely ignored. In fact, throughout my whole elementary school career, I do not recall one mention of Italy or the Italian language or what famous Italians had done in the world with the possible exception of Columbus, who was pretty popular in America. We soon got the idea that Italian meant something inferior, and a barrier was erected between children of Italian origin and their parents. This was the accepted process of Americanization. We were becoming Americans by learning how to be ashamed of our parents. (43)

Covello's words help us to understand why so many first- and second-generation Italian Americans sought economic and popular cultural paths on the road to becoming American. These choices enabled success without strong identification with what was considered a sometimes anti-American immigrant culture.

Assimilation used to be thought of as a melting-down process, a process by which each immigrant group reached the same common denominator: the American citizen. As early as 1922, John Valentino wrote an essay encouraging assimilation: "Immigrant children may yearn for freedom to live untrammeled American lives; but they can do so only by abandoning, physically as well as intellectually their own households" (355). Going to college required such an intellectual abandonment; attending any American institution, be it the military, the library, or even the insane asylum, enabled such a physical abandonment. But by asking immigrant children to abandon their cultural foundation or at least exchange it for one that was "American," those who longed for a single American culture were denying the utility of cultural diversity. Whether because of a need to find more economically secure work or pressure to avoid identity with *Italianità*, few early Italian Americans ventured into the field of literature as writers or critics.

Early twentieth-century immigrants from Italy to the United States did not at once refer to themselves as Americans. Most of the early immigrants were sojourners or "birds of passage," primarily men who crossed the ocean to find work, make money, and return home. This experience is well presented in books such as Michael La Sorte's *La Merica: Images of Italian Greenhorn Experience* (1985). In addition to language barriers, these immigrants often faced difficult living conditions and often encountered racism. In *Wop! A Documentary History of Anti-Italian Discrimination* (1999), Salvatore LaGumina gathers evidence of this racism from late nineteenth- and twentieth-century American journalism appearing in the *New York Times* and other major publications.

In response to this treatment, many of the Italians referred to Americans as "merdicani" short for "merde di cane" (dog shit). Italians also used the word as a derogatory reference by Italians to those who assimilated too quickly and readily into American culture. Most novels published prior to World War II depicted the vexed immigrant experience of adjustment in America: Louis Forgione's *The River Between* (1928), Garibaldi LaPolla's *The Grand Gennaro* (1935), Valenti Angelo's *Golden Gate* (1939), Guido D'Agostino's *Olives on the Apple Tree* (1940), Mari Tomasi's *Deep Grow the Roots* (1940), and Jo Pagano's *Golden Wedding* (1943).

In spite of a substantial presence in literature Italian Americans had little visibility in American popular culture other than the Rudolph Valentino romantic exotic types and a few gangster films. Norman Rockwell paintings and illustrations, considered in the 1930s and 1940s to be typically American, never included images of Italians. Even the works of Italian American artists themselves were conspicuously void of direct references to the immigrant experience. Filmmaker Frank Capra, who emigrated from Sicily with his family in 1903, managed to include the Martini family in *It's a Wonderful Life* (1946) as a marginal reference to the poor helped by George Bailey. In the literary arts, becoming an American is the focus of much of the early artists such as John Fante, whose "The Odyssey of a Wop," appeared in H. L. Mencken's *American Mercury*, a popular magazine of the 1930s and 1940s. Fante, a self-proclaimed protégé of Mencken, wrote novels and became a Hollywood screenwriter. His *Full of Life* (1957), a mainstream Hollywood comedy starring Richard Conte and Judy Holiday, was based on his novel of the same title, which helped bring this experience into the American mainstream.

Immigrant struggles, beyond trying to make a living and feed self and family recounted in such novels as Pietro di Donato's *Christ in Concrete*

(1939), John Fante's *Wait until Spring, Bandini* (1938), Mari Tomasi's *Like Lesser Gods* (1949), Julia Savarese's *The Weak and the Strong* (1952), and autobiographies such as Jerre Mangione's *Mount Allegro* (1943), included coping with the prejudice and discrimination that reached extremes in the 1891 New Orleans lynchings and later with the trial and 1927 executions of Sacco and Vanzetti. The literature produced during this period provides great insights into the shaping of American identities and into the obstacles that these immigrants faced in pursuing their versions of the American dream.

A history of the Italian American intellectual is yet to be written, but when it is, one of the stories it will tell is the tension between what Antonio Gramsci has identified as the organic and the traditional intellectual. It will present a gallery of rogue scholars whose voices are vulgar and vital and whose place in American culture has never been stabilized by political lobbies, cultural foundations, or endowed chairs. It will tell the tale of the pre-Christian paganism of Italian culture that has resurfaced in popular culture through the antics of Madonna and the controversial cultural analyses of Camille Paglia. While both of these American women of Italian descent seem to be innovators in interpretation, they are in fact, popularizers of ideas that have long remained submerged in the shadows of Italian American culture. One need only look to Diane di Prima's *Memoirs of a Beatnik* (1969) or the cultural criticism of Luigi Fraina and Robert Viscusi to find their antecedents. The major problem facing Italian American intellectuals is not a lack of preparation for or sophistication in their critical methods, but a lack of self-confidence that the culture they come from can be used to express themselves to the American mainstream audience. The lack of this self-confidence is one result of the immigrant experience.

In these days, when cultural differences are exploited more than similarities are explored, when the idea of working-class unity is clouded by the competition for leisure time and credit card possibilities, imagining that there was a time when what happened to the working class mattered to intellectuals is difficult. But these days, as increasingly radical intellectuals are reclaiming their working-class backgrounds, we must remember the cultural work done by those immigrant intellectuals who dedicated their lives to the working-class cause. The earliest voices of Italian America heard publicly were those of political and labor activists such as poet-organizer Arturo Giovannitti, Frances Winwar, journalist-organizer Carol Tresca, and Luigi Fraina. Following is a brief look at some of those immigrant intellectuals.

Although Luigi Fraina did not develop an identity that strongly connected to his Italian ancestry, he certainly stayed true to his working-class origins. Fraina was born in Galdo, Italy, in 1892 and came to America with his mother at age three to join his father, a republican exile. An early participant in the DeLeon socialist labor movement, Fraina was involved in the founding of the American communist party after experience in both the socialist labor party and the Industrial Workers of the World (IWW). In the early 1900s Fraina was one of the earliest to publish Marxist literary and cultural criticism in the United States. By age thirty, he had disconnected himself from any political group, changed his name to Lewis Corey, and became a leader of the anticommunist liberal movement. Working as a proofreader and editor as Charles Skala, Fraina began writing as Lewis Corey. During this period he was a union activist and a prolific Marxist critic and journalist; despite never having been formally educated beyond grammar school, he wrote several books about U.S. capitalism. His *The House of Morgan* (1930), *The Decline of American Capitalism* (1934), and *The Crisis of the Middle Class* (1935), helped fuel the radical movement of the 1930s.

In one of his few directly antifascist articles, "Human Values in Literature and Revolution" (1963), Fraina speaks out against fascism and argues that the only good literature is that which concerns "itself primarily with consciousness and values, with attitudes toward life" (8). Of the literature of his time that does this, Fraina notes three types: (1) "the literature of capitalist disintegration," (2) "the literature of fundamental human values and defense of those values," and (3) "the literature of conscious revolutionary aspiration and struggle." Fraina sees fascism as "the final proof" that "in any period of fundamental social change, particularly as the old order decays, there is an increasing degradation of human values" (8). Fraina points to the writing of Ignazio Silone as truly revolutionary:

> In one of his short stories Silone (whose *Fontamara* combines the understanding of theory and the sweep of life into a magnificent symphony) tells of a group of radical workers who are destroyed by a fascist spy because of their sense of decency. The moral is: you cannot be decent against the indecent. But Silone conveys more: that it is terrible to abandon decency, even necessarily and temporarily, because our fight is to make life decent. (8)

Fraina dedicated his entire life to theoretical analysis of the impact of capitalism on U.S. democratic culture and to the search for a new social order that would respect and reward human labor. His words in the 1930s were prophetic:

> We must learn to appreciate the underlying unity of events, the logic of historical development. The threat of fascism, of new world wars and a new barbarism, arises out of the class necessity of entrenched interests which cling, at all costs, to the old order. This menace to all other classes can be met only by a struggle for a new social order

capable of creating a new and higher civilization, for capitalism in decay is now capable only of creating reaction and death. (*The Crisis of the Middle Class* 12–13)

Those words have yet to lose their relevance. Fraina believed that the struggle would require education, especially of the middle class as to its historical role in the propagation of the traditions of the ruling class. Only through education, he believed, could "the dispossessed elements of the middle class" (19) understand their role in creating a new national order. But Fraina was not one to advocate revolution from an office. He also worked on the front lines.

During the Great Depression he worked as an economist for the Works Progress Administration (WPA) and then became educational director of Local 22 of the International Ladies' Garment Workers' Union (ILGWU) from 1937–1939. In the early 1940s, as a result of the German–Soviet Pact of 1939, Fraina broke from his belief in Marxism and struggled to find ways of creating a more democratic economy and expressed his thoughts in *The Unfinished Task* (1940). He went on to teach from 1942–1951 at Antioch College, and from there became the educational director of the Amalgamated Butcher Workmen, American Federation of Labor (AFL) in Chicago. From this experience came his *Meat and Man: A Study of Monopoly, Unionism and Food Policy* (1950). The U.S. government attempted to deport him for being in the country illegally and for having been a communist. Two days after Fraina's death in 1953, the U.S. Department of Justice issued him a certificate of lawful entry.

The rise of fascism in Italy in the 1920s, 1930s, and 1940s had a tremendous effect on the identity and behavior of Americans of Italian decent, and this effect became a prime subject in their literature. Jerre Mangione captured this experience in his memoirs *Mount Allegro* (1943) and *An Ethnic at Large: A Memoir of America in the Thirties and Forties* (1978):

In my years of becoming an American I had come to understand the evil of Fascism and hate it with all my soul. One or two of my relatives argued with me on the subject because they had a great love for their native land and, like some men in love, they could see nothing wrong. Fascism was only a word to them; Mussolini a patriotic Italian putting his country on its feet. Why did I insist on finding fault with Fascism, they asked, when all the American newspapers were admitting Mussolini was a great man who made the trains run on time? (*Mount Allegro* 239–40)

Trapped between two countries (their parents' homeland and their own), Italian American writers tended to stay aloof of the current international political situation. Not until after the fall of Mussolini did Italian Americans, in any significant way, address fascism in their fiction and poetry. The earliest antifascist writings dared to contradict the pro-fascist posture the U.S. government assumed as well as leading figures of the American literary scene such as Wallace Stevens, Ezra Pound, and T. S. Eliot, who as proponents of modernism were also, interestingly enough, if not outright pro-fascist, at least sympathetic to Mussolini's fascism (Diggins 245). Those Italian Americans who opposed Mussolini from the beginning did so at the risk of being attacked or labeled communists by the larger American public as well as their own pro-Mussolini countrymen.

One of the earliest Italian Americans to voice his opinion of Italian fascism in his poetry was Arturo Giovannitti, who with Joseph Ettor, organized the famous 1912 Lawrence Mill Strike. In his poem "To Mussolini" he accuses the Father of Italian Fascism of winning "fame with lies." And he tells il duce that:

No man is great who does not find
A poet who will hail him as he is
With an almighty song that will unbind
Through his exploits eternal silences.
Duce, where is your bard? In all mankind
The only poem you inspired is this. (72)

In "Italia Speaks," Giovannitti depicts the United States as a child of Italy who can rescue its mother from "The twin ogres in black and brown [who] have polluted my gardens" (76). Giovannitti composed poems that echo Walt Whitman's patriotic odes during the American Civil War. In his "Battle Hymn of the New Italy" we find a synthesis of Giosue Carducci and Whitman, as Giovannitti calls for the Italian people to rise up against Mussolini and Hitler.

Along with Giovannitti, those most prominent antifascists whose writing appeared most frequently in U.S. publications were the *fuorusciti*, Italian intellectuals who left Italy and found refuge more often than not in U.S. universities: Gaetano Salvemini at Harvard University in Cambridge, Max Ascoli at the New School for Social Research, Giuseppe Borgese at the University of Chicago, and Lionello Venturi at Johns Hopkins in Maryland (Diggins 140). These *fuorusciti* were responsible for several influential antifascist publications. Their presence made "the universities one of the few anti-Fascist ramparts in America" (Diggins 261). Constantine Panunzio, a professor at the University of California at Los Angeles and author of *The Soul of an Immigrant*, one of the earliest book-length autobiographies by an Italian American, contributed to the understanding of the plight of Italian Americans in this period through his article "Italian Americans, Fascism and the War" published in 1942 in the *Yale Review*. Panunzio explained the relationship between Italian Americans and the Italian government, arguing that although Italian Americans might have nibbled the bait of fascism "as mainly a diversion or a means of escape from the feeling of inferiority which the American community imposed on them" (782), they never swallowed the hook, and "now that the test of war has come, there is no question as to where almost one hundred per cent of our Italian immigrant population stands" (782).

The fiction of Mangione contains similar antifascist sentiments. Mangione's interactions with activist Carlo Tresca became the material on which he would build his second novel, *Night Search* (1965). Based on Tresca's assassination, *Night Search* dramatizes the experience of Michael Mallory, the illegitimate son of antifascist labor organizer and newspaper publisher Paolo Polizzi, a character based on Tresca. Through investigating his father's murder, Mallory learns to take action, and in doing so comes to understand contemporary politics. Mallory very much resembles Stiano Argento, the main protagonist in Mangione's earlier and more strongly anti-fascist novel, *The Ship and the Flame* (1948).

Although immigration to the United States from Italy slowed between the 1920s and 1940s due to political maneuvers such as the 1924 U.S. quota restrictions, several Italian intellectuals were allowed to immigrate to the United States to flee fascism. Most prominent among those included scientists such as Enrico Fermi, who has come to be called father of the atom bomb, and writers Arturo Vivante, P. M. Pasinetti, and Nicolo Tucci. Vivante, a physician, contributed frequently to major publications such as the *New Yorker*. His fiction includes a collection of short stories, *The French Girls of Killini* (1967), and three novels, *A Goodly Babe* (1966), *Doctor Giovanni* (1969), and *Run to the Waterfall* (1965). Pasinetti came to study in the United States in 1935 from Venice and first published fiction in *The Southern Review*. He earned a Ph.D. at Yale University in New Haven in 1949 and went on to teach at the University of California at Los Angeles. Pasinetti published three novels, *Venetian Red* (1960), *The Smile on the Face of the Lion* (1965), and *From the Academy Bridge* (1970); his work earned him an award from the National Institute of Arts and Letters in 1965. Tucci, who came while a student, published two autobiographical novels, *Before My Time* (1962) and *Unfinished Funeral* (1964), using European settings to depict a liberation from the history that the emigrant experiences. For these writers, their sense of the literary was significantly shaped by the prominence in 1930s Italy of *Americanisti* such as Elio Vittorini and Cesare Pavese, both translators and influential editors who helped introduce American literature to Italian culture.

So what has all this to do with the Italians in America? The myth of Italian America was founded at this time by immigrants from southern Italy who did not wait for others to answer the southern question for them. Those who immigrated to the United States eventually created a myth ritualized each October on Columbus Day. Robert Viscusi's booklength poem, *An Oration on the Most Recent Death of Christopher Columbus,* helps us to see the establishment of early Italian American identity in relation to the creation myth of Italian America.

> the fact is columbus day will go the way of the dinosaur
> along with everything else
> meanwhile what about garibaldi
> who was fighting for the poor in italy
> but after the revolution
> lives to see the rich steal italy
> and starve the poor
> selling them to labor gangs in suez
> shipping them to new york to dig subways
> in return to cheap american grain
> they brought back in the empty ships
> the italians went to america in steerage
> that means they slept down below
> all in one room seasick for weeks
> another room would carry wheat the other way
> the italians didn't know where they were going
> when they got there the people spit at them
> and garibaldi lived to see all this begin to happen
> which was his reward for helping the rich steal italy
> he should have come to new york to fight in the civil war
> and march in the columbus day parade (1–2)

One of the great answers to the southern question was the creation of Italian America, which Viscusi has suggested was founded on the myth of the rich throwing the poor out of Italy, and it was inside the Little Italys of Italian America where former Italians became the very intellectuals that Gramsci had hoped would lead his country in a revolution ("Literature Considering" 270). And although Italian immigrants wasted no time in making physical Little Italys, much time would pass before they would create a self-conscious cultural notion called Little Italy, for that, they would have to invent Italian America.

Chapter 2

Inventing Italian America

America was an idea long before it became a place, and as an idea it enveloped all hopes of complete freedom, real equality, absence of persecution, and unlimited potential for living life to its fullest. As Djelal Kadir glossed the word in his *Columbus and the Ends of the Earth; Europe's Prophetic Rhetoric as Conquering Ideology*, America just might mean "nowhereland," a place that can only exist as an idea. Once that idea took residence in a land called the United States, it fell victim to the wiles of reality that make the perfect practice of theory impossible. Kadir calls for moving beyond traditional boundaries of America and American studies, past what he calls the American-American studies, past New American studies, and into a place we might best call Americas' studies. The following incidents help to clarify what I mean.

Recently my family was to travel to Italy to visit, together for the first time, our ancestral homeland—the birthplace of my grandparents. The terrorist attacks on September 11, 2001, greatly concerned most of my relatives and so the trip was cancelled. In our discussions, one of my uncles commented on Italy's response to President Bush's call for help. "Those damned dagoes. Can you believe they had the *coglioni* to say they weren't going to send any troops? Who do they think they are? I'm ashamed to say we came from there. And after we saved them in two wars and kept them from becoming communist. What kind of way is that to respond?" This response indicates the failure of American-American studies and the success of the United States in assimilating Italian immigrants and their offspring. My uncle's response, couched later in religious fluff, shows not only his own ignorance about the reality of Italy's relationship to the United States in two wars, but also the success of the master narrative of U.S. mediated history. The problem with American-American studies is that it has lifted the United States into the center of the world around which all other cultures must focus their attention.

A second instance comes from an editorial that appeared in the October 7, 2001, *St. Augustine Record*. Author Hansen Alexander writes: "Tomorrow's

Columbus Day Celebration will go forth undeterred by the fact that the Genoese mariner helped Spain, not Italy stake a claim to the Americas." Then begins his lament, "The holiday has come to celebrate that which is Italian, or more specifically, that which is southern Italian." Having made this distinction is interesting, but why is another story. Alexander characterizes southern Italy as an area more impoverished than the rest of Italy and the birthplace of "tomato based foods like thin pizza, the notorious Mafia, and poor fishermen like Joe DiMaggio's father" (1). He complains that we do not celebrate northern Italian qualities such as "the industrial might of Milan, the intellectual heritage of its great universities at Bologna and Padua," or the genius of da Vinci, Michelangelo, Galileo, Dante, and Boccaccio. "No," he continues, "tomorrow will be about cheap wine and stereotypical visions of Italians as a congregation of vigilantes."

Unlike my uncle, whom I know well enough to realize there is almost always a bit of irony in what he says, I continued reading the editorial hoping that this was someone's idea of a joke. But it only got worse from there. Although the publisher of the paper later apologized for publishing the editorial and it has been pulled from its online archives, it represents more than the ignorance of one man. Both my uncle and Alexander suffer from the same affliction that is traceable to the difficulty of interpreting the various metaphors that have come to be associated with the United States.

America as Metaphor

To the Italian immigrant America first existed as a metaphor and there was virtually no distinction between North and South America. America meant going west across the ocean where work was available. One needed to compare the American experience to what a fellow Italian could understand. So those who had been to America and returned to their native homelands necessarily used metaphors when relating their experiences to their *paesani*. Far too often exaggerated accounts of their successes and failures were created so that through story the myth of America was created and through metaphor the myth was communicated. Like any good metaphor, America has always been subject to many interpretations; the struggle for identification with America was one of the immigrant's first battles. Even at the entry to America, immigrants were immediately aware of their difference, their un-Americanness.

Now whether the metaphor came to one through song, letters, or conversation it communicated a variety of messages. Much of the metaphor centered on ideas such as freedom, boundless opportunity, and streets paved with gold. A typical Italian immigrant was lured to America by this myth and its promise that life is greener on the other side of the ocean. In Pietro Corsi's novel, *La Giobba* (1982), the real myth was dispelled when the immigrant came to the realization that (1) the streets were not paved with gold; (2) few if any of the streets had been paved at all; and (3) the Italian was expected to pave them. In fact, a contemporary and chauvinistic Italian American T-shirt reads: "America, We discovered it. We named it. We built it."

The early Italian American literature focuses on this dream/reality dichotomy and the coming to terms with the dispelling of the myth/metaphor that lured the immigrant to the United States. To the Italian American, even those born in the United States, America immediately became a metaphor through such myths, and as such it stood for something to strive for. First it was a metaphor of separation: there are those things that are and are not American. This notion is reflected on in much of the early Italian American literature. Jerre Mangione's *Mount Allegro* (1943) for example opens with the exploration of this issue:

> "When I grow up I want to be an American," Giustina said.
> We looked at our sister; it was something none of us had ever said.
> "Me too," Maria echoed.
> "Aw you don't even know what an American is," Joe scoffed.
> "I do so," Giustina said.
> It was more than the rest of us knew.
> "We're Americans right now," I said. "Miss Zimmerman says if you're born here you're an American."
> "Aw she's nuts," Joe said. He had no use for most teachers. "We're Italians. If y'don't believe me ask Pop."
> But my father wasn't very helpful. "Your children will be 'Americani.' But you, my son, are half-and-half. Now stop asking me questions. You should know those things from going to school. What do you learn in school, anyway?" (1)

This confusion over what was and was not American carried over into the next generation. I believed that my maternal grandfather, an immigrant from southern Italy, was not American. I was convinced that the good immigrants were those who struggled to be American with the knowledge that the past contained much of what was not considered to be American. At least, I thought, the good immigrant realized the need to disguise or better yet erase all traces of un-Americanness: stop speaking one's native language, rid one's self of accented American English, start dressing in the latest American fashions, and spurn Italian restaurants and eating Italian food in public. However I would find that all these material things were easier to dispose of than the spiritual. When it came to things such as the family, dignity, and self-respect, my grandparents' *Italianità* could not be smothered. In terms of such Italianate values they revealed *Italianità* in spite of conscious attempts to control or mask it.

To Italian Americans, America as a metaphor communicated denial. It was not a problem of knowing what being American was; rather, the problem came in trying to avoid everything that common knowledge said being American was not. As a kid, I thoroughly despised any mark of *Italianità* and did my best to rid myself of evidence such as darker skin (I would not go shirtless in the summer). Once relatives from Italy visited us and I ignored them. I told my non–Italian American friends (the ones who had pointed them out in my yard as though they were some circus oddity) that those "wops" were strangers who had missed a plane and my family was putting them up until the next plane left for Italy.

Even for those of us who had been educated in U.S. schools, hiding the more instinctual aspects of *Italianità* that had somehow survived our parents' conscious renunciations was difficult. Being American meant talking without using hands. Once a speech teacher wrapped string around us so we would not gesticulate during a speech presentation. Without hands, the job of communicating through kinetics was taken over by shoulder shrugging, facial twitching, and waist turning. Some aspects of *Italianità* were destined to betray my Americanness in spite of all I could do.

To be American was to be what others were, and so we modeled ourselves after those to which the media gave their attention. We made heroes out of others—astronauts, sports figures, media stars, and assassinated presidents. Italian American literature is filled with this desire to be the "other," as the following selection from John Fante's *Wait until Spring, Bandini,* novel demonstrates: "His name was Arturo, but he hated it and wanted to be called John. His last name was Bandini, and he wanted to be called Jones. His mother and father were Italians, but he wanted to be an American. His father was a bricklayer, but he wanted to be a pitcher for the Chicago Cubs" (33). To be American, to be the "other," we needed to defy our parents, our grandparents, and anyone or anything else that reminded us of our non-American ancestry. We needed to turn our backs on what was our past, to melt the mold of our heritage, and hope that it was ice: melt and evaporate without a trace.

Italians learned about America through television, schools, newspapers, and through Irish American–administrated religion and politics. Those media portrayed the United States as sleek, fashionable, material, and present and future oriented. History played a minor role (if any at all) in the life of the average American. History was facts, figures, and military victories in which the losers were always the non-Americans. Those victories represented the conquering of enemies that were inhuman or cowards; especially we learned, that Italians were cowardly soldiers. Italy was fine until Rome fell, but then again the Roman Empire killed Jesus Christ; after that it was all downhill.

Even Great Britain, the basis of much of America's early development was viewed as a quaint land of cottages and castles, a place more romantic than realistic. All that were not Americans were weak and needed American assistance to stand up to enemies. Nothing was complete unless America had had a hand in developing it. America was the metaphor of glory, and as such, its antithesis, Russia, necessarily became the metaphor of doom. As we grew older we realized America was a misread metaphor, but there had been clues all along . . . foreigners never fared well in the novels taught in schools and Italians, if they had written any American novels at all did not count; Boy Scout uniforms did not fit the peasant stock frames that we of Mediterranean ancestry were issued at birth that needed grandma's magic needlework to make us presentable, and that needle often embellished the interiors of the uniforms with stitched crucifixes and crocheted symbols that would protect us from *mal occhio*, the evil eye.

America's imperialistic commercial and military ventures forced an increased awareness of other cultures: first, those who were aided in the battles against Nazism and fascism; then those who were threatened by the Iron Curtain; then when they started blacklisting Italian artists who associated with foreign elements, it became obvious that many people were confused about what was and was not American. The House Committee on Un-American Activities scared everyone whose name fell short of Anglo-Saxon simplicity. By the time the 1960s came along the spotlight revealed the un-American activities that were being perpetrated by the United States: attempts to assassinate Castro and meddling in the affairs of smaller countries.

As Guido D'Agostino's novel *Olives on the Apple Tree* warned, nothing was to be done about not fitting into America. How can you expect an olive to grow from the apple tree? But the culture of the 1960s changed such fatalistic immigrant attitudes. It was as though life in America had been a masquerade party in which everyone in attendance had been wearing American costumes, and in the 1960s came the unmasking, and many of us found that most were not really Americans at all. A once-strong American identity was found to be a fragile façade, a surface, like ice, strong and reflective until the heat comes upon it. And the heat of the 1960s proved to be too much. Breaking the surface we find, like the analysis of any metaphor will prove, that its origins were much more complex than we had thought. The early metaphor was a primitive reaction between self and other. We would soon find out that Indians were the real Americans—the first Americans—and so they would be renamed Native Americans; and this carried over to Black Americans, Jewish Americans, and so forth, until it seemed the hyphenation craze would never end. But this still was not quite what we were hoping for. Although we were now better connected by a bridge of punctuation to the word and thus to the metaphor, we were still without accounts of us in history. What we had learned in history classes was not the real us, but the us that others saw and depicted. So many of us fell for those portrayals that when something like Mario Puzo's *The Godfather* came along in 1969, we were forming "Godfather clubs"; so we did not think we mattered; what mattered was what was historical and that meant it had to be red, white, and blue.

More than a few who were brave thinkers did not fall for such nonsense, realizing they had always been in involved in history and so started documenting their participation in it. Now many books have been published about Italians in the United States—novels, plays, and poetry that show the creation of the metaphor, the interpretations of the metaphor, and the alternatives to the metaphor. The United States is experiencing a cultural renaissance that has come from the reawakening, the researching, and recasting of its ancestors' roles in the development of this land called America.

America typically took the past, renamed it, hid its origins, and made us think it was so brand new, but the same education that was hoodwinking many of us, enlightened enough of us to begin learning for ourselves. Metaphor was responsible for the identity crisis of the children of immigrants and the search though the metaphor for the real basis of the American signs. Once the immigrant lost the original idea of America and some of its early metaphorical associations were dispelled, Italians needed to replace it with another ideal, which is when the notion of the "old country" came to life.

Italy became a metaphor for the postimmigrant generations, and through stories told by immigrant relatives, the images began building. With that image in mind we went off to find that place called "bell'Italia." But it was nowhere to be found. Italy had changed; the metaphors of the past no longer could be found in the present reality. So that they could live on, writers captured them in literature. So the metaphor becomes the map, and once that map is used, the metaphor is no longer useful to the few who used it to control. America was not a foreign language, yet the answer to what America is was always right there in front of our eyes, in the very name. The process by which America was named should have told us that America had its roots in foreign countries. So those who learned to use the language of the land that imperialized and colonized us were also learning to use other languages that gave new words, new meanings, and new dimensions to the American metaphor, and with all this came new interpretations of the metaphor. The irony is that America was built by metaphor, and the American myth is destined to be dismantled by the very language that created its metaphor.

History is catching up quickly with America. As soon as the idea became a place it was eventually doomed to succumb to the realities of every other place in the world. And those who fell prey to the myth and the metaphor, once they had become a part of the place, realized that it was not all it was cracked up to be. It was not the utopia they had hoped for. And once they became a part of the place, they began losing the original idea of the place. That is the threat that we face today: the loss of the original idea of the

United States of America. As long as we refuse to face histories, we are destined to continue denying rights and freedoms to minorities. Individuals, brave creative individuals, must be different, stand up, and refuse to turn on each other and feed our greed and selfishness on the weaknesses of others.

This is how we can work with the myth and use it to study the history of the United States in the context of the history of the world, to study the idea of America in the context of the ideas of the worlds. A history of the metamorphosis of America as metaphor needs to be written, to be studied, and to be acted on. That history is there, somewhere in our culture, and it needs to be identified and examined for truths to extract and use toward the rebuilding of the metaphor. The tension between the metaphor of Italy and the metaphor of America is at the foundation of this study: through that tension Italian America was created.

For many years, Italian American culture has been preserved in the Little Italy neighborhoods, and over the years, more likely than not, in the basement of those homes, where grandpa made wine, where grandma had a second kitchen, and now material legacies and memories are stored. Outside celebrations such as religious festivals became the most important public presentation of Italian American culture, but these annual events were never frequent enough to protect Italian American culture from the regular mass media bombardment of negative stereotypes.

Where Italian Americans have never organized as a cultural group is in the mainstream institutions of education. The public programs that might have taught Italian Americans the value of their own culture and subsequently fortified future generations, the public programs that would have challenged media-made impressions, were never created. Italian Americans have kept their heads in their basements, in what they fondly refer to as the *basciuments*, where Italian American culture is safe inside family celebrations.

Now is the time to move beyond the basements of yesterday and out into the streets of today. The romance and tragedy of early twentieth-century immigration can no longer serve as models for identity. The key to creating a meaningful sense of Italian American culture that means something to today's youth is first to ensure that they have access to the histories of their families and their communities. They need to be exposed to historical and contemporary models in the areas of arts, business, and education that they can study, emulate, and transcend. The Little Italys that once served as the source and haven of Italian American identity, where Robert Orsi's notion of "the domus" was nurtured and enacted, have become little more than cultural theme parks in a gentrified land. With the move to the suburbs, Italian Americans have created scholarships for higher education, but they have done little to help those applicants understand what it means to be Italian American once they enter those institutions. This knowledge comes best when it is found in the very materials those students study, in the very stories they hear and read from childhood through graduate school. Writers such as Pietro di Donato, John Fante, Helen Barolini, Louise DeSalvo, Maria Gillan, and countless others have been writing and publishing those stories, but how many of their wonderful works can be found in the homes and in school libraries where they can serve as models for present and future writings.

Tradition and the Individual Italian

Tradition . . . cannot be inherited, and if you want it you must obtain it by great labour.
        —T. S. Eliot, "Tradition and the Individual Talent"

A literary tradition is built when writers read each other and learn either to extend or escape what has come before. This process requires literary models, something Italian Americans such as Louise DeSalvo could not find. As she tells us in *Vertigo: A Memoir* (1996), "Though I had read scores of books, not one had been written by an Italian American woman. I had no role model among the women of my background to urge me on" (9). For DeSalvo and other Italian Americans born in the 1940s, a sense of Italian American culture and identity would come from one's family and perhaps one's neighborhood, but certainly not from school. Without Italian American models in educational institutions, those such as DeSalvo who would choose to become teachers and writers, would need to look elsewhere. As Alice Walker tells us in her essay, "Saving the Life that Is Your Own": "The absence of models, in literature as in life, . . . is an occupational hazard for the artist, simply because models in art, in behavior, in growth of spirit and intellect—even if rejected—enrich and enlarge one's view of existence" (4). And this is what these writers did for me; they enlarged my view of existence as an American of Italian descent. Toward the end of this essay, Walker writes: "It is, in the end, the saving of lives that we writers are about. Whether we are 'minority' writers or 'majority.' It is simply in our power to do this" (14).

But the artists are not the only ones who suffer when stories are not read or heard. Everyone suffers. At the end of a section of her novel, *Umbertina*, Helen Barolini has the matriarch of a family sitting alone near a tree during a family reunion picnic. She looks around and is proud of what she and her husband created out of the nothing that they brought with them to America. But then, there is a sadness that overcomes her to the point of tears, which is when she comes to realize that of all the relatives here, there is no one to whom she can tell her story. Not one of her daughters or sons, granddaughters or grandsons, can or ever will they know her story: "She had won, but who could she tell her story to? At times the doubt came to her whether she had really won, after all. All her life had been a struggle for family, and now in her old age she saw some signs that made her uneasy" (145).

It is not long before this uneasiness becomes a dis-ease of sorts, and many of you know that it is not simply the stuff of novels. This occurs in every family in which the experience of one generation was denied entry into the consciousness of the next. More often than not this occurred when the language of the immigrants was not passed on to their children. We cannot forget that the immigrants' experiences were processed in Italian and if they were not recorded, not passed on from one generation to the next, it was mostly like due to the impossibility of communicating such complex thoughts and feelings in a new language.

By the time I had learned to speak, read, and write Italian, my grandparents were dead and my parents had long stopped speaking the language. What was lost I could only imagine, so I went in search of those stories. What I found was that although they could not control how they passed down a heritage through conscious stories, they did pass down some unconscious elements that we must understand before we can succeed as a culture. Most of our stories have been stolen by others to make money. When we wish to tell our stories, no one wants the ones that will not make money. A publisher told me that although my novel was a good story, I should make my characters Jewish because Jews read and Jews buy books. I was appalled and that spurred me to become the writer you are reading. I have come to believe that if we do not tell our stories, if we do not preserve them, then we will not have a culture either to protect or promote. When we do not tell our stories, we lose our souls. When someone else tells our story, they steal our souls. When we let them steal our souls, we are accomplices in an ethnic and cultural suicide.

As a community, Italian Americans are just beginning to understand the value of the written word. For years publishers have been saying that the Italian American is not the target audience for most books—they do not buy books because they do not read. However, something is happening to Italian American culture that is changing this stereotypic notion. This "something" emerges as Italian Americans transfer dependence on oral tradition to one of a written tradition.

I am often approached by people who have asked me to write their life stories. Why, all of a sudden, are these Italian Americans searching for writers? I believe this is caused by the disintegration of the traditional Italian American community and the dissemination of Italian individuals into American society. The life stories of our ancestors were part of the common knowledge of those who lived communal lives. In small villages, where contact with others was almost daily, the topics of conversations could be expanded to include history. And history, in terms of origin stories, was kept alive from generation to generation by memory and word of mouth. The past was always a part of the present. This method was sufficient as long as a family did not move away from its place of origins. Even today, all you need to do to learn about your ancestral past is to spend some time in the *piazze* of the southern Italian villages amidst the old pensioners. However, things began to change even though Italian immigrants settled in areas called Little Italys.

In these "old" neighborhoods, the oral traditions were kept alive through the constant interaction among families and friends. Even though my father died when I was young, there was never a lack of people in my neighborhood who, over a beef sandwich and a bag of cecci or some homemade wine, could tell me stories that made my father live. This oral transmission system worked because of the continuous contact we had with the extended family and *paesani*. And as long as the oral system operated, the need for reading and writing was limited to the demands of social and economic factors of the larger society. We had little need to record history as history lived in the minds and words of those who surrounded our lives. But as the old neighborhoods dissolved with migration to multicultural settings and to the far-away places where jobs had taken us, that everyday contact with the past gave way to occasional encounters in which, at best, very few stories were then passed on. One result of this communal disintegration was the loss of an access to a past that could not only inform but also enhance the present. This loss surfaced in questions that need to be answered and an emptiness that needs to be filled.

All good writing begins with good questions, and all great writers begin by filling the great voids in their lives. For Italian Americans, the number of questions and the size of the voids are no doubt growing. This is especially true as the original pioneers disappear without having been listened to, and this is precisely why we are entering a time in which our writers will be recognized. Their recognition will be due to their ability to listen and to respond to what is heard by creating literature.

Any advanced literate society typically depends less and less on its elders. After all, the past is recorded in books, in films, on tapes; the dependence on the elder's memory is exchanged for the dependence on the expert. The problem with Italian Americans is that we have yet to understand this function of a print-oriented society, a society that separates past from present. As we advance, we exchange our personal histories for a public history that has distorted our communal presence through the presentation and preservation of stereotypes.

In short, as Italian Americans move into the fourth and fifth generations, they find that in spite of the predominance of mass media, they are depending increasingly on the written word for the recording of their history and common institutions beyond the family for dissemination of that history. The evolution of Italian American culture depends very much on the ability to produce history. Without these histories they will find that future Italian Americans will, in spite of the best intentions of individual family influence, lose their connection to their ancestral roots. No matter the occasion, whenever a speaker is called on to address an Italian American issue, he or she inevitably points to an illustrious past filled with great works of art. But Renaissance artists are not directly related to the Italian experiences that form bases for Italian American culture. Only when the present interacts with the past can we say that a tradition is being created. The stories of the past, especially when told by elders, have been the major vehicle by which a heritage is transmitted from generation to generation. But this process became endangered when Italians migrated to the United States. Loss of shared primary languages and lack of shared environments (as children leave not only the homes, but also the neighborhoods and often the states of their upbringing), impede the development of a sense of tradition. As T. S. Eliot knew, the task of organizing a literary tradition belongs to the literary critics and historians, but the task of recognizing one belongs to the individual reader and writer.

As a poet in an exile of sorts, Eliot knew well the importance of staying connected to a tradition and keeping that tradition alive. Fortunately for him, the tradition of English literature had no geographical boundaries. Wherever one reads and writes English, the possibility of knowing the best of what literature is produced always exists. This may be the same for Italian American writers, but theirs is a double duty: to know the cultures of Italy and the United States. For as their stories may come from the Little Italys of the United States, they go out to the entire English-speaking public and thus cannot depend on the audience of Italian Americans alone. This, of course, requires a thorough familiarity with literature past and present produced in the English language—a daunting task indeed, but one the greatest writers will accomplish. Eliot told us that the creation of significant verse requires the poet to "extinguish personality," in other words to shift one's attention from self to other, but what many Italian American writers have done is to create their personality through writing. For many, they have acted as Americans through their writing.

Being Americans

American studies came into being in the post–World War II era, as, in part, an expression of American nationalist objectives.
          —Paul Lauter, "Reconfiguring Academic Disciplines"

Prior to the U.S. entry into World War II, Congress passed the Alien Registration Act (the Smith Act), which required all noncitizens older than age fourteen to be fingerprinted and registered at the local U.S. Postal Service. At the outset of the war the Federal Bureau of Investigation (FBI) identified many Italian Americans as dangerous enemy aliens. As the oral history and exhibition project entitled "Una Storia Segreta" (A Secret Story) has revealed, many Italian Americans suffered civil rights violations that seriously affected their lives and livelihoods. Due to political pressure, some of the restrictions were removed on Columbus Day 1942. In all, 10,000 Italian Americans were restricted to certain areas or held in 46 detention camps in Texas, California, Washington, Montana, North Dakota, Oklahoma, New York, and New Jersey. The government confiscated the fishing boats and radios from the father of baseball great Joe DiMaggio. Although such violations were not as severe or pervasive as those enacted against the Japanese Americans, they did significantly disrupt the lives of those imprisoned. In 1999 the U.S. House of Representatives passed Resolution 2442, which acknowledged the wartime violation of Italian American civil liberties.

Pietro di Donato, John Fante, Jerre Mangione, and Frances Winwar (Vinciguerra) are four American writers of Italian descent who were most prominent during this pre–World War II period. Of these, Mangione and Winwar were the most politically committed. Di Donato, author of the 1939 national best-seller *Christ in Concrete*, was conspicuously silent about fascism as was Fante, an established literary figure by the 1940s. Whereas di Donato's writing was not specifically antifascist, his life's work was very critical of established political authority. Fante, who refers to Mussolini and fascism in his letters to his mother and H. L. Mencken, the publisher of Fante's early stories, never discusses the subject in his stories or novels. Unlike Fante and di Donato, Mangione wrote extensively about the effects of fascism on Italy and of those who fought fascism in Europe. In fact, nearly all his fiction and much of his literary criticism is devoted to antifascist themes. One of his earliest book reviews is of Ignazio Silone's *Fontamara*. The review, "Happy Days in Fascist Italy," appeared in the October 2, 1934, issue of *New Masses* and represents Mangione's earliest attempt to explain fascism to a U.S. audience. Henry Hart published an interesting interview with Pirandello, titled "As Benito Desires Me," also in *New Masses*.

The power of Mangione's antifascist writing comes from his ability to depict the effects of fascism on the common people. The theoretical arguments of writers such as Salvemini and Borgese take on flesh and voice through Mangione's anecdotal portrayals of relatives and former Americans living in Italy. Nowhere is this more obvious than in two short stories that Mangione published in *Globe* magazine. In "Sicilian Policeman" (May 1937), Mangione profiles a distant cousin who is a policeman. The story depicts the abuse the Italian authorities take from civilians. In "A Man's Best Audience Is His Horse" (April–May 1938) Mangione presents a strong antifascist perspective through Giovanni, a Neapolitan horse-and-buggy taxi driver who is believed to be crazy because he criticizes the fascist government in conversations with his horse named Garibaldi. Giovanni will not talk philosophy and politics with his wife, Assunta because she considers Mussolini to be a "good-looking genius" (33). In these two stories, Mangione created parables that portray the antiauthoritarian nature of the common Italian people.

He presents a more sophisticated overview of the effects of fascism in his novel *The Ship and the Flame* (1948). The protagonist, Stiano Argento, is one of several characters fleeing fascist and Nazi powers. Argento, a professor of Italian history and literature in Sicily, unjustly accused of antifascist activities, escapes the fascist authorities with the help of local Sicilian people and is smuggled aboard the Portuguese ship *Setubal*. Aboard the ship is Austrian anti-Nazi writer Josef Renner and several refugees from other parts of Europe. The ship, piloted by a fascist-sympathizing captain, is headed for Mexico. On the way from Lisbon, a Nazi submarine stops the ship and three men are to be taken off, including Renner, who is wanted by the Nazis for his earlier anti-Nazi actions. After escaping, Renner, a friend of Stiano since their college days, finds he is unable to further resist the Nazis and commits suicide. Among Renner's papers is a draft of a novel based on Argento's antifascist activities, which Argento burns after reading.

Denied entry into Mexico, the *Setubal* heads for Nazi-controlled Casablanca, where Stiano believes the captain will turn over his passengers. Stiano, a liberal Catholic, realizes that the prayers his wife urges him to make will not be enough; he must act to save the passengers from the captain, a Mussolini-like figure who is determined to return his cargo to a place where many will face death or internment in concentration camps. Argento, inspired by Renner's death and his writing, takes control of the situation and is able to douse the flame of fascism that threatens to engulf the ship. Argento's decision to act comes from the guilt he feels about having let the flame develop the power that virtually destroyed his Sicilian homeland. Through his actions and those of Renner's Polish mistress, Tereza Lenska, the entire group, except for Peter Sadona, a Yugoslavian accused of being a revolutionary, are allowed to enter the United States.

Mangione, aware of the dilemma of the liberal and the fate of the revolutionary in the world, created a microcosm of the larger world of his time that, while suggesting that the struggle against fascism can be won through heroic action, reminds us that intolerance and persecution of those who think and especially act differently than those who enforce the order of other forms of government still remains.

Another strong Italian American public voice of antifascism was Frances Winwar, who Anglicized her Italian name Vinciguerra at her publisher's suggestion so that it would fit on the spine of her first book. Winwar is the only Italian American writer besides di Donato to speak at an American Writers' Congress. At the Second American Writers' Congress in 1937, her

presentation, "Literature under Fascism," described the effects of fascist repression on Italian literature of the 1930s and suggested that unless fascism
is fought, similar consequences would face writers in other countries. Winwar
concludes her survey of contemporary Italian literature by announcing that
"The dark 'Seicento' has come again over intellectual Italy. Fortunately there
are exiles. Wandering from land to land, from country to country, they and
their works are the living proof that the best of Italy cannot be destroyed"
(91). Winwar echoed these sentiments a few weeks later in her review of a
translation of Alberto Moravia's *Wheel of Fortune* in the *New Republic* in
which she berates the novel and most of contemporary Italian literature not
coming from fascist exiles for seeming to "have been written in a vacuum . . . in
some Never Never Land . . . far removed from the Italy of dictatorships and
Ethiopian conquests . . . " (165).

Whereas Winwar unabashedly displayed her antifascist beliefs in her
critical articles, she displaced these direct attacks by devoting her time to
literary biographies: *Poor Splendid Wings: The Rossettis and Their Circle*
(1933) concerned Italian expatriate artists. *The Romantic Rebels* (1935) cov-
ered the revolutionary spirit found in the lives and works of Byron, Shelley,
and Keats, Englishmen living in Italy. In *Farewell the Banner: Coleridge,
Wordsworth and Doroth*y (1938), she creates, as in her other books, an allegory for the contemporary period. In essence, with these books, Winwar
keeps alive the notion of better times in Italy while reinforcing the idea that
great writers can indeed affect history. For a more detailed look at what effect
fascism had on Italian art, see Bianco Capraro's "Art under Mussolini."

Like Frances Winwar, novelist and critic Hamilton Basso kept Italian
history and politics out of his fiction; however, he did contribute to the cause
of antifascism through a few of his articles. His most important and interesting contribution is "Italian Notebook" (1938), published in the *New Republic*,
in which he sketches the dark life that fascism has brought to the Italian
people that he experienced through his trip to Italy.

> There is more in Italy than this regime. But slowly, little by little, it
> sinks into your awareness. It is not only the soldiers and the uni-
> forms and the little boys drilling. It is not only the banners and the
> inscriptions on the walls and the vast domed forehead of Il Duce. It
> is something you cannot touch and cannot hear and cannot see. It is
> some dark blight on the human spirit. It is a cold black shadow on
> the land. Slowly it sinks into you, little by little, and in the end you
> are cold all over. You ache for the American sun. (147)

Basso debunks any comparison of Mussolini to Caesar and sees Mussolini as
" . . . an Italian Kingfish . . . a bigger and better version of Huey Long" (149).

Antifascism becomes a major theme in the memoirs of American writers of Italian descent. As we have seen in the writing of Mangione, the fascist movement required public reaction by many Italian American writers who identified both with their homeland and their parents' homeland. Angelo Pellegrini, in *American Dream: An Immigrant's Quest* (1986), one of his book of memoirs, includes a discussion of fascism in his recollections of life in the United States during the Great Depression and concludes after reading *Fontamara* that "America in the depth of the Great Depression was an earthly paradise compared with the many Fontamaras of southern Italy" (163). Pellegrini devotes considerable space to his discussion of *Fontamara* and sees it as "a prelude to the revolutionary literature of the thirties and an inspiration to the new generation of proletarian writers in America" (165). So moved by this novel was Pellegrini that he joined the communist party believing it was an important enough cause to place his "own security in jeopardy in behalf of the common welfare" (168). Pellegrini, who died in early 2001, saw his antifascist activities as the turning point in his life in which the immigrant became the American. He soon, like Fraina and di Donato became disenchanted with the communist party dogma and left.

Not until after the 1940s do antifascist ideas find their way into the fiction of Italian American writers. I once asked poet Felix Stefanile why this happened and he replied, "We were busy working in unions and when the war broke out, a lot of us were busy fighting it through our muscle and not our words." However, in spite of the absence of works published during the period of the rise and fall of Italian fascism, fascism looms large in the literary imagination of American writers of Italian descent. Its presence as a theme and a force that inspired stories, novels, and poems is something that demands further consideration and analysis. Two prime examples are Michael DeCapite's *No Bright Banner* (1944) and Ben Morreale's *Monday, Tuesday, Never Come Sunday* (1977). Such consideration is essential for the understanding of the role that Italian fascism played in both Americanizing immigrants and Italianizing their children.

One way of proving unquestionable loyalty to the new country would be serving in the military during World War II, and nearly 500,000 Italian Americans served in the armed forces, a higher proportion than any other ethnic group. Poet Felix Stefanile captures the motivation of the young Italian American in "The Dance at Saint Gabriel's:" "In those hag-ridden and race conscious times / we wanted to be known as anti-fascists, / and thus get over our Italian names" (11). The films of Frank Capra during this period celebrated American democratic ideals. *Mrs. Deeds Goes to Town* (1936) and *Meet John Doe* (1941) established a reputation for Capra that would equal Norman Rockwell's for making art that typified American life of the times. Capra put the Italian inside the American. Most of his films deal with the

relationship between the community and the individual, and the moral usually drawn is that without the community, the individual has no identity.
Capra's films are about nobodies who are destroyed when they become
somebodies, and he learned that from southern Italian sensibilities where
the community depends on contributions for survival. To be alone in southern Italian culture is not a positive attribute as some of the proverbs point
out: "Chi non beve in compania, è un ladro o una spia." (He who drinks
alone is either a thief or a spy.) Everything about Capra's films displays his
Sicilian sense of the world transposed to America. But he created those
images on film in an American way, much more so than many later films
that claim to have Italian American themes but miss the mark. From 1935–
1941 Capra served as president of the Academy of Motion Picture Arts and
Sciences. During the war he produced a series of documentary films with
the Signal Service Photographic Detachment titled, "Why We Fight" (1942–
1945). Because of Italy's alliance with the Axis powers, World War II was
not a time to assert one's Italian ancestry. If nothing else, the war turned
Italians into Americans. As Ben Morreale recounts in his autobiographical
novel, *Sicily: The Hallowed Land* (2000): "The army, the war, was the final
assimilation . . . for the second generation Sicilian. It was the good war to
which they all willingly sacrificed themselves and it became the source of
passionate patriotism for many of the second generation. America, after all,
had asked them to serve 'their' country" (186).

Through their participation at home and on the front lines, Italian immigrants proved they could be good Americans and the postwar period saw
the rise of those new Americans in action. Italians continued to play a major
role in what historian Reed Ueda has so aptly called "the cycle of national
creation and re-creation through immigration" (4). After the war, Italians
were among the larger groups of foreign or mixed parentage with 3.3 million. As with other children of immigrants, Italian American artists reflected
the major themes expressed in postwar literature, such as the soldier's return, the generation gap, the sexual revolution, the focus on education, the
struggle for civil rights, interest in jazz, the rise of Catholicism, the creation
of suburban culture, and the rise of mass culture and the consumer society.
As Ueda notes:

> Encouraging the individualist pursuit of pleasure and novel sen-
> sation, [American] consumerist mass culture was at odds with
> certain aspects of their [foreign-born parents'] tradition that
> emphasized moralistic and ascetic values, the stoical acceptance
> of self-denial and abstention for the sake of family propriety. . . .
> Mass culture became a part of their developing a sense of self as
> "ethnic" Americans. (108)

Through mass culture Italian America presented two figures who would become "super Americans." Joe DiMaggio and Frank Sinatra looked on as "secular saints" of sorts became examples of how important the offspring of Italian immigrants could become in the United States. Like the saints through which Italian Americans fashioned examples of how to live their lives, Sinatra and DiMaggio served as examples of Italian American success, promising the same to those who followed in their footsteps. The 1940s and 1950s saw the arrival of more children of immigrants as serious producers of American art. Many of the early writers were returning soldiers and the first of their families to be literate and attend U.S. schools, especially with the help of the G.I. Bill.

John Ciardi, as poet and critic, added new dimensions to *Italianità* in America in 1965 with his translation of Dante's *The Divine Comedy*, which surpassed the 1 million copy mark in paperback. Author of more than forty books of poetry and criticism, Ciardi has done more to popularize poetry than perhaps any other American. Born in the United States, Ciardi traveled to Italy during World War II and in 1956 he received the Rome Prize. Ciardi published more than twenty-five volumes of poetry, some of which dealt with current Italian events. "S.P.Q.R.: A Letter from Rome," published in 1958 in the prestigious *Poetry*, portrays Italian fascism and Mussolini's attempt to re-create the Roman Empire. Ciardi's writing, his work with the *Saturday Review*, and his national radio programs made him a driving force in American poetry, and he was elected to the American Academy of Arts and Letters.

Long before the appearance of his first book of poetry, *River Full of Craft* (1956), Felix Stefanile labored quietly and effectively in the field of American letters. In 1954, with his wife Selma, he founded *Sparrow*, a journal of poetry that is still published nearly 50 years later. His major collections include *A Fig Tree in America* (1970), *East River Nocturne* (1976), and *The Dance at St. Gabriel's* (1995). Winner of the John Ciardi Award for lifetime achievement in Italian American poetry and professor emeritus of English at Purdue University, Stefanile has written some of the most powerful poems depicting life as the child of immigrants caught between two worlds; he gathered many of them in *The Country of Absence: Poems and an Essay* (2000).

The prose fiction of the period just after World War II focused on the struggle to create and enjoy the American Dream. George Panetta, with *We Ride a White Donkey* (1944), *Jimmy Potts Gets a Haircut* (1947), and *Viva Madison Avenue!* (1957), used humor as a means of dealing with his movement from a Little Italy to the advertising world of Madison Avenue. Two of the earliest novels that recount growing up as a daughter of immigrants are by Julia Savarese and Octavia Waldo. Savarese, a playwright and television writer wrote *The Weak and the Strong* (1952). This dark account of life in a

New York Little Italy deals with an Italian American family's struggle to survive immigration and the Great Depression. Waldo's novel, *A Cup of the Sun* (1961), is a powerful coming-of-age story during the World War II and deals with the traumatic experience of familial incest. Rocco Fumento's *Devil by the Tail* (1954) defies the idea of the stereotypic "nice Italian family" by dramatizing a young boy's confronting his father's tyranny as he attempts to forge his own identity. Antonia Pola in *Who Can Buy the Stars* (1957) presents a rare view of how a woman becomes a bootlegger to provide for her family. Michael DeCapite's first two novels portray the evolution from immigrant to ethnic and the effects that assimilation have on three generations of Italian Americans. In *Maria* (1943), the protagonist is an immigrant woman whose marriage to a local bootlegger was arranged by a broker and ends with her being abandoned. *No Bright Banner* (1944) is the coming-of-age story of an Italian American who uses education to escape the destiny of his ancestors. In *The Bennett Place* (1948), DeCapite begins moving away from the Italian American subject to create a novel that focuses on the transition from one social class to another. His early death in a car accident at age forty-three ended what was proving to be a prominent career as an American novelist. As if picking up where his brother left off, Raymond DeCapite wrote *The Coming of Fabrizze* (1960), a wild tale told in the tradition of Mark Twain about an immigrant who starts his Americanization with shovel in hand and ends up playing the stock market, affecting his whole neighborhood. In *A Lost King* (1961), he uses the father-son relationship that is the subject of much of the writing of Italian American men, to dramatize the struggle between generations.

While many of the writers were busy capturing the disappearance of the immigrant generation, others were continuing the radical traditions. Government investigations into communism, launched by U.S. Senator Joseph McCarthy and the House Committee on Un-American Activities, sparked the ire of many Italian American artists. Entertainers such as Frank Sinatra spoke out: "Once they get the movies throttled, how long will it be before we're told what we can say and cannot say into a radio microphone? If you make a pitch on a nationwide radio network for a square deal for the underdog, will they call you a Commie? . . . Are they going to scare us into silence?" (quoted in Patterson 189). Pietro di Donato refused to allow Frank Capra to film his classic *Christ in Concrete* and instead worked with blacklisted director Edward Dmytryk and created a film adaptation of the novel entitled *Give Us This Day* (1949).

Carl Marzani, author of a novel entitled *The Survivor* (1958) and several studies of American Cold War policy and Eurocommunism, suffered a persecution quite similar to Luigi Fraina's. Marzani, who, until his recent death had been writing his memoirs, which reflect a social conscience formed by his political activism of the 1930s, has spent his life fighting injustice through his writing. Born in Italy in 1912, he was just ten years old when he published parodies of fascist songs. In the past seventy years, he had written six books and dozens of pamphlets and film documentaries. In each case, his goal was to make the United States a better place to live by keeping a vigilance over corporate capitalism's fascist tendencies. In 1957 he published *The Open Marxism of Antonio Gramsci*, a translation and annotation of several of Gramsci's prison notes including "Preliminaries to a Study of Philosophy," "Base and Superstructure," "What Is Man," "Marxism and Modern Culture," and "Translation of Philosophic and Scientific Idioms."

Late in his life, the writer, whom Italo Calvino called "the only man truthfully and completely in love with the United States" (xi), shifted his focus to recount the story of his life in a series of books. Marzani had used some of this material in *The Survivor*, his only novel, published in 1958. That was seven years after he was convicted of "defrauding" the government by concealing a reluctant, one-year membership in the communist party. In the novel, Marc Ferranti, a Marzani-like character, is acquitted—a verdict achieved with the help of a senator who reads Ferranti's unpublished autobiography. This story within a story depicts Marzani's response to fascism and his family's flight from Mussolini's fascism and to U.S. democracy. During a scene of a bitter coal miner's strike, Giordano Aurelius, the fictitious name given to Ferranti's father, explains the miners' situation to his son:

> A man doesn't crawl, that's what he means. Mussolini and Fascism are like all the companies and all the Sor Panunzios [a padrone] sitting on top of the Peppones [a strike leader]. By fraud and by force, and a man can't speak, only to say yes sir and thank you sir. They trick and force the people into slavery, beat them into submission so that we bend our backs, walk on four legs, until we are sick with fear and sick with shame and rage. . . . (135)

It is this strong sense of what happened in Italy to his father that leads Ferranti to stand strong against injustice, even if his actions are seen as un-American. This theme replays itself consistently throughout the critical writings of Marzani.

Toward the end of his life, Marzani wrote an autobiography that appeared in volumes. The first, *Roman Childhood* (1992), opens with an "Appreciation" of Marzani by Italo Calvino, who met Marzani during a 1960 visit to the United States. Marzani's firsthand experience of fascism enabled him to recognize it approaching the United States "The key to an understanding of fascism," he writes, "is its destruction of 'existing' democratic institutions" (137). Marzani saw the 1947 loyalty oaths for public servants, ordered by

U.S. President Harry Truman and the American Cold War policies, as the first steps toward fascism in America. He joined the Spanish partisans in their battle against Fascism. "I knew then that if Spain fell the world would be drawn into another war" (Gardaphe, *Dagoes Read* 146).

In *Spain, Munich and Dying Empires* (1993) Marzani recalls his student days in 1936 at Oxford University. Out of curiosity and strong antifascist beliefs, the young scholar visits Spain and finds himself fighting fascism alongside the anarchists in the Spanish Civil War. At the suggestion of his new wife, he reluctantly joined the communist party, an action that he had not given much thought to at the time. "It never crossed my mind that joining the party might embarrass or harm me by jeopardizing my future or making me an outlaw in American society. Given Spain and the CIO [Congress of Industrial Organizations], most Communists and Communist sympathizers were accepted and even respected" (49–50). An honored veteran of World War II for his work in the Office of Strategic Services, Marzani was indicted as a former communist under the Smith Act and spent more than one year in jail as a political prisoner. During this time he wrote a history of the Cold War. Marzani's study, *We Can Be Friends* (1952), introduced by W. E. B. Dubois, argues that the Truman Doctrine and the Korean War were merely "a plan for cold-blooded aggression" (14). The last volume of his memoirs, *From the Pentagon to the Penitentiary* (1995), deals with his persecution by the U.S. government. In the 1970s Marzani continued his study of Eurocommunism and wrote *The Promise of Eurocommunism* (1980), a thorough and critical analysis of Eurocommunism in the 1960s and 1970s.

Because of its dominance during the war, the United States had become a leader in international politics and began using immigration "as a tool for shaping foreign relations to further American self-interest" (Ueda 42). Postwar restrictions on immigration from Italy were relaxed through legislation such as the War Brides Act (1945), the Displaced Persons Act (1948), the McCarran-Walter Act (1952), and the Refugee Relief Act (1953). One beneficiary was Joseph Tusiani who immigrated to the United States shortly after the war so that his family could join his father. Although his first novel, *Envoy from Heaven*, appeared in 1965, he is perhaps best known for his translations of the poetry of Michelangelo and Tasso. He was the first Italian American to be named vice president of the Catholic Poetry Society of America (1956–1968). His "Song of the Bicentennial," written in celebration of America's two hundredth birthday questions the meaning of *Italianità* or Italianness in America and its relation to the immigrant's identity: "Then, who will solve this riddle of my day? / Two languages, two lands, perhaps two souls . . . / Am I a man or two strange halves of one?" (*Ethnicity* 5). Through his poetry Tusiani gives voice to those who preceded his arrival:

I am the present for I am the past
of those who for their future came to stay,
humble and innocent and yet outcast.
. . . For this my life their death made ample room (6)

Giose Rimanelli is another postwar immigrant who helped redefine Italian America. Rimanelli's first novel, *Tiro al piccione* (1950), the publication of which was fostered by Cesare Pavese, is a fictionalized autobiographical account of his early years in Molise and his experiences during World War II in Italy. This novel, translated into English by Ben Johnson as *The Day of the Lion* (1954), received critical praise and became an American best-seller. Six years and several novels later, Rimanelli came to America to give a lecture at the Library of Congress, after which he was invited to teach and travel throughout North and South America. Even before moving to America, Rimanelli was beginning to examine the American influence on life in Italy. In his second novel, *Peccato originale* (*Original Sin*, 1957) he gives us the story of a Molisani family and the father's (Nicola) obsession with the dream of coming to the United States. Early in the 1970s he wrote his first novel in English, *Benedetta in Guysterland* (1993), which parodies the Mafia stories of Mario Puzo and Gay Talese. The novel won an American Book Award.

The continuation of a radical heritage Giovannitti, Sacco and Vanzetti, and New York congressman Vito Marcantonio began can be found in the poetry of Vincent Ferrini, *No Smoke* (1941), *Injunction* (1943), and *Know Fish* (1980). A labor activist, Ferrini carried on the worker-writer tradition using the experience of work and injustice to dignify the world of American workers. The same heritage is celebrated by those who would gain recognition as members of the Beat movement. America's beatniks arose in response to an apolitical complacency that seemed to set in directly after the war. As precursors of the 1960's "hippies," the Beats fused art and politics to raise American consciousness about the politics of life and the life of humanity.

Lawrence Ferlinghetti, Gregory Corso, and Diane di Prima were key figures during this period and profoundly affected America's literary scene. Ferlinghetti, well-known founder of City Lights Books and Bookstore of San Francisco (the first paperback bookstore in the United States), published Allen Ginsberg's *Howl* (1956), the subject of a precedent-setting censorship trial in the late 1950s. Ferlinghetti became San Francisco's first poet laureate. His classic, "The Old Italians Dying" is a testament to the dying immigrant culture and was first published on the op-ed page of the *Los Angeles Times*. The driving force behind the poetry and prose of Diane di Prima is a gender- and culture-based tension created between men and women and between Italian and American culture. Her *Memoirs of a Beatnik* (1969) was the first major autobiography by an Italian American woman, and the poetry in her

Revolutionary Letters (1971) acknowledges a strong connection to her grandfather's leftist politics. *Recollections of My Life as a Woman* (2001), a memoir, returns to the troubled times before she left home (when *Memoirs* begins) and struggles to uncover and process the family secrets that have haunted her.

Government investigations into organized crime, led by Estes Kefauver, brought Italians to the attention of millions of Americans through the new and pervasive medium of television. "Television," wrote cultural critic George Lipsitz, "provided a forum for redefining American ethnic, class, and family identities into consumer identities" (47). Plots of shows such as *The Goldbergs, Life with Luigi,* and *I Remember Mama,* offered purchasing products as a way to assimilate into American culture. However, the only major Italian presence on American television, beyond performers such as Perry Como, Frank Sinatra, Dean Martin, and Connie Francis, were televised U.S. Senate hearings on crime and the gangsters on the popular program *The Untouchables.*

Mario Puzo, whose earliest works, *Dark Arena* (1955) and *The Fortunate Pilgrim* (1964), received critical acclaim without financial success, took advantage of the nation's new obsession with Mafia and wrote *The Godfather* (1969). Not since Pietro di Donato had a U.S. author of Italian descent been thrust into the national spotlight. The timing of the novel's publication had much to do with its rapid climb to number one and its long sixty-seven-week stay on the *New York Times* best-seller list. The effect of *The Godfather* was tremendous; since its publication, and especially since its film adaptations in the early 1970s, Italian American novelists have been writing in its shadow.

Gay Talese is a noted journalist and pioneer of the New Journalism style of writing nonfiction. His work, which has invited comparisons to Truman Capote and Tom Wolfe, explores some of America's postwar social preoccupations. He explores the Mafia phenomenon through the Bonanno crime family in *Honor Thy Father* (1971). His memoir, *Unto the Sons* (1992), captures the forces of history that have shaped modern Italy and the United States as he tells the story of his father's immigration to the United States.

Ben Morreale's first novel, *The Seventh Saracen* (1959), depicts the return of an Italian American to his ancestral homeland in Sicily. *A Few Virtuous Men* (1973), is a literary thriller about Sicily and what living on the other side of the Mafia is like. Its main character, a priest, recounts his life among Mafiosi. In *Monday Tuesday . . . Never Come Sunday* (1977) Morreale explores America in the 1930s through the eyes of a young Sicilian American protagonist. Set in Brooklyn's Bensonhurst, on a block called "Lu Vaticanu," the novel portrays a young man's coming of age during the tough times of the 1930s.

The war and education in U.S. schools brought Italian American writers in contact with the world outside of Little Italy and opened up their imaginations and creativity to the modernist experiments. Increasingly postwar Italian Americans were making their way into and through U.S. universities. Diana Cavallo, a professor of creative writing at the University of Pennsylvania, once worked as a psychiatric social worker, and from these experiences she created her novel *A Bridge of Leaves* (1961). Joseph Papaleo, once the director of creative writing at Sarah Lawrence College, began his writing career by publishing short stories in major periodicals such as *Dial*, *Epoch*, *Harper's*, and *New Yorker*. His two novels, *All the Comforts* (1967) and *Out of Place* (1970), both deal with the psychological struggle of the second-generation Italian American to find a respectable place for himself in U.S. society. *Streets of Gold* (1974) by Evan Hunter, whose real name is Salvatore Lombino, was an example of the autobiographical fiction that appeared during this period. Hunter also used the pseudonym Ed McBain, among others, to pen hundreds of detective and science fiction novels. The fiction produced in the 1960s and 1970s fashioned a number of myths that would be explored, exploited, and challenged by later generations of Italian American writers.

Chapter 3

Mythologies of Italian America
From Little Italys to Suburbs

In 1971 Michael Novak's *The Rise of the Unmeltable Ethnics: Politics and Culture in American Life* woke up Americans to the realities that "white" ethnicities were not lost in a fog of assimilation. Novak pointed to the ambivalent attitude of progressive intellectuals toward the early-twentieth-century immigrant as one example of the effect of a melting pot mentality. Their ambivalence, said Novak, resulted from their privileging individual accomplishments over those of the family and community. For Italian Americans, the fifth largest ethnic group in the United States, the years since the publication of Novak's book have been challenging in terms of developing leaders on all fronts, but most especially in terms of developing intellectuals, those Novak describes as creators of, rather than distributors of, intellectual culture. Those Italian Americans who have become intellectuals have followed a model in which alienation from one's birth community and often birth class was, more often than not, a requirement for acceptance into the club.

In the process of assimilating into American culture, the children and grandchildren of Italian immigrants fashioned a mythology of Italian America that would become the foundation of the visual explorations of Italian American life found in films of Francis Ford Coppola's *The Godfather* (1972) and *The Godfather Part II* (1974) and Martin Scorsese's *Mean Streets* (1973). These films contributed several character types to postwar American culture including the gangster and the uneducated urban blue-collar worker. Prior to the 1960s very few American writers of Italian descent had been educated through college. As a group, Italian Americans would not surpass the national average of the college educated until the 1990s; an increasing number of those who were becoming writers would be those who had graduated from college. Political activists Mario Savio, a leader of the free speech movement at the University of California at Berkeley; Daniela Gioseffi, *In Bed with the Exotic Enemy* (1997), who worked in the civil rights movement; and Father

James Groppi were products of the new awakening of the children and grand-children of immigrants.

During a time when the very definition of *American* was being challenged and changed, Italian American writers were busy exploring their own American histories. Helen Barolini's novel *Umbertina* (1979) appeared during American ethnic revival period just after the publication of Alex Haley's *Roots* (1976). *Umbertina* tells the story of four generations of Italian American women focusing on the immigrant matriarchal grandmother, her granddaughter, and her great-granddaughter. *Umbertina* is a novel of self-discovery, a bildungsroman that spans four generations, but that can be read as the historical evolution of the Italian woman into the American woman, as the feminization of the Italian woman as she becomes the Italian American woman.

America's postwar feminist movement had a strong effect on the daughters of the immigrants. Social activist Eleanor Curtri Smeal became president of the National Organization of Women and a spirit of similar social action and the redefinition of the American women became subjects of several novels by Italian American women. Dorothy Calvetti Bryant explored a specifically Italian notion of feminism in her novels *Ella Price's Journal* (1972), *Miss Giardino* (1978), and *Anita, Anita* (1993), a historical recreation of the life of the wife of Italian risorgimento leader Giuseppe Garibaldi. Under the impetus of urban renewal programs, many Italian ghettos throughout major U.S. cities were razed, forcing those residents who could not flee to the suburbs to find homes outside their traditionally ethnocentric Little Italys. Tina De Rosa's *Paper Fish* (1980) tells the story of a young girl who comes of age in a disintegrating Little Italy. De Rosa's tale achieves a timeless quality through her creation of a world unaffected by any history beyond that of the personal history of the family. The author, who can only imagine the southern Italian culture into which her grandmother was born, disconnects her characters from historical time and suggests that the journey toward self is a continuous quest, uninterrupted by the passing of generations. By creating the archetypal figure of the grandmother, the image of Italy will remain inside Carmolina as long as the memory of her grandmother is kept alive. De Rosa, an eyewitness, recorded the experience of the death of place and the inevitable dissolution of an accompanying culture in a language that she has said was impossible for her ancestors to articulate. Similarly Tony Ardizzone, who turned from student protester to creative writer and professor of creative writing at Indiana University, captured this experience in "Nonna," a short story in his Flannery O'Connor award-winning collection *The Evening News* (1986). His novels include *Heart of the Order* (1986) and *In the Garden of Papa Santuzzu* (1999) which depicts the immigration of a Sicilian family through different points of view.

The shift from urban to suburban ethnicity is the subject of the writing of many young Italian Americans who watched as their families moved from working-class to middle-class life. Anthony Giardina's novels *A Boy's Pretensions* (1988) and *Recent History* (2001), and collection of short fiction, *The Country of Marriage* (1997), exquisitely capture this experience. George Veltri's *A Nice Boy* (1995) explores the impact drug use has on the grandson of immigrants. The myth of Italian identity and its reinvention is the subject of Carole Maso's *Ghost Dance* (1986), a novel that tells the story of a third-generation ethnic who, unlike earlier generations, has the option of picking and choosing from the many traditions comprising American culture. The Italian characteristics the protagonist, Vanessa Turin, does not inherit directly through experiences with her grandparents, she imagines and reinvents to fulfill her needs. Few novels capture so well the effects of the fragmentation that occurs when solid cultural traditions are fractured. Maso's subsequent novels, *The Art Lover* (1990), *Ava* (1992), *The American Woman in the Chinese Hat* (1993), and *Defiance* (1998), explore lesbian themes as central to the American experience and are all daring steps into new forms of narrating fiction.

The myth of the dominance of the macho Italian American male is challenged by many of the women writers, but none as effectively as Josephine Gattuso Hendin in *The Right Thing to Do* (1988). This critically acclaimed novel of a young woman growing out of the shadow of her immigrant father earned an American Book Award. Hendin vividly presents the drama of a young woman's attempts to make her own way outside of her family and her father's expectations. As the daughter Gina rebels, her father weakens in health; as he moves closer to death, she comes closer to understanding his life and the legacy she will inherit.

Robert Viscusi, one of the foremost critics of Italian American literature and culture, president of the Italian American Writers' Association and director of the Ethyle R. Wolfe Institute for the Humanities at Brooklyn College, has captured what it means to be Italian American in a time when that identity is challenged as never before with his novel *Astoria* (1995), winner of an American Book Award. In his imaginary autobiography he presents an extended meditation on the meaning of cultures European and American, mother and madonna, father and padrino, on one's love of the lost and the lost loves of one's past.

The rise of the minority political power during the postwar period is reflected in the novels of the late Robert Ferro, *The Family of Max Desir* (1983), *The Blue Star* (1985), and *Second Son* (1988), which explore the complex relationships among gay Italian Americans, their families, and straight and gay communities. Felice Picano has proven to be one of the most prolific writers of the Italian American gay community through his stories, novels, and literary leadership. Rachel Guido deVries's *Tender Warriors* (1986) and

How to Sing to a Dago (1995) and Mary Saracino's *No Matter What* (1993) and its sequel *Finding Grace* (1994) speak in lesbian voices that affirm ethnic identity and community inclusion as strongly as they attack the myth of the normal, patriarchal, and heterosexual Italian American family. A collection of autobiographical essays, *Fuori* (1996), and an anthology of writing collected by Giovanna (Janet) Capone, Denise Nico Leto, and Tommi Avicolli Mecca titled *Hey Paesan!* (1999) attest to the variety of gay and lesbian experiences in Italian America.

Although some of the most powerful presences of Italian Americans on the U.S. stage can be found in Tennessee Williams's *Rose Tattoo* (1951) and Arthur Miller's *A View from the Bridge* (1955), Italian Americans such as Michael Gazzo, Mario Fratti, and Albert Innaurato have had a great impact on American theater. Gazzo's *A Hatful of Rain* (1955), dealing with drugs and family, emerged from improvisations at New York's famous Actors' Studio. Fratti, who immigrated to the United States in the 1960s as a respected and established playwright, has been a consistent presence in the New York theater scene with productions such as *The Cage* (1966), *The Victim* (1968), and *Nine* (1982), his stage adaptation of Federico Fellini's film *8¹/₂*. Innaurato, born in 1948 in South Philadelphia, studied at the Yale School of Drama and has written several influential plays: *The Transformation of Benno Blimpie* (1973), the Broadway hit *Gemini* (1976), and *Coming of Age in Soho* (1984), all of which have helped paved the way for a more direct recognition of the realities and fantasies of Italian American culture when the worlds of Little Italy and the Ivy League collide. Joe Pintauro, whose early work as a novelist included *Cold Hands* (1979) and *State of Grace* (1983), has had numerous plays produced off-Broadway and at Long Island venues. *The Moon Dreamers* (1969) by Julie Bovasso, the first Italian American female playwright, paved the way for contemporary works by female playwrights such as Jo Ann Tedesco's *Sacraments* (1978) and Teresa Carilli's "Dolores Street" and "Wine Country" published in *Women as Lovers* (1996).

Contemporary poets who have had an impact on American culture include Lewis Turco, whose *A Handbook of Poetics* (1968) and *Poetry: An Introduction through Writing* (1973) established Turco as a promising young talent in teaching poetry; he fulfilled that promise with *New Book of Forms* (1986), *Visions and Revisions of American Poetry* (1986), and *The Public Poet, Five Lectures on the Art and Craft of Poetry* (1991). Besides his scholarly and critical books, Turco has amassed a healthy body of his own poetry from *First Poems* (1960) and *Awaken, Bells Falling: Poems 1957–1967* (1960) to his *The Shifting Web: New and Selected Poems* (1989). Maria Mazziotti Gillan, professor of English and director of creative writing at SUNY, University at Binghamton, is founder and director of the Poetry Center at Passaic County Community College, editor of *Footwork: The Paterson Literary*

Review, and co-editor of acclaimed anthologies, *UnSettling America* (1994), *Identity Lessons* (1999), and *Growing Up Ethnic in America* (1999). Her collections include *Flowers from the Tree of Night* (1982), *Taking Back My Name* (1989), *Where I Come From: Selected and New Poems* (1995), and *Things My Mother Told Me* (1999). Dana Gioia, who published *Daily Horoscope* (1986) and *The Gods of Winter* (1991), is a leading poet in the language school. David Citino, a professor of English at Ohio State University, author of *The Appassionata Doctrines* (1985), and W. S. DiPiero, author of *The Dog Star* (1990), are among the best of younger poets. Sandra Gilbert, a pioneer of feminist theory and scholarship, has written poetry about her identity as an Italian American in *In the Fourth World: Poems* (1978), *Emily's Bread: Poems* (1984), and *Blood Pressure* (1988). Jay Parini's *Anthracite Country* (1982) and *Town Life: Poems* (1998), reflect life thoughts about Italy and America. Noted editor and translator Jonathan Galassi's poetry is collected in *Morning Run: Poems* (1988). Rose Romano's *Vendetta* (1992) and *The Wop Factor* (1994) unite the personal and the political in strong poetry. Thom Tammaro's *When the Italians Came to My Home Town* (1995), combines prose and poetry to explore the impact an immigrant past has had on his identity.

Fiction produced in the 1980s and 1990s began recreating the immigrant experience from the perspective of the grandchildren. Among the major texts reflecting this point of view are Gilbert Sorrentino's *Aberration of Starlight* (1980), George Cuomo's *Family Honor* (1983), Michael Anania's *The Red Menace* (1984), Kenny Marotta's *A Piece of Earth* (1985), Jay Parini's *The Patch Boys* (1986), and Denise Giardina's *Storming Heaven* (1994). Key writers of short fiction who deal with similar themes are Mary Bush in *A Place of Light* (1991); Anne Calcagno in *Pray for Yourself* (1993); George Cuomo in *Sing Choirs of Angels* (1969); John Fante in *The Wine of Youth* (1985), and Agnes Rossi in *The Quick* (1992). Flannery O'Connor awards for short fiction collections have gone to Salvatore La Puma for *Boys of Bensonhurst* (1987) and Rita Ciresi for *Mother Rocket* (1993). Renee Manfredi earned an Iowa Short Fiction Award for her story collection *Where Love Leaves Us* (1994).

Several scholars have turned from critiquing to creating literature. A professor of English at Duke University, Frank Lentricchia has created a trilogy of works focusing on his experiences of growing up in a Little Italy, *Johnny Critelli and The Knifemen* (1996); growing out of Little Italy, *The Edge of Night* (1994); and returning to a Little Italy in *Music of the Inferno* (1999). In these works Lentricchia draws breath from Mario Puzo, Edgar Allan Poe, and James Joyce, and blood from filmmakers Federico Fellini, Martin Scorsese, and Brian De Palma to create his own approach to familiar themes. For example, in *The Music of the Inferno*, Robert Tagliaferro, an orphan child of unknown racial background, makes a grim discovery shortly after his eighteenth birthday and leaves his hometown of Utica, New York. The young man takes refuge in a bookstore in New York City where he lives like Ralph Ellison's *Invisible Man*. His book learning replaces his family as he tells us, "In the absence of my father, I acquired knowledge. My knowledge is my memory" (72).

Don DeLillo, who is perhaps the most accomplished living American writer of Italian descent, was born to Italian immigrants. His early life was spent in the urban settings of the Bronx and Philadelphia where he most likely experienced the type of neighborhoods he writes of in a few of his early stories. He attended Fordham University. Of his entire body of published work, only two of his earliest stories are set in Little Italy and these are the only works that overtly use Italian American subjects as protagonists. In his first novel, *Americana* (1971), the American middle-class values that DeLillo infuses in his protagonist David Bell are the very values that become goals for the ethnic who wishes to become American. By exploring the "other," DeLillo issues a warning to those who would covet Americanness and attempt to remake themselves in the image and likeness of the stereotypical American. Although his writing has earned some of the most prestigious prizes the United States offers (a Guggenheim, a National Book Award, and the Pen Faulkner), it was not until *Underworld* (1997) that he created a protagonist of Italian American descent. The natural move for the child of immigrants is away from the world of the parents and toward the larger world of mainstream America. *Underworld* maps these steps from Nick Shay's origins in Bronx to his later life in Arizona. Along the way DeLillo tells the story of the transition of a Cold War America into a postmodern present.

Perhaps the most eloquent tragicomic Italian American fiction can be found in Anthony Valerio's *Valentino and the Great Italians, According to Anthony Valerio* (1986). In this collection of twenty-two literary essays, Valerio elevates regular Joes and Josephines as easily (and as wittily) as he levels the stature of household names such as Enrico Caruso, Frank Sinatra, and Joe DiMaggio. He has been called the Philip Roth of Italian American literature. His earlier fiction in *The Mediterranean Runs through Brooklyn* (1982) wove imaginative chiaroscuro flights into Italian American history and his own life. In *Conversation with Johnny* (1997; republished as *Lefty and the Button Men*, 2000), he pushed even further ahead by tackling two stereotypes that have plagued Italian Americans: the gangster and the lover. In this sometimes parodic, sometimes sardonic, but always entertaining look at crime and culture, Valerio attempts a literary hit on those stereotypes. Even though he might not eliminate them, he certainly paralyzes both of them long enough for us to see that "the cult of *The Godfather*" is over.

One of the best novels reflecting the working-class experience is Chuck Wachtel's *Joe the Engineer* (1983), which tells the story of Joe Lazaro, a Vietnam War veteran who has returned home ready to enter the traditional American working-class life. Wachtel, who is half Italian American and half Jewish American, has portrayed the idea of the hybrid American in his 1995 novel, *The Gates*, in which Primo Thomas is born to an African American father and an Italian American mother.

Postmodern experimental writing in an Italian American vein can be found in Gilbert Sorrentino's later work and the experimental fiction of Mary Caponegro's *The Star Cafe* (1990) and *Five Doubts* (1998). Mark Ciabattari has created two novels that might be considered quintessential postmodern fiction, *Dreams of an Imaginary New Yorker Named Rizzoli* (1990) and *The Literal Truth: Rizzoli Dreams of Eating the Apple of Earthly Delights* (1994), and Dennis Barone's poetry *Forms/Froms* (1988) and fiction *Abusing the Telephone* (1994), *Echoes* (1997), and *Temple of the Rat* (2000), provide evidence that the Italian American experience is varied, plural, and very much capable of reinventing itself as it moves further away from the immigrant experience.

Richard Gambino wrote in a 1983 article, "If any of the traditional Italian values are to survive, they can no longer rely solely on the custom of family education. Italian Americans must become conscious of their traditional values through formal education" ("Measure for Success" 15). Only recently have Italian Americans entered schools of higher education in numbers approaching the national average, in spite of the fact that for two decades Italian Americans have earned incomes well above the national average. But attending college is no guarantee that Italians could become conscious of what might be their traditional values, unless those values created conflicts with the system. The answer for Italian American culture then is to find ways of transmitting their culture through American educational and cultural institutions, and for this to happen, Italian American intellectuals must work both inside and outside Italian American communities.

And so we must look to the margins of mainstream culture, away from the centers in which traditional American cultural critics such as Lentricchia, Paglia, and Gilbert have achieved a powerful cultural currency, to observe attempts to create new power centers from which Italian American culture might develop. Italian American intellectuals such as Robert Viscusi, whose work on Italian American literature has paved the way for critics such as myself, has built a foundation on which an Italian American discourse can be staged. For a long time Viscusi was on his own, producing some of the most interesting criticism of Italian American literature. In many of his articles he offers a different critical approach that relies heavily on the reader's need to understand Italian culture and the context it creates for interpreting Italian American narrative. I think of him as the Leslie Fielder or the Henry Louis Gates of Italian American criticism. In his important essay "Breaking the Silence: Strategic Imperatives for Italian American Culture," Viscusi sets forth a program designed to realize a distinctive discursive power that would allow "its possessors to grapple directly with the problems that confront them" (3). Viscusi's tripartite program calls for the development of three possessions that discursive power requires: (1) the creation of a language; (2) the creation of a narrative, or the articulation of a "collective purpose"; and (3) the creation of a dialectics that would "proceed from a double tongue and a double narrative of passage." Such a narrative would enable the deconstruction of "the monotone discourse of weakness that has led us to repose so much tacit faith in the forms of ethnic self-enclosure" (9). In his article "Narrative and Nothing," Viscusi has begun to observe the replication of Italian archetypes (found in the works of Dante, Boccaccio, and others) in Italian American literature. Viscusi's work as president of the Italian American Writers' Association and as director of the Ethyle R. Wolfe Institute for the Humanities at Brooklyn College, in which he has begun to provide Italian American writers and intellectuals with long-awaited forums for dissemination of their thought, identifies him as a leading force in the attempt to institutionalize Italian American culture.

Raymond Belliotti, a professor of philosophy at SUNY College at Fredonia and a seasoned scholar of ethics and public policy, has linked his Italian American upbringing to his latest analysis of the interaction between family and community influences on individual behavior. In *Seeking Identity: Individualism versus Community in an Ethnic Context*, (1995) Belliotti presents the dilemma of growing up Italian in the United States. Belliotti's narrative style reveals the tension between being an intellectual and being an Italian American. His writing combines static professional jargon and a fluid autobiographical narrative. Alternately didactic and dramatic, Belliotti reveals that there is a personal in the political, reminding us that the intellectual, whether artist or critic, is shaped by his or her relationship to the family, community, and the nation-state. What is unique about Belliotti's study is that it considers and responds to ideas presented by other Italian American intellectuals, especially in his chapter, "The Gendered Self Struggles with the Family," in which he critiques both Richard Gambino's and Helen Barolini's ideas of the image of the woman in Italian American culture. Belliotti also draws extensively from the work of sociopolitical historian Nunzio Pernicone to present a historical survey of the relationships between anarchy, Italian style, and political theory.

Literary critic and scholar Anthony Tamburri is representative of the best of contemporary Italian American intelligentsia. Born in the working-class ethnic community of Stamford, Connecticut, Tamburri worked his way through college Southern Connecticut State College, Middlebury College, and the University of California at Berkeley. One of his earliest forays into the field of American studies was a manifesto-styled essay, *To Hyphenate or Not to Hyphenate: The Italian American Writer—An "Other" American Writer* (1991), which drew out pertinent questions regarding any literature we consider ethnic and developed a theoretical model for the basis of future studies. In this essay, Tamburri questioned the arbitrary construction of rules that most of us take for granted. In that questioning he revealed how they contribute to the distance our society has created among its cultures.

Tamburri's essay serves as a vital challenge to sociologist Richard Alba's notion of the "twilight of ethnicity." As he examines the marginalizing process and its effects, Tamburri comes to the conclusion that Italian American writers are re-covering as they discover their pasts and add it to their self-identities. From here, he moves into a discussion of the hyphen. Using a paradigm Daniel Aaron established in "The Hyphenate Writer and American Letters," Tamburri presented the evolutionary stages that occur within an author as well as among generations. He elaborated on this evolution in his recent *A Semiotic of Ethnicity: In (Re)cognition of the Italian American Writer* (1998). Using Charles Sanders Peirce's notion of "firstness," "secondness," and "thirdness," Tamburri complicates earlier readings of the Italian American writer and enables us to examine the evolution of ethnic consciousness that takes place within a writer's artistic development.

Scholar and poet Mary Jo Bona makes an observation in an important essay that brings awareness to a double burden carried by Italian American women writers: "Italian American women writers have explored the vital connection between being a woman and being ethnic in a world (America) which traditionally has valued neither" ("Broken Images" 91). Because of this burden, many Italian American women writers have had to take on the dual role of creator and critic of Italian American literature. In the process they have become strong leaders in the development and advocacy of Italian American literary culture, an accomplishment historians and scholars of American literature have not formally recognized. Consequently, Italian American female writers, much more so than their male counterparts, have become the organic intellectuals of their ancestral culture.

Italian American female writers are struggling against the constraints placed on them from both inside and outside of their ethnic culture. Add to these cultural constraints the usual issues of negotiating one's place in the vast array of English and American literary history and the struggle to find a style, a voice, a publisher, and one begins to see why becoming writers is so difficult for Italian American women. Perhaps this is why so many Italian American women take on a dual burden in their work as writers. It is this dual requirement that makes writing into extremely challenging work for Italian American women as they attempt to reconcile past and present, old world and new.

Typically, women were not expected to attend college; but when they did go, it was often with their parents' hopes that they would just find husbands. Faced with such restrictive barriers erected by family and tradition, the Italian American woman who would be a writer could only become one by directly challenging the forces that attempted to keep her tied down to traditional roles. And part of that challenge required fighting the image that the larger society had created for her to emulate. Shortly after the publication of *The Dream Book* (1985), Rose Romano, a poet, editor, and freelance typesetter, undertook a pioneering literary project when she launched *la bella figura*, a literary journal devoted entirely to writing by Italian American women. The first issue, entitled "Omertà," featured poetry, short fiction, and reviews from both well-known and first-time published writers. Maria Mazziotti Gillan and Rachel Guido deVries are two of the better known writers featured in the debut issue.

Romano started the journal after literary magazines began publishing work in which she was using what she called "this ethnically unspecified presumed to be WASP persona" (Gardaphe, "Romano" 194). When she started writing about being Italian American, all of a sudden nobody wanted to publish her work, which led her to start her own magazine. Thus, Romano joined other Italian American women, such as Helen Barolini, who have taken the wheel when it comes to directing the promotional drive of Italian American writers. Romano's motivation comes from her feeling that Italian American women were not taken seriously. In an interview, she says, "We're not considered real; we're Europeans, and Europeans run the world; it seems that no matter where we go we get it for being something; you're never the right thing. Now it's like we're American enough that we can afford to be Italian. We're not foreigners anymore" (195). Through her own writing and the publications she created with her malafemmina press, Romano helped create a sense of a distinctive culture and tradition of Italian American women writers that would serve as models.

Marianna DeMarco Torgovnick, an established critic and scholar, has documented her story of assimilation in *Crossing Ocean Parkway: Readings by an Italian American Daughter*. "What I tell here," she wrote, "is different from the story of arrival. It is the story of assimilation—one that Italian Americans of my generation are uniquely prepared to tell, and that females need to tell most of all" (x). Although Torgovnick has acknowledged her ancestral culture in writing, she has only indirectly taken on the responsibility of contributing to the institutionalization of that culture.

With *Claiming a Tradition: Italian American Women Writers*, Mary Jo Bona joins Olga Peragallo, Rose Basile Green, and Helen Barolini as one of the great advocates of Italian American literature. What separates Bona from the others is her command of cultural and literary theories that help place Italian American women's writing in the context of U.S. history. Hers is a most important contribution to the field of American literature in general and women's studies and Italian American culture in particular.

Claiming a Tradition is the first book-length study of Italian American women writers, and Bona's clear writing and lucid arguments make it accessible to the casual reader as well as the professional scholar. From the opening, a strong, authoritative, and confident voice guides us along. A solid introduction places the literature in the context of U.S. literary history and ethnic studies. Bona does an excellent job of setting up the background against which her readers are projected. She writes, "claiming a tradition for Italian American women writers is an act of assertion in the face of possible resistance" (1). She then shows us the many sites that generate that resistance in mainstream U.S. culture and from within Italian American culture itself. Furthermore, she includes a good summary of earlier critical work on the literature so that we know we are listening to someone who has done her homework.

The bulk of the study explores elements of *Italianità* that Bona finds inside each of the works she reads. These include the role of the mother, "l'ordine della famiglia," "destino," "la via vecchia," "comparaggio," and "omertà." She structures her chapters by pairing texts that highlight concepts such as family in Mari Tomasi's *Like Lesser Gods* (1949) and Marion Benasutti's *No Steady Job for Pappa* (1966); coming-of-age in Octavia Waldo's *A Cup of the Sun* (1961) and Josephine Gattuso Hendin's *The Right Thing to Do* (1988); personal identity in Diana Cavallo's *A Bridge of Leaves* (1961) and Dorothy Byrant's *Miss Giardino* (1978); and recovering ancestry in Helen Barolini's *Umbertina* (1979) and Tina DeRosa's *Paper Fish* (1980).

In many cases the authors she covers have received little, if any, critical attention. We are witnessing an original contribution to the field of literary criticism and history that advances earlier thinking and scholarship. The study is well integrated; each chapter builds on the previous one the way a narrative might build a plot, except that her story is composed of critical arguments. Her organization helps us witness a tradition evolving. Bona's keen sense of what has been missed by previous scholars stems from the thoroughness of her preparation, the precision of her execution, and her passion for the material. *Claiming a Tradition* represents a mature rethinking and immense reworking of the ideas and the language that were ahead of their time even in the early stages of the development of her thesis. Bona has revised her earlier writing to reflect both her continued passion for literary expression and her mastery of the field. Her methodology of pairing authors works well to bring out commonalties as well as differences. This technique advances her argument that these women are, whether they realize it, creating a real literary tradition. Beyond giving us insight into the past, this study serves the future development of Italian American literature. Her final chapter, "Recent Developments in Italian American Women's Literary Traditions," is a survey of contemporary writers such as Rachel Guido deVries, Renee Manfredi, Agnes Rossi, and Carole Maso and provides us with a good sense of what will be happening in the decades to come. Bona, an accomplished and award-winning poet, has given up much of her career as a creative writer to criticizing and historicizing the writing of Italian American women. Bona's powerful study was published in "Ad Feminam," a series edited by Sandra Gilbert. And while Gilbert may have not yet written critically about Italian American women writers, she became a powerful advocate of Italian American women's writing by publishing this fine study.

Poet and memoir writer Edvige Giunta has managed to bring a great light to many American women writers of Italian descent and, at the same time, establish herself as one of the leading critics of ethnic women's writing in the United States. *Writing with an Accent: Contemporary Italian American Women Authors* collects much of what this leading critic had previously published on Italian American women writers. Included are her afterwords to the reprints of Tina DeRosa's *Paper Fish* and Helen Barolini's *Umbertina*, an essay on Agnes Rossi and Nancy Savoca first appearing in The *Canadian Journal of Italian Studies*, papers delivered at the 1996 and 1997 conferences of the American Italian Historical Association and gathered in the proceedings, and a number of other essays, book chapters, and reviews.

Giunta is able to avoid the traps of a simple recollection of previous work by weaving the pieces together with a strong thread of personal memoir. From her acknowledgements to the last word of her epilogue, she connects the works of the writers she has read by looping their contributions with hers. Many of these writers have depended on Giunta for public exposure, and she continues to carry them with her. Although each chapter may focus on a different writer, Giunta, ever conscious of the collective nature of the women's writing community, reminds us that the work of one is the work of many. She typically includes Louise DeSalvo, Mary Cappello, Maria Mazziotti Gillan, Rosette Capotorto, Kym Ragusa, Nancy Savoca, and Nancy Caronia in many of her chapters.

Categorizing this book is impossible. Is it criticism? Is it a memoir? It is both—and more. This hybrid jumps genres and forms as Giunta connects her life story with the stories that have captured her critical attention. She left her Sicilian home in 1984 to study English literature at the University of Miami. Under the guidance of the eminent scholar and critic John Paul Russo, she completed a dissertation on James Joyce and went on to teach at Union College and New Jersey City University. Readers will not be able to discern this by reading her book. It is her speech, and not her writing style, that betrays her biculturality. Her dedication to the writing of Italian American women signals an embrace of that accent that lesser critics have avoided. One of the limits of this juxtaposition of history, criticism, and memoir is that we too often learn more about the writer than the written: something we expect in the memoir, but not in scholarship. But Giunta finds honor in defiance of tradition.

This book is a triumphal monument to her dedication to the accented subjects of her writing. Risking banishment to the shadows and side streets of literary and cultural discourse, Giunta's work owes a debt to that of Olga Peragallo, Rose Basile Green, Helen Barolini, Mary Jo Bona, Mary Frances Pippino, and Mary Ann Mannino, and she earns unique status for connecting these writers to both Italian and American traditions that enrich us all.

Other writers provide even more evidence of this dual responsibility taken on by Italian American women writers. Maria Gillan publishes writers and gets their books reviewed in the *Paterson Literary Review*; she also sponsors contests, organizes readings, and edits anthologies with major presses—all this in addition to doing her own award-winning writing. Rita Ciresi takes time both from her teaching and her award-winning fiction writing to comment regularly on writers in the journal *Italian Americana*. Mary Ann Mannino, in addition to publishing fiction and poetry, recently published her dissertation on women writers (*Revisionary Identities*, 2000), and Maria Fama has begun making Italian American women poets accessible to readers of Italian through her translations.

The women, more so than the men, have a strong sense of community and of the need to support that community in any way possible. This was not the case, as Helen Barolini so strongly recounts in her essays, with Gay Talese, Mario Puzo, and Jerre Mangione. The development of this work of creating, cataloguing, and criticizing Italian American literature is by nature a collective project that requires the interaction of all concerned so that Italian American writers can achieve the cultural impact they so rightly deserve. The Italian American female writer has taken on this double burden and has showed us best how to get this done.

Contemporary Italian American literature demonstrates a growing literary tradition through a variety of voices. Critical studies, reviews, the publication of anthologies and journals, and the creation of new publishing houses are ample evidence that Italian American culture has gained understandings of its past as it develops a sense of a future. Through organizations such as the American Italian Historical Association, The Italian American Women's Collective, reborn in 2002 as MALIA, and the Italian American Writers' Association, American writers of Italian descent are meeting and exchanging ideas. Contemporary critics of Italian American literature who have produced exciting and vital histories and interpretations are Mary Jo Bona, Thomas Ferraro, Edvige Giunta, Fred Gardaphe, Louise Napolitano, Camille Paglia,

Robert Casillo, Mary Frances Pippino, Justin Vitiello, Luigi Fontanella, and
Paolo Valesio. These are the major voices of contemporary Italian American
criticism who represent the development of an indigenous criticism and the
advancement of a culture that epitomizes the evolution of ethnic identity in
American postwar history.

All these efforts by organic intellectuals have allowed the more traditional, and in some ways more powerful, intellectuals such as Sandra Gilbert, Camille Paglia, Marianna Torgovnick, and Frank Lentricchia to shift
their critical gaze inward to the project of Italian American cultural analysis. The development of this work is by nature a collective project that
requires the interaction of three groups of intellectuals: the Italian
Americanists, the Americanists and the Italianists; cooperation (and in many
cases, collaboration) of all three groups is essential to fashion a discourse
in which the work of Italian American writers can achieve the cultural
power they so rightly deserve. The responsibility then of all intellectuals is
to create knowledge that will not only nurture the next generation, but also
enable intellectuals to connect to, and not shy away from, the communities
that have created them. For as we will see in the next chapter, gaining
recognition as American writers was not always easy for writers of Italian
American descent.

Part II

Thematic Essays

Chapter 4

Left Out
Three Italian American Writers of the 1930s

The project of creating a literary history of the texts American writers of Italian descent produced is a recent development in American cultural studies.[1] The difficulties the historian faced attempting to place these contributions in any historical context are many and compounded by the absence of significant references to and legitimate analyses of these writers in the literary histories that have been produced thus far. Although several reasons exist why contributions of this American subculture have never been adequately documented and examined in the context of American literary history, this chapter considers three possibilities and applies them to three writers whose careers began in and whose perspectives were shaped by the 1930s.

By 1940 three American writers of Italian descent had established an important and respectable presence in American literature. John Fante, born in 1909, had already published half of his lifetime production of short stories in national magazines such as *American Mercury, Atlantic Monthly, Harper's Bazaar,* and *Scribner's Magazine.* He had also published two novels and a collection of his stories. Pietro di Donato, born in 1911, had published "Christ in Concrete," his first short story, in the March 1937 issue of *Esquire*; the story was reprinted in Edward O'Brien's *Best Short Stories of 1938* and expanded into a best-selling novel that was chosen over John Steinbeck's *Grapes of Wrath* as a main selection of the 1939 Book of the Month Club. Jerre Mangione, born in 1909, had numerous articles and book reviews to his credit, and more important, served as national coordinating editor of the Federal Writers' Project. In 1943 Mangione completed a book that Malcolm Cowley lauded as having "more lives than any other book of our time."[2] The bulk of the subsequent writing of these three authors documented the 1930s and 1940s from an ethnic perspective that has received little critical attention.

Although most scholars are familiar with Sacco and Vanzetti—two major figures and objects of left writing of the period—documentation and close reading of Italian participation in American culture has been omitted from most studies of the 1930s.[3] Only Warren French's *The Social Novel at the End of an Era* (1966) includes a brief discussion of di Donato; however, although French acknowledges the "fresh and vigorous viewpoint" that di Donato's novel *Christ in Concrete* (1939) "brought to the American social scene," di Donato is portrayed as an example of "the very irresponsibility that destroyed the age" (17). French includes di Donato, along with Richard Wright, in an epilogue subtitled "Beginners Luck."

This absence is quite characteristic of scholarship even today that has either ignored or outright dismissed the contributions of American writers of Italian descent. The lack of formal experiment in their writing, which would have attracted attention of the New Critics, and their attitudes toward communist party politics, which prevented their being taken up by left-wing critics, have combined to keep these writers out of the major studies of the period. More often than not these writers, if considered at all, are not read in the context of their Italian American heritage and with consideration of ethnic-specific concerns that they addressed in their work. When their writing is recognized, they are usually (mis)read as members of the dominant white Anglo/Saxon culture. Although this practice might please those who wish to erase the stigma of an immigrant past and thus pass as whites, it distorts (if it does not ignore or erase) the social and political problems encountered by Italian Americans and overshadows the contributions they have made to U.S. culture.

America's lack of exposure to the accomplishments of these writers and their impact on the development and evolution of Italian American literature can be attributed to three claims I present with the goal of helping us understand the absence of these three writers in historical accounts and critical writings of and about the 1930s. The first claim concerns the construction of historical categories scholars and critics use to frame the study of this period; the second is based on the interpretative theoretical models that have been traditionally applied to works of this period; the third concerns the religious orientation of these three writers. All three of these claims apply, in varying degrees, to each of the writers presented here. And although other reasons may exist but not considered in the scope of this chapter, I offer these as possible reasons why these three writers have been omitted from every major literary and cultural history produced thus far.

The historical categories that have been constructed by critics and scholars to characterize this period of U.S. history have framed the way we see and study this important period in U.S. history; unfortunately, until only recently, most of the approaches developed and employed have excluded from consideration those cultural products produced by members of minority cultures such as the Italian Americans. One of the problems occurs when the definition of the period is limited to the writing published between the years 1930 and 1939. John Fante, Pietro di Donato, and Jerre Mangione all began their publishing careers in the 1930s and matured during the 1940s and 1950s. The constraints of periodization that have been constructed and applied by readers of the period have contributed to their being left out, as evidenced by Warren French, who writes that "1939 and 1940 marked not only the end of an era in social and political history, but the end of a literary generation, especially in the creation of the social novel" (*Social Novel* 17). From this perspective, these writers could only be viewed as latecomers, stragglers in a cultural parade who pass the viewing stand long after the critics have left. In actuality those years mark the very birth of a generation of Italian American writers, who as children of Italian immigrants, wrote stories and novels depicting their social environments. These are writers who would go on to produce what in retrospect can be labeled as classics of Italian American literature.

The traditional American Marxist criticism that is a characteristic, if not *the* dominant, critical approach to literature of the 1930s privileges class-conscious texts over those texts that emphasize ethnic, gender, or racial issues. As we know through the experience of Richard Wright, it was one thing to have one's writing accepted, and quite another to have one's self accepted in social situations.[4] The communist party's attempts to establish a sense of a shared class identity among its writers, while important, was complicated by racism and xenophobia in the United States. While the desire to be supportive of a class struggle is important to such writers, their writing necessarily reflects other struggles created by racial and ethnic differences. Thus, by writing novels that did not follow important criteria major Marxist literary critics of the period such as Granville Hicks established, literary critics and historians could easily ignore or overlook these writers.[5] However, by placing these writers into a culturally specific context (that is, one that identifies and analyzes the Italian American signifiers found in their writings), we can recover their works and acknowledge them as vital contributions to the literature of the 1930s.

None of these three writers identified strongly with what they perceived as the ideology of American communist party politics. Fante, a loyal follower of H. L. Mencken, stayed out of politics and described his attitude toward party-line politics and Marxist aesthetics in a letter to his literary mentor:

> I haven't sucked out on Communism and I can't find much in Fascism. As I near twenty-six, I find myself moving toward marriage and a return to Catholicism. Augustine and Thomas More knew the answers a long time ago. Aristotle would have spat in Mussolini's

face and sneered at Marx. The early fathers would have laughed
themselves sick over the New Deal. (*Moreau* 103)

Fante's "return to Catholicism" and his choice not to align himself with left-
wing ideology hindered his reception and consideration by cultural critics
adhering to Marxist aesthetics. Fante never committed himself to any political cause. He registers his disappointment with those who mix politics and
literature in one of his many letters to Mencken in which he recounts his
experience at the 1939 Western Writers' Conference in San Francisco:

> My experience with writers is invariably disillusioning. The more I
> meet them the less I think of the profession. There is always the
> man's work—and then the man. That is excusable in hacks and to
> be expected, but it seems to me the messiah on paper should not step
> out of his role in real life. Mike Gold for example turns out to be
> a platitude carrying a cross. He's so god-awful paternalistic, and yet
> so unmistakably adolescent. (*Moreau* 106)[6]

In his resurrection of the late di Donato's contribution to the Third
American Writers' Congress, Art Casciato helps us to understand why the
established critics and scholars of the period have ignored writers such as
di Donato. As Casciato points out, di Donato, in his brief speech that Malcolm
Cowley asked to be rewritten so that it would conform to Cowley's expectations, refused to adopt "the prescribed literary posture of the day in which
the writer would efface his or her own class or ethnic identity in order to
speak in the sonorous voice of 'the people'" (70). As Casciato explains, di
Donato's style resisted the modern and "thus supposedly proper ways of
building his various structures." The result is that he is "less the bricklayer,
than a bricoleur who works not according to plans but with materials at
hand" (75–76). Di Donato was the only one of these three writers to join
the communist party, which he did at age sixteen on the night that Sacco
and Vanzetti were executed. The following excerpt from his contribution to
the Third American Writers' Congress reflects di Donato's attitude that
Cowley found troublesome:

> I am not interested in writing for class-conscious people. I consider
> that a class-conscious person is something of a genius—I would
> say that he is sane, whereas the person who is not class-conscious
> is insane. . . . In writing *Christ in Concrete* I was trying to use this
> idea of Christianity, to get an 'in' there, using the idea of Christ.
> (*Casciato* 69)

Needless to say, di Donato's use of "comrade-worker Christ" (173) as a metaphor for the working-class man was quite problematic from a Marxist perspective.

Although sympathetic to the communist party in the United States, Jerre Mangione never formally joined because he recognized in it a constraining dogmatism that reminded him of Catholicism. His memoirs *Mount Allegro* (1943) and *An Ethnic at Large: A Memoir of America in the Thirties and Forties* (1978), along with *The Dream and the Deal* (1972)—a study of the Federal Writers' Project—present a thorough accounting of the 1930s from an ethnic perspective.[7] His interest in writing and his encounters with American avant-garde artists of the 1930s lead him to dismiss the art-for-art's-sake cult and to realize that "no writer worth his salt could turn his back on social injustice" (*An Ethnic* 49). For a brief time he attended meetings of the New York John Reed Club and taught literary criticism at the New School in New York. Although uncomfortable with party-line politics, he became a dedicated antifascist and contributed to the antifascist cause through news articles, book reviews, and social and political satire through publications in the *New Republic*, *New Masses*, *Partisan Review*, and *Daily Worker*, many of which he published under the pseudonyms Mario Michele and Jay Gerlando. However, in spite of his left-wing activity and his strong antifascist beliefs, Mangione's work has never been adequately acknowledged in histories of this period.[8]

The writings of these authors were considered neither politically charged nor stylistically innovative. Thus, when the traditional modernist/formalist standards of this period, which proponents of the New Criticism established, are applied to their works, Fante, di Donato, and Mangione are, at best, relegated to minor figure status. Much of their writing could be overlooked for their lack of experimentation that was typical of the modernist movement.[9] All three writers wrote episodic bildungsromans in the naturalist or realist tradition—more obviously influenced by Dreiser and Dostoyevsky than by Eliot and Joyce. Thus caught between the two dominant reading modes traditionally applied to texts of the period, their work falls through the critical cracks into an oblivion that would only be detected long after their publication. However, when cast in the spotlight of a culturally specific reading, their work can be read as the foundation on which an Italian American literature can be and is being created.[10]

My third claim is based on the issue of religion. The writing of Fante, di Donato, and Mangione is heavily imbued with an Italian Marianist Catholicism that is in many ways distinctly different from an American Catholicism institutionalized and controlled by Irish Catholics.[11] Discussion of their work thus requires new interpretative frameworks that identify and include such contexts.[12] Such frameworks are only now being constructed. In a paper presented in a special session at MLA's 1991 meeting, Thomas J. Ferraro proposed reexamining the period by focusing on the relationship of Mediterranean Marianist Catholicism to American culture.[13] Such an approach would make ignoring the writings of Italian Americans impossible, both proponents and opponents of American Catholicism, who documented what the Catholic Church referred to as "The Italian Problem" (Malpezzi and Clements 108). In most of the works of these three writers, a variation of Catholicism is presented and represented that is often anti-institutional and often referred to as un-American. The Italian Catholic backgrounds of all three writers, which strongly roots their works, is an area of U.S. literary history that has yet to be adequately examined.

To examine these claims, I now turn to examples of the work of these three writers and examine their content, style, and religious orientation to offer readings that enable them to be included in revised histories of the period. Space limitations in mind, the following is more of a historical orientation to, rather than a detailed analysis of, representative works of these three writers.

Unlike the few Italian immigrant writers who preceded them, whose work essentially argued for acceptance as human beings and pleas for recognition as Americans, the children of Italian immigrants used their writing both to document and to escape the conditions under which they were born and raised. Recovery and consideration of their works will aid us in recreating a literary history that is sensitive to the process by which the children of immigrants create American identities. A common thread in the works of these three writers is the difference in life between the generation of the parents and the child. Their parents' generation, characterized by hard work and the acceptance of injustices as destiny, would give way to the child's ability to fight injustice through writing. Although these three writers' works all deal with the experiences and exploitation of the working class, none of them follow any of the expected and often perceived as prescribed formulae for the creation of proletarian literature. In fact, they all focus on what Richard Pells calls "a crisis of identity." But unlike writers who "spent an inordinate amount of time worrying about whether they had completely suppressed their bourgeois attitudes, whether they had truly been converted to the revolution, whether they were permanently immune to the temptations of the old world" (166), these Italian American writers struggled with personal issues that complicated their sense of class identity. Analyzing their writings enables us to realize that when ethnicity intersects with class, it changes the dimension of one's perception of and identification with class struggle. Unlike 1930s intellectuals V. F. Calverton and Michael Gold, whose name changes could be seen as attempts to avoid direct confrontation with their ethnic identity, di Donato, Fante, and Mangione chose to deal with their struggle to be perceived and accepted as Americans of Italian descent first. Because these writers begin their careers in the 1930s, the writing produced during these years is necessarily focused on personal development; this struggle is the essence of these writers' contributions to 1930s culture.

H. L. Mencken's desire to combat the Anglocentric hegemony of New England literary establishment helped John Fante, the earliest of the three to publish. Among the books published in the 1930s, James T. Farrell recognized Fante's 1938 bildungsroman, *Wait until Spring, Bandini*, as one of the "few [novels] of genuine merit and value" ("End of a Literary Decade" 208).[14] Most of Fante's works concern the development of the social and aesthetic consciousness of a child of Italian immigrants. The subject of much of his writing is the relationship between the individual and his family and community and the subsequent development of a single protagonist's American identity that requires both an understanding and a rejection of the immigrant past that parental figures represent. Fante's early writings focus on the development of an American identity through attempts to distance his characters from their Italian and working-class identities. Because of this Fante's work reflects the more personal and thus ethnic aspects of his characters' experiences, rather than the political or class-based dimensions of his characters' lives.

Fante's four-book saga of Arturo Bandini, of which *Wait until Spring* is the first, tells the story of a young man who sets out for California with the intent of escaping his family and its ethnicity. In the second novel, *Ask the Dust* (1939), Bandini abandons his Italian American home and makes his way to California. In the process he denies his ethnicity and calls attention to the ethnicity of others, such as Camilla, the Mexican waitress with whom he falls in love and whom he continually calls a "greaser." Bandini believes the only way to become American is by identifying others as non-Americans.[15] However, after he does this, he identifies with their reactions and offers apologies with explanations such as:

> But I am poor, and my name ends with a soft vowel, and they hate
> me and my father, and my father's father, and they would have my
> blood and put me down, but they are old now, dying in the sun and
> in the hot dust of the road, and I am young and full of hope and love
> for my country and my times, and when I say Greaser to you it is
> not my heart that speaks, but the quivering of an old wound, and I
> am ashamed of the terrible thing I have done. (47)

Through episodes such as this Fante provides us with insight into the process by which a child born of Italian immigrants struggles to fashion an American identity. Fante's characters do this through the process of denying other immigrants

and their children the same possibilities, that is, to become an American one
needs to identify the un-American and separate himself from it. For Arturo
Bandini, the development of this offensive behavior is a necessary defense,
especially for one coming-of-age during the rise of Italian fascism.

During this period, Fante was at work on his first novel, *The Road to Los
Angeles* (1985), which had been contracted by Alfred Knopf.[16] In the novel,
the protagonist, Arturo Bandini, uses references to the thought of European
bourgeois intellectuals to set himself apart from the masses: "I said to Mona
[the protagonist's sister], 'Bring me books by Nietzsche. Bring me the mighty
Spengler. Bring me Auguste Comte and Immanuel Kant. Bring me books the
rabble can't read'" (85). The key conflict in this novel, and one that separates
Fante from the proletarian writers of this period, is the attempt of a young
writer to gain a sense of superiority over the working class by identifying
with the literary models of bourgeois culture. Throughout the novel, Bandini
comically regurgitates his readings in rebellion against his home environment. He uses his identity as a writer to separate himself from the working
class which reminds him of the past he is trying to escape. In *1933 Was a Bad
Year* (1985) Fante depicts a young boy's desperate struggle to assimilate into
American culture. The protagonist, Dominick Molise attempts to separate
himself from his poverty and ethnicity and rise above the masses through
baseball. Fante juxtaposes the experiences of Molise's dream of "making
America" through sports with the reality of the life of leisure led by the
protagonist's wealthy best friend.

One impediment that continually keeps Fante's protagonists from identifying themselves completely with mainstream U.S. culture is their strong
connections to Italian Catholicism. More than half the stories of his collection
Dago Red (1940) deal with this subject. In *1933 Was a Bad Year* the protagonist writes an essay on the mystical body of Christ (14) and believes he has
been visited by the Virgin Mary (37). Although Fante strays from this strong
identification with Marianist Catholicism in *The Road to Los Angeles*, a novel
in which Bandini constantly mocks the Christianity of his mother and sister
in his attempt to separate himself from his background, he nevertheless does
so through a character who is more comical than serious. In spite of the fact
that Fante shares some of the concerns of those traditionally identified with
the modernist movement, his ethnic and religious orientation combine to
create philosophical obstacles that prevent critics and historians from including him in the Marxist and New Critical studies that have shaped the definition
and thus our awareness of the modernist American literary tradition.[17]

While Fante was busy portraying characters who took to the road traveling west and away from Little Italy, Pietro di Donato was documenting the
struggle of an Italian American family with the threat of disintegration posed
by the U.S. capitalist system. Di Donato, who died in January 1992, left

behind a considerable body of work dealing with the 1930s that deserves more attention than it has received. Born in Hoboken, New Jersey, in 1911 to Abruzzese parents, di Donato became a bricklayer like his father after his father's tragic death on Good Friday, 1923. Unlike Fante, di Donato never dreamed of becoming a writer, but *Christ in Concrete*'s success placed him in a national spotlight that many critics believe blinded his literary vision for life. In an early review, E. B. Garside, called him "a shining figure to add to the proletarian gallery of artists" (*Atlantic* 7). Garside then went on to predict that di Donato:

> would never create a prose *[sic]* equal of Leopardi's *A Silvia*, nor will his latter-day rebellion rise to the supple power of *Pensieri*. But it must be understood that the Italian soul is essentially 'thin.' The Italian peasant and work man live themselves out fully as part of a family, or of an aggregate of some sort all committed to the same style. (7)

Louis Adamic, more sensitive perhaps to di Donato's immigrant characters, saw that *Christ in Concrete* was unlike the staple fare of the laboring class that were "reflections of the economic treadmill on the tenuous cheesecloth fabric of an ideology" (5). Yet, in spite of this sensitivity, his review betrays a stereotypical notion of immigrant *Italianità* when he characterizes the writing as:

> robust and full-blooded and passionate, now and then almost to the point of craziness; and also like Fante he has imagination and a healthy sense of the source of poetry in the Italian. . . . Sometimes one feels as though bricks and stones and trowelfuls of mortar have been thrown on the pages and from them have risen words. (5)

Italianità is vitally important to nearly everything di Donato has written. Through his work we can gain insight to the mysteries of Italian immigrant life and Italian Catholicism. Di Donato's style of writing is a strange synthesis of Theodore Dreiser's naturalism and James Joyce's stream of consciousness that rings with biblical echoes. His innovation can be found in his diction and word order, which re-create the rhythms and sonority of the Italian language. Whether he is describing a work site or a bedroom, di Donato's imagery vibrates with the earthy sensuality that early Italian immigrants brought to their American lives.

By directing his characters' rage at the employers who exploit immigrant laborers, di Donato argues for solidarity among American workers, and thus *Christ in Concrete* could be read in the tradition of the proletarian novels of

James T. Farrell. Indeed, as Halford Luccock has noted, it was "written by a workman resembling more nearly the much heralded actual 'proletarian' author than any other [labor writer]" (*American Mirror* 174). Unlike much of the proletarian literature of the period, di Donato continually inserts Italian Catholicism as a force that controls the immigrants' reactions to the injustices of the capitalist system that exploits as it maims and kills the Italian immigrant. Di Donato's Catholicism has its roots in pre-Christian, matriarchal worship.[18] Annunziata, the mother in *Christ in Concrete*, controls her son's reaction to the work site "murders" of his father and godfather by calling on him to put his trust in Jesus, the son of Mary. By the end of the novel, Paul's faith is nearly destroyed as evidenced by his crushing of a crucifix offered to him by his mother (296–97). However, the final image of the novel suggests that the matriarchal powers still reign. The image we are left with is an inversion of the *Pietà* in which son is holding a mother who is crooning a lullaby depicting her son as a new Christ, one that her children should follow (303). Thus, while di Donato's novel depicts the injustices the immigrants faced, no revolutionary solution is offered to the reader. The absence of such a solution, combined with the novel's Roman Catholic philosophical underpinnings, keeps *Christ in Concrete* out of the historical purview of proletarian literature and thus outside those literary histories devoted to such literature.

Jerre Mangione's contributions to American letters are fueled by a social conscience formed by the 1930s. Although his literary works were not published during the 1930s, they were certainly written in response to his experiences of this period. Unlike di Donato, Mangione wanted to be a writer since his college days during the late 1920s. As Mangione writes in *An Ethnic at Large*:

> My true ambition, which I tried to keep secret from my parents as long as possible, was to be a writer. It seemed to me that I had no talent for anything else; that, moreover, it offered the fastest avenue of escape to the world outside that of my relatives. (19)

Mangione left that ethnocentric world of his family when he entered Syracuse University, and during the 1930s he wrote extensively about the effects of fascism on Italy and about those who fought fascism in Europe. In fact, nearly all his fiction and much of his literary criticism is devoted to antifascist themes. One of his earliest book reviews is of Ignazio Silone's *Fontamara*, "Happy Days in Fascist Italy." It represents Mangione's earliest attempt to explain fascism to an American audience. "Fascism," Mangione wrote:

contrary to the impression it tries to give to the world has made his [the peasant's] lot considerably worse. It has borne down on him in many instances the naive faith the ignorant peasant had in 'his government' and depriving him of his means of livelihood. (37)

Mangione uses this opportunity to present an alternative view of fascism, that of the illiterate Italian peasant who was "tricked" into accepting the veiled offer of hope and progress extended by Mussolini's black-shirt movement:

Silone's canvas takes in the whole of Fontamara, the money-mad, tyrannical officials; the politician who calls himself "friend of the people" and then betrays them at every turn; those peasants who, before they realized the true implications of Fascism and implicit faith in God and "their" government. . . . Fascism has wiped Fontamara off the map, but Silone has put it on again in such a way that no Fascist bullets can destroy its significance. (38)

During this early stage of his writing career, unlike di Donato and Fante, Mangione begins the task of interpreting Italian culture and life under Mussolini. He reviewed translations of Pirandello's books *Better Think Twice about It* and *The Outcast* in the August 28, 1935, issue of *New Republic*. The review, "Acrobat to Il Duce," points out Pirandello's influence on fascist literature:

Long inclined to emphasize the cerebral and anti-realistic aspects of writing, Fascist literature needed only an impetus like Pirandello's to give it direction; that he has succeeded in giving it, is shown by the sheerly psychological and fantastic themes used and abused by modern Italian writers in every branch of literature. . . . It is hard to read very far in his two latest books without seeing Pirandello, the acrobatic metaphysician, jostling aside the characters and stealing the stage for his own pet somersaults. (82–83)

During the same year, Mangione, using the pseudonym Jay Gerlando, reviewed *Mr. Aristotle*, a translation of Ignazio Silone's collection of short stories. The review's title, "Pirandello Didn't Know Him," comes from the fact that when Mangione interviewed Pirandello during the playwright's visit to the United States, Pirandello said he had never heard of the author of *Fontamara*. "This ignorance," wrote Mangione, "indicates that Italy has been more subtle than Germany in her suppression of intelligent books. Instead of making a bonfire of them, she has simply buried them, leaving no obituaries. . . . [Silone] is an intellectual who can see clearly the plight and frustration of the peasant living under fascism" (23–24).

The predominance of Italy as a subject in Mangione's writing can be attributed to his travels there during Mussolini's regime. Mangione first visited Italy in 1936 and was an eyewitness to the methods of fascist control. He first documented this trip in articles he published during 1937 and 1938 in *New Masses, New Republic, Travel,* and *Globe* magazine and *Broun's Nutmeg,* and later it would become a significant portion of his first book, *Mount Allegro* (1943). His left-wing publications and his friendship with publisher and activist Carlo Tresca proved to haunt his first trip to Italy, during which facist authorities censored his mail and monitored his movements. In 1936 Mangione traveled through Italy and Sicily with the fear that at any time Fascist authorities could arrest him and force him into military service. This trip is recounted in his classic memoir *Mount Allegro.*[19] In it he describes the effects of fascism on Italy and Sicily as observed through contact with his encounters with Italians and his Sicilian relatives.

In 1937, Mangione left a New York publishing job to work for the New Deal. In the course of this period of politicization he came to understand the terrible threat that European fascism presented to the world. As he worked to understand it better he befriended Tresca, an Italian antifascist and anarchist who came to the United States in the early 1900s to aid the exploited Italian immigrant laborers. His interactions with Tresca became the material on which he would build his second novel, *Night Search* (1965). Based on Tresca's assassination, *Night Search* dramatizes the experience of Michael Mallory, the illegitimate son of antifascist labor organizer and newspaper publisher Paolo Polizzi, a character based on Tresca. Published in 1965, this novel follows Mallory as he searches for his father's murderer. Mallory is an apolitical public relations writer inclined toward liberalism who, through an investigation of his father's death, learns to take action, and in doing so, comes to understand where he stands in relation to contemporary politics. Mallory very much resembles Stiano Argento, the Catholic protagonist in Mangione's earlier and more strongly antifascist novel, *The Ship and the Flame* (1948). During this same period Mangione also read Sicilian writers, interviewed Luigi Pirandello, and convinced the publishing firm that employed him to accept the translation of Ignazio Silone's now classic antifascist novel, *Bread and Wine.* Mangione, using the pseudonym Mario Michele, explored in greater depth the effects of fascism on his relatives in "*Fontamara* Revisited" in which he describes a visit to Realmonte, his ancestors' homeland in southern Italy. In a later publication, based on his European experiences of the late 1930s, Mangione presents a more sophisticated overview of the effects of fascism. In *The Ship and the Flame* he creates an allegory for the sorry state of political affairs in Europe prior to the United States' entry into the World

War II. Aware of the dilemma of the liberal and the fate of the revolutionary in the world, Mangione created a microcosm of the larger world of his time, suggesting that the struggle against fascism could be won through heroic action that would not compromise one's Catholic beliefs.

Beyond the insights into Italian American ethnicity that we can gain by reading their representations of the struggles of immigrants to "make America," to overcome prejudice and discrimination, and to negotiate an American identity without totally abandoning their *Italianità*, closer readings of their writing will reveal aspects of the mainstream writing of the 1930s. The radicalism of di Donato, the liberal pragmatism of Mangione, and the political apathy of Fante represent three political positions available to writers at the time. In spite of their different political beliefs, their works are united by the social criticism of the larger American scene that comes from their positions at the banks of America's cultural mainstream. These three writers are but a few of the many unstudied voices who can reward a revisionist history of the 1930s from the perspective of Italian American ethnicity.

A thorough examination of the works that these writers produced during and about the 1930s, would be, in most cases, a first critical and historical consideration. The next step, after analyzing their works as individuals and looking at the Italian American aspects, is to compare their work to those created by other marginalized writers. Investigations of their contributions, especially when compared to the work that other marginalized writers—women, African Americans, Mexican Americans, and others—can provide us with new ways of seeing the past and subsequently with new ways of organizing the present, especially in terms of developing multicultural approaches to literary history and criticism.

Chapter 5

The Consequences of Class in Italian American Culture

> *To dare write about working-class literature in a culture where the working class itself is denied a name, never mind a literary category, is to plunge in over one's head.*
>
> —Janet Zandy, "Introduction" to *Calling Home*

The vast majority of American writers and artists of Italian descent have come from, if not remained in, working-class families. Luigi Fraina and Carl Marzani are two examples of Italian American intellectuals whose Americanization included both an intellectual examination of the consequences of class in the United States. Rather than abandon their working-class origins, they focused nearly all their life energies on understanding it and working for change. The challenge for those born into working-class families, according to Janet Zandy, is to "resist assimilation into bourgeois sensibilities and institutions" (*Liberating Memory* xi). This resistance requires the sustenance of personal histories through memories that are not erased through class mobility. Zandy envisions this happening by a reconstruction of "the ways in which working-class identity moves in time, with change and continuity, and with the concomitant development of a critical class consciousness that recognizes the value of this identity to collective struggle" (*Liberating Memory* 1).

To date virtually no examination has been made of their work for what it has to say about that experience. This chapter begins the task of examining the relationship of key Italian American critics and artists to working-class culture with the belief that, as Janet Zandy suggests in her "Introduction" to *Liberating Memory: Our Work and Working-Class Consciousness*, we can locate "the missing identifying principle," which can help us "see each other's history" and "construct a viable paradigm that addresses multiple oppressions" (10). This chapter reunites Italian American authors and artists through the idea of class and in this way enables their work to reach out beyond the narrow confines of Italian Americana. Writers discussed in this chapter include fiction writers Pietro di Donato, Mari Tomasi, and Tina De Rosa, and the poets Arturo Giovannitti and Joseph Malviglia.

In the Italian American writer's presentation of work a poetic relationship exists between work and the working-class writers of the earlier generations. These writers neither explore nor do they emphasize the political relationship between an individual and his or her community. Instead, they focus on what I will call a poetic idea of work as it is connected to one's self and work as it becomes one's art. Work, for these writers, never becomes solely a means of transforming self from one class to another, but a way of making meaning out of life.

From my readings I have observed that a continuum exists among the literary works of Italian American working-class writers and that continuum reveals a sometimes conscious, sometimes unconscious "relationship between individual and community" (Lauter 65). Thus, one of what Paul Lauter calls "center of gravity" of working-class art produced by Italian Americans is the concrete representation of work in, if not a poetic language, then certainly through a poetic relationship of simple symbolism that elevates the common worker to the status of a deity; in essence such representation becomes a way of dignifying the plight of the worker. In line with Lauter's thinking, these working-class artists, "have produced ideas about social relationships crucially distinct from those of the bourgeoisie" (66). Like the jazz musician of Paul Lauter's analogy in his essay, "Caste, Class, Canon," Italian American working-class artists "ring variations on melodies the listeners know and love" (64), and one of the most common, if not fundamental, sources of melodies for Italian American writers and the one I will focus on is the Catholic religion. Other sources include pre-Christian elements in Italian and American folk and popular cultures.

In "Professions and Faiths: Critical Choices in the Italian American Novel," Robert Viscusi introduces the ideas that the Italian American novelist "brings to an American theme an orientation that is particularly Italian. . . . The American theme is professional life, and the Italian orientation grows out of the imaginative form that Christianity takes in the culture of the Southern Italian" (41). Viscusi identifies a suspicion that Italian Americans have fostered toward the idea of middle-class professionalism, which he attributes to a "special brand of Christianity." This suspicion surfaces in the portrayals of working-class characters who enter professions and turn their backs on their ancestral communities. One example he uses to illustrate his point is a doctor in Guido D'Agostino's *Olives on the Apple Tree,* but Viscusi could have used any number of novels. Beyond this idea of suspicion planted by these novelists, in terms of the consequences of assimilation and class mobility, Viscusi points to a more interesting notion in the later essay, "A Literature Considering Itself: The Allegory of Italian America," in which he introduces the idea that the "allegorical destiny of Italian American heroes, [is] to endure ritual death and processional re-identification in the process of becoming divinities" (272). In speaking about Italian American literature, Viscusi tells us, "It was clear to the discourse, if not to its explicators that no other role was open to Italians in the American imagination except that of divinities. The Puritans had preempted the role of moralists, [what R. W. B. Lewis called the American Adam] and the Blacks the place of the victim" (274–75)." Although Viscusi means well, his unfamiliarity with the literature beyond the Anglo and Italian American cultures has lead him into a dead-end discourse, out of which I believe I can extract him like some literary roadside towing service by building on his notion of Italian American working-class heroes as gods.

Throughout southern Italian and Sicilian history is a consistent theme of the transformation of labor and the elements of labor into artistic and religious material and vice versa. One example of this is the former communist party's appropriation of St. Joseph, the carpenter, as the patron saint of the worker, so that the Catholic celebration of his feast day, March 19, has become an occasion for workers' marches. Whereas the connections between work and religion are quite common, the rewriting of common religious texts to verify, dignify, and unify the worker is one way the earliest Italian American writers responded to their experience in the United States through poetry and prose. Although poetry by Italian American immigrants has yet to be documented historically, the most significant work was done by labor activist Arturo Giovannitti, whose participation in the great 1912 strike in Lawrence, Massachusetts, landed him and Joe Ettor, president of the IWW, in jail for murder. As a worker-poet, Giovannitti edited *Il Proletario* and the political and literary magazine *Il Fuoco*. His first collection of poetry, *Arrows in the Gale* (1914), introduced by Helen Keller, gave a voice to the hundreds of thousands of Italian immigrants who worked their way into status as Americans. In one of his early poems, we find the idea of a god of work presented in a poem that formalistically imitates the "Our Father":

Te Deum of Labor
Our Father Labor stern and kind
Who art wherever life has birth,
Thy will be done among mankind,
Come thy republic on the earth;

Give us this day our daily bread
Our daily task, our daily song,
Deliver us from all blood shed
From greed and hate, from right and wrong,
Save us from envy and discord
And when our day is done and when
Thy final whistle blows, O Lord,
Spare us the fear of death. Amen. (45–46)

Giovannitti replaces the sacred god of the original prayer with Labor, the profane god, and introduces the idea that that work, like religion, is an institution that controls lives. Many critics might see this poem as a straightforward imitation of prayer without any sense of originality or irony, but just as Henry Gates sees Phyllis Wheatley signifying on English literature in her poems, I see Giovannitti signifying on the New Testament and the teachings of the Catholic Church. Knowing that the Italian American working class contained a great number of if not anticlerical then certainly agnostic members who were nevertheless quite familiar with the New Testament, helps us to see the parody at work in this poem. This appropriation of common religious forms is prevalent in Giovannitti's poetry. In *Arrows in the Gale* he revises the Sermon on the Mount to "The Sermon on the Common," which he delivered to striking workers on the Lawrence Common. The speaker of the poem is an organizer who tells the crowd: "Think not that I am come to destroy the law: I am not come to destroy, but to fulfill through you what the prophets of mankind have presaged from the beginning. For verily I say unto you, While man lives and labors, nothing can destroy the eternal law of progress which after each advancing step bids him further" (194). His rewriting of Christ's sermon fosters non-Christian behavior:

> Blessed are they that mourn their martyred dead: for they shall
>   avenge them upon their murderers and be comforted.
> Blessed are the rebels: for they shall reconquer the earth.
> Blessed are they which do hunger and thirst after equality: for
>   they shall eat the fruit of their labor. . . .
> Blessed are ye when the scribes of the press shall revile you,
>   and the doctors of the law, politicians, policemen, judges
>   and priests shall call you criminals, thieves and murderers
>   and shall say all manner of evil against you falsely, for the
>   sake of Justice. (193)

Another early example of this worker-as-god conceit appears in the poetry of Pascal D'Angelo, which we find primarily in his 1924 autobiography, *Son of Italy*. D'Angelo's metaphors shift from the world of nature as represented by his poems about Italy, to the world of man as represented in his poems about his experience the United States. For D'Angelo, the United States becomes a land in which man struggles with nature, a place where man's imprint on the world destroys the natural relationship of his past and create in its place a tension that often results in confusion.

"Night Scene," the first poem that appears in the "American" section of *Son of Italy*, demonstrates the intensity of the struggle in men's lives when they become disconnected from nature. In this poem D'Angelo contrasts a man walking home from work as a storm approaches. He characterizes the storm as "an unshaped blackness," a "mountain of clouds" that "rises like a Mammoth" (75). The black clouds are illuminated by the fires of a foundry. The man is characterized first as a "form" nearly indistinguishable from the black clouds, but as it nears the figure on the road becomes a man—a man who, oblivious to the beauty of the world around him, curses something, perhaps, his life, his fate as a worker. This experience is like a storm in nature when elements clash to disrupt the peace of the pastoral world. This poem comes at the end of chapter six in which D'Angelo recounts his first jobs and the "endless, continuous toil" as a pick-and-shovel man and comes to the realization that such work is getting him, materially and spiritually, nowhere. He needs more than work and the meager life it brings. He tells us in his autobiography that he needs poetry, which lives longer than manual labor.

> Who hears the thuds of the pick and the jingling of the shovel. All my works are lost, lost forever. But if I write a good line of poetry— then when the night comes and I cease writing, my work is not lost. My line is still there. It can be read by you to-day and by another to-morrow. But my pick and shovel works cannot be read either by you to-day or by anyone else to-morrow. (74–75)

D'Angelo keeps the beauty of the world of his past alive through his poetry, but his present world is filled with hard work and the terrible work accidents he witnessed. Work, he says, "was a war in which we poor laborers—Poles and Italians—were perpetually engaged" (117). In "Accident in the Coal Dump" D'Angelo presents a narrative of a man who has died "in crushed splendor under the weight of awakening" (117). The worker had been a friend to D'Angelo and a family man now transformed by death into "an extinguished sun still followed by unseen faithful planets / Dawning on dead worlds in an eclipse across myriad stars" (118). After they have dug out his body they leave. A "youngster who was trying to fool himself and his insistent thoughts" attempts to joke about "the dead man (118). Snow begins to fall "like a white dream through the rude sleep of winter night," and "a wild eyed woman came running out of the darkness" (118). This juxtaposition of darkness and light is characteristic of D'Angelo's depictions of his American experiences. Most of his imagery is presented in this chiaroscuro fashion. But unlike the dark/light portrayals of Italy in which man is connected organically to the natural world, those of America present man in conflict with nature and the ruling divinities. This shift comes through clearly in "Omnis Sum," a Whitmanesque lyric that opens the chapter in which he recounts a work accident. The injury forces him out of his job and brings him the opportunity to begin learning English language. In this poem D'Angelo juxtaposes the image of himself as Christ in the darkness of thought. Light is created by a Thor-like god who rules the night. Like Christ, D'Angelo suffers a terrible wound to his hand after following a foreman's order against his and other workers' advice. After the accident, which renders him unable to work, D'Angelo meets Michele, a fellow worker who speaks good Italian and who talks to him of Dante—whom the illiterate D'Angelo thought "was an ancient king" (132). When D'Angelo shows him his wounded hand, Michele says, "Boy, a stupid world drove nails through other hands—other hands." D'Angelo's literal-minded protagonist does not understand the allusion to Christ (132), but certainly the writer does.

The themes of class war and the exploitation of workers found in the poetry of Giovannitti and D'Angelo become the foundation for Pietro di Donato's highly mythic and poetic *Christ in Concrete*, in which work becomes personified as "Job," the antagonist to the worker-as-Christ protagonist. This idea of a poetic relationship between man and his work comes through most clearly in this novel in which work becomes a living, monster against which the worker-hero must battle to survive. Job becomes the antagonist to the worker-as-Christ protagonist. When speaking of a worker's relationship to his job, di Donato writes: "The great God Job, he did not love" (8). This idea of a poetic relationship between man and his work comes through most clearly in this novel in which work becomes a living monster that the worker-hero must battle to survive.

> Whistle shrilled Job awake, and the square pit thundered into an inferno of sense-pounding cacophony.
>
> Compression engines snort viciously—sledge heads punch sinking spikes—steel drills bite shattering jazz in stony-stone excitedly jarring clinging hands—dust swirling—bells clanging insistent aggravated warning—severe bony iron cranes swivel swing dead heavy rock high-clattering dump—vibrating concussion swiftly absorbed—echo reverberating—scoops bulling horns in rock pile chug-shish-chug-chug aloft—hiss roar dynamite's boomdoom loosening petrified bowels—one hundred hands fighting rock—fifty spines derricking swiveling—fifty faces in set mask chopping stone into bread—fifty hearts interpreting Labor hurling oneself down and in at earth planting pod-footed Job. (46)

For these early Italian American writers, then, work as a concrete entity replaces the abstract notion of God as presented in the Christian religion. Workers, in giving their lives for their jobs, become, as the title of a novel by Mari Tomasi says, *Like Lesser Gods*.

Pietro Dalli, the protagonist of Tomasi's 1949 novel, sees his work as his art. She describes him as a man with two hearts, one for his work, the other for his wife, and his love for his work drives his wife into a fit of jealousy in which she destroys a granite monument he has carved believing that its destruction would lead him to give up his job. Although Pietro's death does not come from one of the many job-site accidents that occur in the quarry, he contracts tuberculosilicosis and dies young. When his doctor asks him why he stayed so long in the stonecutting business he says:

> "You have to cut it to know. It is hard stone. Beautiful. Lasting. Always when I carve a name on a memorial, I feel, well, important." A half smile wiped the earlier fear from Pietro's face. It was as if for a moment, he had forgotten the grim reason for this visit to Gino's [the doctor's] office. "I carve the name and I say to myself, 'From up there in heaven the Dio creates new life; and when He sees fit to take it away, then we stone cutters on earth take up where He left off. We take up the chisel, we carve the name, we make a memory of that life. Almost, boy, it is being like—like—' "
>   In Gino's mind tiptoes a sentence from an old mythology book: "On Olympus live the greater gods; and below, the lesser." He nodded to Pietro, understanding him, and he murmured quietly—"like lesser gods." (166)

The message of Tomasi's novel is that a worker's immortality can be achieved only through one's work; just as work can give one life and provide for the lives of one's family, it can also take life away, and so, work is the Greater God. Similar ideas about work and its role in life and death come through contemporary novels such as Jay Parini's *The Patch Boys* and Denise Giardina's *Storming Heaven* and *The Unquiet Earth* and the poetry of Joseph Maviglia.

Maviglia, the son of Calabrian immigrants to Canada, is a poet and Juno Award-winning singer-songwriter. His first collection of poetry, *A God Hangs Upside Down* (1994), appeared shortly after his first record CD, "Memory of Steel." Many of the poems in *A God Hangs Upside Down* deal with the idea of the worker as a greater god than Christ and reveals a strong influence by Pietro di Donato. The collection contains a section titled "The Song a Shovel Makes," which features poems about his experience as a construction worker. One is titled "Job," another, dedicated to di Donato is titled "Dust and Gravel." In the latter poem, Maviglia reminds the worker:

> Christ in all his forgiveness
> does not know the taste of dust.

> His gold
> his purpled robes his saints
>
> know nothing of the dust against
> six men in battle against time
> against the needs of company owner
> against the threat of being left at home
> if you refuse to pull your weight. (57)

This theme of work as religion, job as God, worker as Christ, or better than Christ, appears throughout the literature of Italian America. John Fante's *Brotherhood of the Grape* and Don DeLillo's *Ratner's Star* have scenes of fathers taking sons to work sites to show their children concrete examples of what they did with their lives. The idea of achieving not only an identity but also dignity through a job is important for the immigrant who has few other ways to achieve a sense of self in a new country. In Pietro Corsi's *La Giobba* Italian immigrants believed that where there was work there was hope and often referred to a man out of work as "un povero cristiano nudo"; being without work was as degrading as being without clothes. Unemployment reduces men such as Corsi's protagonist Onofrio to a level of physical and spiritual life that is lower than the one they left in Italy. Through much of Italian American literature we learn that although the early immigrants make art of their work, later generations make work of their art.

Thom Tammaro pays tribute to the working-class culture he grew up in through "On Being Asked if There Was Art or Culture in the Town Where I Grew Up," "Union Meeting, 1959" and "Workers." In these poems he revives the spirit of working-class life through the sights and sounds of work and uncovers a rich culture too often snubbed by those seeking to be artists. The poet's strong sensory perception and linguistic presentation, especially in "Workers," are reminiscent of the powerful portrayals of construction workers in Pietro di Donato's classic short story "Christ in Concrete." And in "Union Meeting, 1959" Tammaro revives both the chiaroscuro imagery and the worker's struggle against nature conceit found in the poetry of Pascal D'Angelo.

> Beyond these fences, nothing else mattered.
> The whole world was here. Later, we felt
> sleet turn to snow as we made our way along
> the dim streets above the frozen river,
> catching glimpses of ourselves
> in store windows, watching our shadows
> go before us into that long night,

those fires burning deep and bright
into the center of our lives. (13)

The fires of the U. S. Steel furnaces become the sun at the center of the worker's universe. The artificial world of man has taken precedence over the world of nature, and in this world the worker becomes involved in a heroic struggle for his life.

The idea of writing as work, of academia as job, runs throughout such writers as early as Pascal D'Angelo's *Son of Italy,* Jerre Mangione's memoirs in which writing becomes the job in the form of book editing, advertising, and the Federal Writers' Project, and in Frank Lentricchia's *The Edge of Night* where he writes:

My job is teaching (annotation from the mouth) and critical writing (annotation from the pen). "My job": hard for me to say those words. They had jobs. Anna Mary, my mother: the textile mills, then the assembly lines of General Electric. Wires, bits of metal, I don't know the names, she never taught me the names, small hard things with sharp edges, in bare hands, into radios. (146)

Marianna Torgovnick's *Crossing Ocean Parkway: Readings by an Italian American Daughter,* Sandra Gilbert's poetry, and Janet Zandy's work with autobiography and working-class women's writings all point to the importance of work in the writing of Italian Americans. Thus, perhaps because so much of Italian American literature deals with work and working-class lives, it has been so long ignored, so long unwelcomed by the publishing houses, so long overlooked by critics, and so long misunderstood by everyone.

At first glance, *Paper Fish,* a novel by Tina De Rosa, does not seem to be a narrative even remotely connected to working-class culture. The powerful and poetic prose, the disjointed narrative structure, its lack of overt politicization of class issues—all invite most educated readers to set the novel on the pedestal of high modernist tradition, which is often seen as antithetical to, if not working-class culture, then certainly to proletarian culture. In my previous discussions of the novel as an important development in Italian American culture, I never once paid attention to the novel's power as a work of art reflecting the working-class experience. Thanks to Janet Zandy's contributions to the development of theoretical approaches to examining working-class literature, I have begun to find the way, as well as the words, to express how express how this novel makes art of working-class life.

Paper Fish is the first novel by an Italian American writer to be set in Chicago's largest Italian working-class neighborhood known as Taylor Street. De Rosa's style, more impressionistic than realistic, presents working-class

portraits of both the Italian American family and the neighborhood that challenge the stereotypical media portrayals of Italian Americans. What is truly
exciting is that contemporary reviewers are able to see what earlier reviewers
were not. Bill Marx, reviewing the novel in the *Boston Globe* (October 17,
1996), tells us that *Paper Fish:*

> is a remarkable memoir of working-class life in Chicago's Little
> Italy of the 1940s and '50s . . . a slice of life with multicolored
> metaphorical layers. The book's disjointed narrative and impression-
> istic imagery not only undercut familiar sentimental caricatures of
> immigrants—salt-of-the-earth stereotypes revered by the political left
> and right—but reject the unholy alliance of realistic description and
> baby-boomer self-absorption that fuels the current solipsistic rage
> for confessional fiction and nonfiction. De Rosa realizes that psy-
> chological grandstanding leaves no room for beauty or mystery, that
> style makes the memory. (E3)

That Marx sees the novel as a memoir is an interesting discrepancy that
points to the need for moving beyond mere recognition and into serious
analysis of working-class art.

Florence Howe and the Feminist Press have rescued this novel, and
through Janet Zandy we can learn how to examine it as a working-class
artifact. In her "Introduction" to *Calling Home: Working-Class Women's
Writings, An Anthology,* Zandy begins to teach us how to theorize about
working-class literature. She writes: "Consider thinking of working-class literature as analogous to documentary photography. At its best, documentary
photography is artistic expression and social commentary, the aesthetic and
the political intertwined" (9). Zandy tells us that the subject of photographers
such as Lewis Hine "stare back at the viewer and force an emotional and
intellectual engagement" creating images that:

> have a particular context connected to larger history, as do the char-
> acters, narrators and writers of working-class literature. Their indi-
> vidual stories become *la storia* (in Italian, history), and the artist,
> writer, photographer, becomes the mediator. In this literature, social
> and economic class shape, and sometimes determine, that history. (9)

Although Marx correctly sees *Paper Fish* as a "chronicle of tough times
among the Italian underclass [that] contains the usual domestic pressures and
economic tribulations" (E3), the larger discussion, not within the range of a
review, needs to focus on the relationship of the "mediator" to both the
subject and audience. If we accept Zandy's analogy to documentary photog-

raphy, then we should see *Paper Fish* not as a realistic, but an impressionistic, depiction of the working-class experience.

De Rosa's achievement as a literary artist is the creation of a novel that documents the disintegration of a family and an old Italian neighborhood, not through realistic narrative, but through an impressionistic and lyrical linguistic meditation. As the community shrinks and trolley tracks disappear, the protagonist, a young Carmolina Bellacasa, grows strong and finds her own image in a mirror that once reflected only her family. This story of life, death, and a young girl'□s redemption reaches the reader soul through poetic rendering of pictures in a gone world. And even when the working-class world disappears, De Rosa never lets go. The demise of the Italian ghetto, as De Rosa knew it, becomes a wound that heals through the writing, but remains a scar in the minds of those who remember, as she tells us in an interview:

> I wanted the neighborhood to live again, to recreate it and so many of the people I was close to, especially my grandmother and father who had both died. I think I was haunted by it all. I wanted to make those people and that neighborhood alive again. I wanted the readers of the book to care about it, to realize that something beautiful had existed and that it was gone. Taylor Street had become a myth of terrible beauty and terrible ugliness. It was a world completed unto itself. The further I got away from it, the more I could see it as a small, beautiful, peculiar world. (*Dagoes Read* 76)

This impulse, to recreate a working-class world gone, is part of what Zandy calls the "process of witnessing." Referring to the contributions of award-winning Working-Class Studies issue *Women's Studies Quarterly* issue, Zandy tells us, "Each writer demonstrates a sense of connection to others across time, and a desire—even a responsibility—to use this occasion to provide a space where the silenced may be heard and seen . . . the connecting tissue is a collective class consciousness and a solidarity with working people" (4). As a witness to a world destroyed by urban renewal, De Rosa preserves, in mythical fashion, the memory of a time and place when immigrant workers, such as Grandpa Dominic and Grandma Doria Bellacassa were heroes whose tales of the old world helped to create new worlds for those who would listen. As Zandy reminds us:

> Often it falls on the will and more privileged circumstances of the next generation, those from working-class families who acquired educations, to see that the experiences of the majority of the people are not forgotten. What is crucial to retrieving and producing working-class culture is the reciprocal and dialogic dimension of the process.

> We are generationally interdependent: the past is given voice in our
> work, but our work would not exist without this class history. It is a
> conversation of multiple voices across time. Working-class histories,
> stories and images and not *taken* to be sold in the marketplace of
> ideas, but rather *claimed* as a valuable inheritance. ("Editorial" 5)

This is the story of *Paper Fish* and its creator. As De Rosa tells us in her essay,
"An Italian-American Woman Speaks Out," "the price you pay for growing
up in one culture and entering another" is the feeling of not belonging to
either. "Always you find yourself running away from one of them. . . . You
say partially goodbye to one, partially hello to another, some of the time you
are silent, and if you feel a little bit crazy—and sometimes you do—then you
write about it" (39). *Paper Fish* becomes the document of that connection
between working-class and middle-class cultures.

De Rosa fashions the tale of that transition into segments that move in
the manner of human memory, and the novel's "Epilogue" is a good place to
see this style in action. Divided into six segments, all illustrating different
angles of the disintegration of the Italian neighborhood, the "Epilogue" more
than describing the destruction of the "old neighborhood," resurrects its
working-class realities through an imagistic language that uses repetition, a
technique that echoes the oral tradition from which she comes rendering a
folktale-like feeling to her narrative:

> Underneath, the street is brick, brick that is no longer whole and red,
> but chipped and gray like the faces of dead people trapped under
> lava. The street heaves up bricks, the guts of the street spit up brick.
> The face of the street cracks open and reveals its belly of brick, the
> gray faces. Squads of men in white T-shirts and hard hats with
> pickaxes in their hands chew into the street's cement face and the
> face cracks and there is no body under the bricks, only the cracked
> cement face. Then the street explodes, explodes in the faces of the
> men with pickaxes who come to take the streetcar line away. . . .
>   The people of the neighborhood sit on wooden benches, eat
> lemon ice in fluted cups, their lips are wet from the ice. They look
> at the clean steel bones of the tracks. (*Paper Fish* 133)

The excavation of the city streets, like the archeological diggings of historical
sites such as Pompeii, might possibly reveal layers of past life, but for the
observer of this scene, there is nothing beneath the surface of this American
setting. What has made this site sacred, is not the life that came before, but
the lives that are being destroyed as the workers remove the streetcar line.
What remains is for the observer-writer to transplant this all into memory

where it can live in the future. The value of any writer to a culture is that she can create illusion out of reality and reality out of illusion both of which affect human memory. De Rosa renders this idea through the poetry of the final segment, which finds Carmolina seated next to her grandmother at a circus, watching a clown sweeping away a spotlight:

> Carmolina, Grandma whispers, you hear the magician? He still there?
> He's there, Grandma.
> *Faccia bella,* Grandma says.
> The clown sweeps the light away.
> The music stops.
> It's only a trick, Grandma, Carmolina says. Don't let it fool you. (137)

Earlier in the novel Grandma Doria had told Carmolina that, unlike her sick sister Doriana, Carmolina had a magician who watched over her and would bring her "good luck like gold" (110). The magician, however, also has the ability to create illusions, the ability to entertain people by making things seem to appear and disappear. Like a magician, the writer creates illusion out of reality, out of the impressions she has fashioned by combining imagination and memory. Grandma Doria, by making Carmolina aware of the magician, helps to develop Carmolina's power of observation so that she will become the documentarian of a culture in transition. While the Little Italy and its people are physically transformed, they remain forever, mentally preserved in the memory of Carmolina as she has fashioned it out of her grandmother's stories. The novel ends with that image of a disintegrating Little Italy, but Italy will remain inside Carmolina as long as the memory of her grandmother is kept alive. This experience, the death of place and the inevitable dissolution of an accompanying culture, is recorded by De Rosa, an eyewitness, in a language that she has said was impossible for her ancestors to articulate:

> Our grandparents and parents were bound to survival; we, on the other hand, have become freer to use our own talents and to rescue the talents of those who came before us. Because we have passed through more time, we have a perspective that gives us the ability to look back and to judge their experiences as treasures that we cannot throw out. (*Dagoes Read* 76)

Critic Edvige Giunta tells us in her "Afterword" that the republication of *Paper Fish* is as much recovery as it is discovery. For some readers, it is the discovery of a world never known; for others, it is the recovery of a world we might have forgotten. In either case, the impressions of working-class life recorded in *Paper Fish* enable us all to examine, in Janet Zandy's words, "the historic markings of class on present circumstances" (*Liberating Memory* 10). Giunta perceptively comments that, "An analogy can be drawn between the separation experienced by the immigrant, and the separation from the family that moving into the middle class entails for the working-class person. Like many other working-class writers, De Rosa views the family as a homeland that can be revisited only through writing" (127). De Rosa's *Paper Fish* joins Louise De Salvo's memoir *Vertigo: A Memoir* and Mary Bucci Bush's short stories in *A Place of Light,* as model working-class narratives, as memory liberated through meditation that make them all important additions to a working-class literary canon.

A simple survey of the place of work in the creations of other Italian American artists reveals similar themes. A young Ralph Fasanella supported antifascism in mind and on the battlefields of Spain in the 1930s. Nurtured by an immigrant mother who was a left-wing activist, Fasanella, like Marzani, also became a victim of McCarthyism. Fasanella, who spent most of his life working with unions until he was blacklisted during the 1950s, began painting in the 1940s. Most of his paintings deal with social and political causes revolving around the lives and deaths of the American working class. The theoretical ideas Luigi Fraina and Carl Marzani wrote about come to life in the works of Fasanella. Whether he is painting a working-class neighborhood, a work site, a union hall, or a ball field, Fasanella's goal is to portray the everyday workers as heroes and their everyday lives as important historical events.

The plays of Albert Innaurato, Michelle Linfante, Richard Vetere, and Teresa Carilli; the music of groups such as Dion and the Belmonts, Frankie Valli and the Four Seasons, and the Young Rascals—all beg for examination through the lens of working-class culture. Although very few films focus on the Italian American working-class experience in a positive light, John Turturo's *Mac* can be read as a rewriting of di Donato's *Christ in Concrete.* These are but a few of the many works which challenge the stereotypical portrayals of Italian Americans in the media.

Micaela di Leonardo, in "White Ethnicities, Identity Politics, and Baby Bear's Chair," has quite appropriately referred to film portrayals of the Italian American working class as minstrelsy.

> The ambiguous "Godfather" phenomenon, which had lent glamour and gravitas to organized crime, gave way to *Moonstruck, Married to the Mob, True Love, Working Girl, My Cousin Vinnie*—all films that represent working-class and better-off Italian Americans as philistines, tasteless boobs, Guidos and Big Hair girls, the kind of people who would have mashed potatoes dyed blue to match the bridesmaids' dresses. White ethnicity, in some venues, at some times,

came to mean the inelegant, disorganized enactment of others' life
dramas for our amusement—minstrelsy. (182)

Although the impact of this minstrelsy on Italian American identity is only
beginning to be studied, we do know that the images of Italian Americans
that are presented in the mass media tend to be aped or avoided. Organized
crime task forces report that criminals, especially those in the lower echelons
of known crime syndicates, began acting increasingly like the gangsters in
The Godfather films only after they had seen the films, that the power the
media associates with the mob is often appropriated by Italian American kids
in the hopes that peers will respect them and "leave them alone" (and it is not
just kids; Frank Lentricchia and Gay Talese are two prominent Italian American writers who do not mind such an association, and in fact at times have
gone out of their way to be associated with gangster mythology); Italian
American professionals and intellectuals must often fend off Mafia jokes as
they advance in their careers. Without positive images of Italian Americans
in the media, many Italian Americans tend to avoid any public association
with Italian American culture beyond necessary family or religious situations.
Such minstrelsy is one impediment in the way of cultural coalition building
that could bring working-class Italian Americans into constructive contact
with their counterparts of other ethnic and racial groups. As Zandy suggests,
working-class study provides us with "the missing identifying principle,"
which can help us "see other's history" and "construct a viable paradigm that
addresses multiple oppressions." Reading works of Italian American artists
through the lens of working-class culture will facilitate a cultural coalition
building that could bring working-class Italian Americans into constructive
contact with their counterparts of other ethnic and racial groups.

Chapter 6

Variations of Italian American Women's Autobiography

And who I am, I found, is almost a hyperbole for all women who write, for that condition is intensified through the Italian American experience: the tension between family and self is greater; the pull of tradition more present; the fear of autonomy and distance more harrowing; the neglect and disparagement by the outside more real.
—Helen Barolini, "Foreword" to *Chiaro/Scuro: Essays of Identity*

The writing of autobiographies by Italian Americans is a quite a recent phenomenon in the scheme of American literary history. Louis Kaplan, in *A Bibliography of American Autobiographies* (1961), identified twenty-eight Italian Americans who are responsible for 30 entries out of more than 6,000 written prior to 1945. Patricia K. Addis, in *Through a Woman's I* (1983), identified fourteen Italian and Italian American women autobiographers out of more than 2,000 between the years 1946 and 1976. And although the number of Italian American autobiographies has increased significantly in the past twenty years, critical study of only a few of those produced during this period is limited to a handful of articles, two dissertations, and one book.[1]

To any one familiar with Italian American culture, what is surprising about this literature is not how few autobiographies have been written especially compared to other major ethnic groups, but that any autobiographies have been produced at all. The small number of self-narratives can be attributed to several cultural obstacles within southern Italian culture, which most Americans of Italian descent have had to confront before they could first publicly speak and then write about the self. Identifying these cultural constraints and then examining how writers either work within or against them is important for understanding the self-fashioning that takes place in Italian American autobiography. This chapter presents a few characteristics of Italian American narrative in general and then analyzes their functions in contemporary autobiographical works by Italian American women.

The idea of speaking of one's self as independent of the community into which one was born is a recent development in Italian American culture. As Georges Gusdorf tells us in "Conditions and Limits of Autobiography":

> The conscious awareness of the singularity of each individual life is
> the late product of a specific civilization. Throughout most of human
> history, the individual does not oppose himself to all others; he does
> not feel himself to exist outside of others, and still less against
> others, but very much *with* others in an interdependent existence that
> asserts its rhythms in the community. (29)

The available literature on Italian oral traditions supports Gusdorf's observations. Telling the story of self in public was not part of any cultural tradition
that can be found south of Rome (the region from which come more than
eighty percent of the Italians who migrated to America). In the Italian oral
tradition, the self is suppressed and is not used as a subject in storytelling in
the communal settings of Italy, where one function of such stories was to
create a temporary respite from the harsh realities of everyday peasant life.
Traditional stories served both to entertain and to inform the young, while
reminding the old of traditions that have endured over the years. Personal
information was expected to be kept to one's self.

The caution against speaking publicly of one's self becomes a strong
warning against writing about the self. Southern Italian culture engendered a
strong distrust of the written word (an Italian proverb warns: *Pensa molto,
parla poco, e scrivi meno*—Think much, speak little and write even less). The
institutions of Italy—the Catholic Church as well as the State—maintained
power over southern Italian peasants by controlling literacy. Hence came the
immigrant's distrust of U.S. cultural institutions, which represented the ruling
classes. Not surprisingly, then, Italians gave little or no parental encourage-
ment of American-born children to pursue literary careers and put great pressure on these children to earn money as soon as they were old enough to be
employed. In her "Introduction" to *The Dream Book*, Helen Barolini hypoth-
esizes why few children of Italian immigrants wrote:

> When you don't read, you don't write. When your frame of refer-
> ence is a deep distrust of education because it is an attribute of the
> very classes who have exploited you and your kind for as long as
> memory carries, then you do not encourage a reverence for books
> among your children. You teach them the practical arts not the imagi-
> native ones. (4)

In spite of the low priority Italian Americans gave to writing on the whole,
several authors have emerged who document their experiences as Italian
Americans. These writers have created the basis for a distinctive literary
tradition that emerges out of a strong oral tradition. In this respect, Italian
American writers have much in common with writers who come from Native

American, Mexican American, and African American traditions. While, more often than not, the models for the structure of Italian American autobiographies come from the dominant Anglo-American culture, the content found in those structures is shaped by a home life steeped in a culture maintained by orality. Thus, the work produced by these writers should be read with an understanding of the inherited oral traditions as well as the American literary tradition that contribute to their cultural formation.

The strong storytelling traditions that we find in Italian American oral culture are filled with tales that explain the reasons for traditional rituals and provide information about how to life one's life. American writers of Italian descent point to oral tales as the impetus for the creation of their own stories. In retrospect, many of these writers have realized that these stories provide the very keys to their self identity. Much of Jerre Mangione's *Mount Allegro* deals with the stories his family told; Diane di Prima recalls in her memoir that her grandfather told her stories that have stayed with her. Gay Talese recounts quite a number of stories told by his family in *Unto the Sons*. Examining the role that oral tradition plays in the development of Italian American literature enables us to trace the evolution of the Italian American's conception of self and its progress into public discourse.

Besides a strong connection to orality, Italian American narrative literature exhibits a number of characteristics reflective of behavior determined by social codes found in southern Italian culture. The act of writing in any culture is a means of connecting one's self to the society that surrounds the self, a means of bridging the public and the private. For any autobiographer, the initial society is the nuclear family, the extended family of grandparents, uncles, aunts, cousins, godparents; the neighborhood; and the larger society outside the neighborhood. The unwritten rules that govern behavior within, between, and among these levels of interaction are manifested in Italian American autobiography.

Essentially, immigrant autobiographies document a remaking of the Italian self into an American self. The foreign born "I" argues for acceptance as the "you" that represents the established American who serves as the autobiographer's model reader. In immigrant autobiographies we find the sources of an autobiographical tradition that contrasts Italian culture with American culture, creating a tension that drives the narrative. This tension is found in the overriding theme of these immigrant narratives which is the flight to a better world or a promised land, a theme found in many immigrant autobiographies and slave narratives. Arrival in the United States brought the immigrant to a new system of codifying cultural signifiers, a system that often conflicted with a previous way of interpreting life. The resulting conflicts are most obvious in the early language encounters between Italian-speaking immigrants and the English-speaking Americans. Arrival in the United States also required that the immigrant develop a new sense of self in the context of the larger society. Many immigrant *cantastorie* shift from recounting traditional tales to telling personal narratives about the immigrant experience. This is the case with the earliest Italian American autobiographies of Constantine Panunzio, Pascal D'Angelo, and Rosa Cavalleri.

Those autobiographies of the children and grandchildren of immigrants, contrasted to immigrant autobiographies, document the remaking of the American self as Italian American. In these works, the more established and Americanized "I" explains, as it explores, the mystery of its difference from the "you" that is the model reader. Thus, for these Italian American writers, there exists the interesting option of identifying or not identifying with the American model reader. Although it is important for the immigrant writer to be accepted as an American, this argument is one that is needed less as the Italian American assimilates into American mainstream culture. However, what does become more important to these later writers is establishing a connection with one's Italian ancestry. When reading Italian American writers we need to observe the ways in which traditions, both American and Italian, both oral and literary, function in their narrative constructions. The evidence used to locate and analyze what Michael M. J. Fischer has called "interreferences" will be found in the Italian and American signifiers produced in these texts.

Several social codes are found in Italian American culture that generate the signs through which Italian American autobiography can be read. The two I focus on are *bella figura/brutta figura*—proper/improper public image and *omertà*—or the code of male behavior, known popularly (and mistakenly) as the code of silence. The code of *bella figura* traces back to the writings of Machiavelli and Lorenzo the Magnificent through their use of the word *sprezzatura*, an oxymoron that signifies the concept of both appraising and not appraising something. *Sprezzatura* explains the ironic quality of Italian culture that has informed the writing of Italian Americans. Until now this irony, which plays a major role in the Italian American narrative, has never been examined through its Italian origins. It is a concept that forms the basis of public representation of the Italian self. Understanding the code of *omertà* heightens the reception of the writings of Italian Americans. This code of manliness, coming from the Spanish *hombredad*, stresses that enduring any suffering to protect the family from outsiders is manly. It is also manly not to make public the family business, especially to those who are capable of using information to harm the family's reputation and thus their standing in the community. Southern Italian culture is replete with aphorisms and proverbs that advise against revealing information that can be used against the self or the family. *A chi dici il tuo segreto, doni la tua libertà*: To whom you tell a secret, you give your freedom. *Di il fatto tuo, e lascia far il fatto tuo*: Tell everyone your business and the devil will do it. *Odi, vedi e taci se vuoi viver in pace*: Listen, watch and keep quiet if you wish to live in peace.

The act of writing creates a more permanent record than conversation and is capable of generating unintended interpretations. In this way, *omertà* is tied to *bella figura*; by keeping silent about personal subjects, one does not reveal one's true self and can continue to maintain a self-controlled presence that is less vulnerable to penetration by outsiders. Often, hyperbolic language and actions are used to simultaneously vent pent-up feelings and disguise the impact new knowledge has on one's self. Any one who has observed a conversation between two Italians that seems to be going out of control—evidenced by intense screaming, threatening gestures, and so forth, and then dissipates into a hug or an arm-in-arm stroll toward a bar—has witnessed *bella figura* in communication. Semblances of this behavior carry over into the writing of Italian Americans.

Autobiography as Piecework: The Writings of Helen Barolini

Le parole son femmine, e i fatti son maschi. (Words are female, and actions are male.)
—Italian Proverb

Traditionally tied to the home, Italian American women often contributed to the family income by bringing work into the home, *ritaglia di tempo*, which literally translates as "time cuttings," which was the Italian phrase for piecework. In a similar light, when Italian American women add the work of writing to the demands of caring for the family, the result is that their autobiographies are more likely to be created in bits and pieces and published as articles in journals, magazines, and newspapers. Long in shadows of the spotlight given to her husband, the late Antonio Barolini, Helen Barolini has struggled to establish her identity as a writer and her writing provides us with an example of this experience. Barolini encourages women to reconsider this "work at home" tradition in terms of creating literature:

> A revolutionary concept could be based on the fact that Italian American women, by preference or not, have traditionally worked at home—taking in lodgers, making artificial flowers, doing piecework and embroidery, cooking for others . . . . Why not, then, work at home as writers? This would be revolutionary in admitting intellectual and artistic endeavors as "work," especially since they seldom produce immediate income. But the *miseria* mentality would finally have been overcome. ("Becoming" 31)

Although Barolini has not written an autobiography per se, she has provided us with a sense of one through her various essays (many of which are collected in *Chiaro/Scuro: Essays of Identity,* two novels, and *Festa: Recipes and Recollections.* Her writings reveal the plight of the woman in the immigrant home and create a sense of how traditions both survived and died in the experience of succeeding generations.

Barolini knows the importance that creating and reading literature plays in one's self-development. "Literature," she says, "gives us ourselves" ("Introduction" 51). Without experiencing models created by Italian American women, Barolini says, we cannot expect Italian American women to pursue literary careers. She believes that the Italian American women can contribute to a revitalization of American literature, which might begin with writing about the self in the manner of keeping journals and writing memoirs and autobiographies:

> ... quite missing, as yet, are the honest and revealing stories of women's inner lives. ... Redefining the self not as mirrored by society's expectations but in one's own authentic terms is essential for an integrated literary expression. Autobiography, when it is honest and not a camouflage, can be a powerful declaration of selfhood and a positive step toward establishing an incontrovertible voice. ("Introduction" 51–52)

What we often find in the autobiographical work of Italian American women, especially in the work of those who are children and grandchildren of the immigrants, is an intense politicization of the self, rare even among men in the old world. Frequently this politicized expression emerges in combative voices, representative of the intense struggle Italian American women have waged in forging free selves within the constraints of a patriarchal system. Although discussing the African American writer, Stephen Butterfield accurately describes the experience of Italian American women writers:

> Every writer must struggle to discover who and what he is; but if you are never able to take who you are for granted, and the social order around you seems deliberately designed to rub you out, stuff your head with little cartoon symbols of what it wants or fears you to be, and mock you with parodies of your highest hopes, then discovering who you really are takes on the dimensions of an epic battle with the social order. Autobiography then becomes both an arsenal and a battle ground. (*Autobiography* 284)

If creating an American identity was difficult for Italian American men, the process for Italian American women, as Barolini explains, would prove even more onerous. ". . . The displacement from one culture to another has represented a real crisis of identity for the Italian woman, and she has left a heritage of conflict to her children. They, unwilling to give themselves completely to the old ways she transmitted, end up, in their assimilationist hurry, with shame and ambivalence in their behavior and values" ("Introduction" 13). This shame and ambivalence often become the very building blocks of Italian American women's writing.

The house that Barolini grew up in was not a shrine to the old country; yet in spite of her parents' attempts to turn their back on their Italian heritage there were experiences that raised questions of identity in the young granddaughter of immigrants:

> I knew very little of my Italian background because it had always been played down. There had been the early confusion in grade school when I didn't know what to fill in on the form when nationality was asked: was I Italian because my name sounded strange, or was I American because I was born here? By the time I was in high school, it was simply a matter of embarrassment to be identified with a people who were the dupes of that great buffoon, Mussolini, and the war intensified our feelings of alienation from Italy and the efforts to be thoroughly American. We didn't want to be identified with the backward Italian families who lived on the North Side and did their shopping in grocery stores that smelled of strong cheese and salamis. Neither the ethnic nor the gourmet age had yet dawned in the states; it was still the time of the stewing melting pot and of being popular by being what everyone else was or thought we should be. ("Circular" 111)

However much the young girl wanted to disassociate herself from her Italian identity, there was always the female figure in black, her immigrant grandmother Nicoletta, "who didn't speak English and had strange, un-American ways of dressing and wearing her hair" ("Circular" 111), reminding her of her family's Italian origins. However, in leaving home to attend college, Barolini did not run away from, but right into an Italian identity. It was at Wells College in a Latin course that she was "first awakened . . . to unsuspected and deep longings for the classical Mediterranean world, and for an Italy from which after all I had my descent . . . " ("Circular" 111).

Later, on a trip to Italy, Barolini met the man she would marry, Italian poet and journalist Antonio Barolini. At first, the marriage upset her parents,

"who felt that in marrying an Italian I had regressed in contrast to my brothers, who had married Irish" ("Circular" 112). After settling into an Italian life,
the couple soon found themselves back in New York, where Antonio was
employed as a consul general for one year. Antonio's career required frequent
relocation between the United States and Italy. While the frequent travel to
Italy of writers such as Mangione served to develop and strengthen an American
identity, the opposite experience was Barolini's, whose life in Italy served to
recreate and nurture her Italian identity, as she explains in her "Introduction"
to *The Dream Book*: "I had to make the long journey to Italy, to see where
and what I came from, to gain an ultimate understanding and acceptance of
being American with particular shadings of Italianità. To say that was at odds
with the dominant American culture is an understatement. It is the essence of
life long *[sic]* psychological conflict" (269). This conflict surfaced in her first
novel, *Umbertina*, an America saga that dramatizes the lives of three generations of Italian American women. Because the first generation turns its back
on the past and looks only forward, it influences the second generation to do
the same; the third generation looks back to the past for keys to its identity.

The opening of *Umbertina*, appropriately enough, finds the granddaughter of the immigrant Umbertina, in a psychiatrist's office recounting a dream.
The psychiatrist analyzes the dream and suggests that she might begin her
search for self by digging into her family's past. This fiction then parallels
Barolini's own experiences of the third generation's return to the past and
recovery of an *Italianità*, that serves to establish a historical context for her
present-day self. This odyssey in search of self takes Barolini back and forth
from Italy to the United States.

In her essays Barolini identifies "conflicting signals" that she was getting
at home, at school, and in the larger world, and many of the essays in her
Chiaro/Scuro: Essays of Identity deal with the experience of receiving those
conflicting signals. In fact, the entire book serves as a map of the journey this
writer has made from her early childhood uncertainty as an Italian American
daughter to her adulthood in which she comes to understand her position as
an American woman writer.

Identity begins at home and Barolini's "How I Learned to Speak Italian"
demonstrates how a path traveled in our youth can become the direction our
future will take. The narrative bent of this essay brings out the connection
between learning Italian and identifying as an Italian American. Her motivation for learning the language was driven by her attraction to an Italian who
was studying at Syracuse University. Learning the language her parents never
taught her enabled her to unearth a past that reshaped her identity. Looking
back at her first lessons with Mr. De Mascoli, Barolini reflects on the fact that
she is now called *nonna* by her grandchildren: "I never knew the word with
which to address my own grandmother when I was a child standing mute and

embarrassed in front of her. Now, if it weren't too late, I would call her *Nonna*, too. We could speak to each other and I'd hear of the spring in Calabria" (37).

In "The Finer Things in Life," she presents a the story of her mother's assimilation into American culture, which is nicely contrasted by the author's assimilation into Italian culture. If ever a life was made for writing about culture clashes, it is Barolini's. "On Discovery and Recovery," "After-thoughts on Italian American Women Writers," "The Case of the Missing Italian American Writers," "Looking for Mari Tomasi," and "Writing to a Brick Wall" are pieces of the intellectual map of the author's discovery that Italian American literature was unknown to mainstream America. As Barolini's own work reveals, writing for Italian American women became not only a means of discovering an American identity, but also a means of discovering and creating a human identity. It is this dual requirement that turns writing into extremely challenging work for Italian American women as they attempt to reconcile past and present, old world and new:

> If not the immigrants, then their children and grandchildren are pre-
> eminently in the process of becoming something else, of making them-
> selves over, of reinventing themselves as an amalgam of old and new
> elements. They must do this for themselves because there is no fixed
> and tested pattern for them in the new environs; the old tradition is not
> perfectly viable or transmittable in the new world no matter what the
> sentimental folklorists of Little Italies say. (Ahearn 47)

In the houses of Italian America were women writers, who, until Barolini gave them *The Dream Book*, often felt they wrote in a void, isolated both from the Anglo-American literary tradition as well as the beginnings of a male-dominated Italian American tradition. Barolini's comments on the desires of second- and third-generation Italian Americans to emulate and adapt a more "American" way of life tells us much about the conflict the women experienced: "We wanted the look of tweed and tartan and not the embroideries of our grandmother's Italian bed linens; we wanted a Cape Cod cottage for our dream house, not some stuccoed *villino* with arches and tomatoes in the back yard" ("Introduction" 20).

Italian immigrant families, in spite of embracing the freedoms the United States provided that Italy did not, kept up the traditional male/female double standard. Women were not expected to attend college; when they did go, it was often with the parents' hopes that they would find husbands. Faced with such restrictive barriers erected by family and tradition, the Italian American woman who would be a writer could only become one by directly challenging the forces that tied her down. Barolini took it upon herself to recast the public image of the Italian American woman in her own likeness. In doing so, she proved not only that an Italian American woman could write, but also that any consideration of Italian American culture would be incomplete if the literary works produced by women were ignored.

In *Festa: Recipes and Recollections*, Barolini faces what is perhaps the riskiest challenge, destroying the stereotype of the Italian woman posed, wooden spoon in hand, slaving over a stove full of pots and pans. Barolini turns the woman's room, the family kitchen, into an embassy of cultural tradition. Although the Italian's relationship to food has been trivialized and reduced to the point of absurd media stereotyping, cooking and eating are important identity-creating acts. Barolini reminds us that cultural traditions are reinforced and transmitted in Italian American kitchens and at their dinner tables. "Starting in her kitchen, my mother found her way back to her heritage, and this, I suspect happened for many Italian American families who were rescued from lives of denial by the ethnic explosion of the sixties" (520).

Although writing about the family festivals in *Mount Allegro*, William Boelhower could just have easily been referring to Barolini's latest book:

> If the festive gathering is the heart of the transindividual subject, then the banquet is in turn the heart of the festive gathering. It is the macrosign of the autobiography just as the gathering is the text's most recurrent and typical and typical narrative sequence. The banquet, more than the gathering, changes linear time into rite and ceremony and individuals into a community. (*Immigrant* 1)

It is in such ceremonies as accompany meals and *feste* that ethnic identities are reinforced.

In *Festa: Recipes and Recollections*, Barolini examines the traditional relationship between Italians and food. She presents a personal monthly calendar the traditional Italian and Italian American celebrations and the foods that are part of those festive occasions. "Italy is as close to me as appetite (1)," she says in the first sentence. Her writing is a combination of memoir and research that demonstrates how food's history and preparation are inseparably bound. To Barolini, the instruments of cooking, the ingredients, whether seen in the wild or on a grocer's shelf, the aroma of a spice, a ragu, or a the sweet bite of a pastry, have the power to evoke endless streams of memories.

> *Mangiando, ricordo. Mangiando, ricordo*, translates as "By eating I remember." My memory seems more and more tied to the table, to a full table of good food and festivity; to the place of food and ritual and celebration in life. Yes, I believe in good food and in festivity.

Food is the medium of my remembrance—of my memory of Italy and family and of children at my table. (13)

By establishing the social and historical contexts for her recipes, Barolini does more than give us another cookbook, she relates personal history to group history and describes how the habits and work of women have been formed in and through the Italian family. With *Festa: Recipes and Recollections,* Barolini takes us into the private world of the Italian American woman, sharing what is often quite secretive authentic family recipes, what Boelhower refers to as the key to ethnic feasts: "Indeed, it would be farfetched to say that without recipes there could be no feast and that both competence and performance are held together by the shared ethnic values that circulate in both" (*Glass Darkly* 113).[2]

Complete with historical references, proper means of preparation, and manners of serving and consumption, Barolini has given her readers vital sustenance, not only for the body, as the caricature of Mamma Mia has been restricted to providing, but also for the mind and the soul. She has also presented us with a new way of reading the role of the woman in the kitchen. Barolini's version of the Italian American house encompasses many rooms, but the heart of what she has to offer lies in the kitchen and the stories that for more than 100 years women have shared as they worked together to whip up family banquets.[3]

To date we have only a few autobiographies by Italian American women that have not been co- or ghostwritten, although as I write many are in the works. And so, we must turn to the literary products produced *ritaglia di tempo* to examine the presence of Italian American women in the genre of American autobiography. In *Festa*, as in Barolini's many autobiographical essays, we find the stories that the men would never hear, stories passed down to daughters, nieces, and granddaughters who would one day turn them into literature. As Helen Barolini explains:

The displacement from one culture to another has represented a real crisis of identity for the Italian woman, and she has left a heritage of conflict to her children. They, unwilling to give themselves completely to the old ways she transmitted, end up, in their assimilationist hurry, with shame and ambivalence in their behavior and values. ("Introduction" 13)

This shame and ambivalence often become the very building blocks of Italian American women's writing. As an illustration I now turn to Diane di Prima's memoirs.

Diane di Prima: Autobiography as Self (Ex)Tension

Italian American women writers have explored the vital connection be-
tween being a woman and being ethnic in a world (America) which
traditionally has valued neither.
                      —Mary Jo Bona, "Broken Images, Broken Lives"

The driving force behind the poetry and prose of Diane di Prima is a gender-
and culture-based tension created between men and women and between
Italian and American cultures. In *Memoirs of a Beatnik* (1969), the first major
autobiography by an Italian American woman, di Prima opens her narrative
with the violation of two traditional taboos based on the two proffered codes:
she *talks* about *sex* in public. *Memoirs*, which begins with di Prima recounting the loss of her virginity and closes with her first pregnancy, represents the
definitive fracturing of silence that, as Helen Barolini best explains in her
"Introduction" to *The Dream Book*, has been the cultural force behind the
public silence of Italian American women. Although *Memoirs* does not con-
stitute a traditional autobiography, it should be considered as a precedent
against which we might better read the sexual personae of Italian American
women such as Madonna and Camille Paglia.

   In one of the few articles that examines di Prima's connection to her
ethnicity, Blossom Kirschenbaum points out that much of di Prima's poetry
defies and yet extends the traditional notion of *la famiglia*: "Poems flaunt
defiance of familial convention, but at the same time enlarge the circle of
quasi-family. . . . Even as she distances her parents, she carries forward an
understanding of her grandfather's legacy. In revolt, therefore, di Prima still
seeks precedents in her own cultural history" (38). Kirschenbaum examines
the Italian content of di Prima's writing and the poet's behavior, which rebels
against the traditional expectations Italian men have of their women; she sees
di Prima as fracturing the centuries-old code of silence, which men have used
in their attempts to control women:

   By rejecting self-sacrifice, and by sexualizing (even bestializing) the
   female goddess, di Prima has moved away from traditional Italian
   values and content. . . . By direct challenge of the concept of legiti-
   macy, by revising the index of who really counts, and by using non-
   English verse forms . . . di Prima has been rewriting history and, by
   implication, genealogy. She widens the concept of common ancestry
   and common progeny. . . . She defines her own usable past to include
   the Italian heritage that does not however limit her. She insists on her
   own definitions of history, country, and self. Confidence in that self

sustains her openness to the world of other selves. This is her legacy
to her children and grandchildren—and to her readers. (38)

This legacy is the result of her gaining control of language, which enables di
Prima to break away from the traditional holds that have kept Italian women
silent. By recreating her life through her art, she gives voice to the selves that
were kept silent in the past and in effect gains control over her self and how
that self is presented to society.

In her most recent memoir, *Recollections of My Life as a Woman* (2001),
she returns to the troubled times before she left home (when *Memoirs* begins)
and struggles to uncover and process the family secrets that have haunted her.
Like many other Italian American women writers, di Prima uses the figure of
the grandmother as a symbolic source from which she draws her ethnic identity.

Di Prima opens *Recollections* by establishing a connection to her immigrant grandparents. In contrast to her grandmother's fatalistic sense of real-
ism is her grandfather's idealism. Through her grandparents she learns at an
early age of the Italian sense of irony that enables her to envision unity in
opposites: "To my child's senses, already sharpened to conflict, there was no
conflict in that house. He was an atheist, she a devout Catholic, and for all
intents and purposes they were one" (1).

She weaves her memoir out of journal entries, unsent letters, accounts of
dreams, quotes from other writers, poetry, grandfather's stories, and a variety
of forms that interrupt the narrative flow and remind us that memory comes
in pieces. Through this structure we get a sense of the many selves that di
Prima has fashioned during her life and how they continue to interact in her
mind. She does it all through the singular sound of a voice that clearly
belongs to a woman looking back on her life, and in this respect, hers reflects
a more modernist approach to writing her life story.

Unlike her mother, who kept silent about her own breakdown until shortly
before her death, di Prima is able to talk about her weaknesses as well as her
strengths. When she confronts her siblings about their perceptions of the past,
she is met with silence. And as she continues to investigate and reimagine her
past, she begins to form the idea that the only thing the silence is covering
is childhood abuse—both physical and psychological. But di Prima is not out
to bare her wounds but to heal them. For di Prima, writing has always been
instrumental in healing the psychic traumas of life. Through the first few
chapters she confronts a number of them, which she first describes and then
reflects on. One key insight is that she has inherited what she calls "immigrant fear," something similar to what Rosa Cavalleri spoke of in her as-told-
to autobiography written by Marie Hall-Ets. Whereas Rosa's fear stemmed
from class divisions in the old country, di Prima's fear extends from the

family into the societal strata of her life in the form of travel timetables and insurance claim forms and manifests in her "not opening the door to the census taker" (42). Di Prima begins to take control of her public image only when she is presented with the opportunity to go to high school; it is the first time she is able to shape her life outside her family's reach, to "reinvent" herself. Later, by going away to college and living on her own, she is able to break away from the domination of her parents completely; yet her parent's attitudes continue to haunt her.

> The week I was leaving for college, my father turned to me, somber, to deliver his deepest message. Summation of his truth, what he had learned. Held me by the shoulder, or with his eyes: "Now don't expect too much. I want you to always remember that you're Italian." Not that we weren't as good, but however good we were, we would be held down. Or back. An underclass. (72)

Although di Prima has overcome the fatalistic sense of destiny communicated by her father, her autobiography reveals the success of an American woman of Italian descent both to overcome and to understand elements of the Italian culture that helped shape her life. In her struggle against the power of the patriarchal Italian American culture, she learns to identify with those oppressed by American culture. Her autobiography, as with much of her poetry, is an attempt to redefine the idea of woman through Italian American eyes. Unlike most earlier Italian American autobiographies, she speaks for herself and in the act of speaking breaks the traditional code of *omertà* in a manner that according to traditional expectations of female behavior would be *brutta* or *mala figura*. She uses the tensions of her life to extend her "self" beyond the traditional constraints that have silenced earlier generations of Italian American women. She also challenges and provides an alternative to what Sidonie Smith has called, the earlier, "official histories of the universal subject" (19). Di Prima uses the tensions of her life to extend her "self" beyond the traditional constraints that have silenced earlier generations of Italian American women.

Louise DeSalvo as Savior of Self

Louise DeSalvo, a professor of English at Hunter College in New York City, has made a career of connecting writers' lives and their works. After two powerful and original studies, *Conceived with Malice: Literature as Revenge* and *Virginia Woolf: The Impact of Childhood Sexual Abuse on Her Life and Work*, and a novel, *Casting Off*, DeSalvo turned her attention toward her own life in *Vertigo:*

A Memoir, a powerful testament to the belief that reading can change your life. "It is as simple as this," she writes. "Reading, and writing about what I have read have saved my life (7)." Reading *Vertigo* helps us to understand why Italian American women have written so few autobiographical works.

> Even as I write, though, I am wary of what I am writing. I am inescapably, an Italian-American woman with origins in the working class. I come from a people who, even now, seriously distract educated women, who value family loyalty. The story I want to tell is that of how I tried to create (and am still trying to create) a life that was different from the one that was scripted for me by my culture, how, through reading, writing, meaningful work, and psychotherapy, I managed to escape disabling depression. It is the unlikely narrative of how a working-class Italian girl became a critic and writer. (xvii)

This "unlikely narrative" is a verbal montage of a life lived in pieces that comes together only through writing. A mother's depression, a sister's suicide, and growing up in a home with a father at war and a mother in an enclave of women-managed households form the basis for DeSalvo's early traumas. She seeks salvation in the local library and fashions her identity through rebellion and pursuit of academic excellence. DeSalvo uses language as a "scalpel" to "exorcise" what has happened in her life. She has learned the secret of writing and how it enables the scribe to live life more fully by living it twice: She writes, "language, I have learned, by writing about this, gives birth to feeling, not the other way around" (105).

Each chapter is a wonderful, personal essay that explores the author's feelings. Chapters such as "Fixing Things," "My Sister's Suicide," and "Combat Zones" set the scene through dramatic recollection of everyday life. In "Finding My Way," "Safe Houses," and "Colored Paper" we learn of her early experiences in school and reading the classics. "Spin the Bottle" and "Boy Crazy" tell of her early sexuality and how her "obsession with sex" made her what she wants to be: "an outsider." As a young girl, DeSalvo suffers from fainting spells, from vertigo caused by the cycle of "loving, loss, grief and mourning" both for the living and the dead. Her encounters with gender and ethnic discrimination, which she overcomes through her power over language, remind us that Italians were not always assimilated. In "The Still Center of the Turning Wheel," she documents the education that enabled her to survive what her mother and sister could not.

Her comments on food, which form a leitmotif throughout the work, enter early: "Life, I have always believed, is too short to have even one bad meal," and are echoed in her chapter "Anorexia," where she recalls her college days and her embarrassment at having nothing to say when she's asked to name her favorite meal: "For years my mother cooked things that I believed no one should eat, things that I certainly couldn't eat. Old World things, cheap things, low-class things, things that I was sure were bad for you, things I was ashamed to say I ate, and that I certainly couldn't invite my friends over to eat. I wanted to pass for American. I wanted a hamburger" (204). DeSalvo's artistry lies in her deft manipulation of point of view. She moves from past to present to future, covering time in what seems to be the wink of an eye. Her style whirls like an amusement park ride in dizzying fun that is laced with a sense of danger.

"Portrait of the Puttana as a Woman in Midlife" is a rewriting of the essay that appeared in *The Dream Book*. A comparison of the two shows the growth of DeSalvo's poetic sensibility, her sense of self, her confidence in her ability to say what she is, what she wants out of life. She comes off as a tough girl who is not afraid to cry: "The way I write this, the 'tough broad' tone I take, is of course, a disguise for how hurt I was, for how seriously betrayed I felt" (*Vertigo* 238). In "Personal Effects," DeSalvo goes through a manila envelope her father gave to her after her mother's death. The envelope contains memorabilia: postcards, articles, and poems from women's magazines. By going through the little bit her mother saved, DeSalvo begins to understand why her mother never fulfilled her own artistic dreams. It is these pieces of others' lives that help the author complete the puzzle of her self: "The most trivial, yet the most important personal effects of the women of my family, come together at last, and mingle in my kitchen drawers and cupboards" (263). She has, at last fit them all into her life, first through language, then through feeling.

Vertigo joins Diane di Prima's *Memoirs of a Beatnik* and *Recollections of My Life as a Woman* and the collected essays of Helen Barolini as the major self-writings by American women of Italian descent. They have all dared not only to speak out, but also to write about their lives. The results are literary models, something DeSalvo longed for early in her life. "Though I had read scores of books, not one had been written by an Italian-American woman. I had no role model among the women of my background to urge me on . . ." (9–10). And her persistence and perseverance eventually paid off: "My work has changed my life. My work has saved my life. My life has changed my work" (12).

Autobiography as Journalism: Maria Laurino

"Were you always an Italian?" once asked former New York governor Mario Cuomo of Maria Laurino, author of a collection of essays that bears that question as its title. Cuomo, in his witty way, was being critical of Laurino's ambivalence about her Italian ancestry. And while the author shook her head no, she has since used that occasion as to come to terms with her Italian ancestry. Perhaps a better question for Cuomo to have asked might have been, What kinds of Italian have you been? The essays in her book *Were You Always an Italian,* subtitled *Ancestors and Other Icons of Italian America,* all feature a different stage in Laurino's development from being self-conscious to being in touch with the subconscious of what it means to call oneself an Italian American.

The nine essays, many of them occasional and previously published in a variety of mainstream venues, combine cultural history, travel sketches, feature journalism, and personal meditations to present the evolution of a consciousness shaped by shame and ignorance and changed by the knowledge and confidence that comes with age and experience. The longer essays are framed by two at the beginning and end that are both titled "Beginnings." This should be the first indication that we are invited to observe the development of an identity that will continue to change. All the essays serve as charms on a literary bracelet, each with its own cache of memories that say one thing to the author and often something quite different to the reader.

In the earlier essays, especially "Scents," "Tainted Soil," "Clothes," and "Rome," Laurino reveals her position deep in the shallow end of Italian culture. In these we find an identity built on the fear of being connected to the "Ginzo Gang" boys who, "Olive-skinned and muscular . . . were sexy in their crudeness; and their faint gasoline scent and oiled-down hair defined the image of Italian Americans in our school" (23). Her inability to translate a native Italian's pronunciation of the word *ships,* which she reads as "sheeps," reveals a lack of contact with the contemporary Italy and a knowledge of things Italian that has yet to transcend the Armani, Versace, and Gucci shops. Her discussion of ethnic self-hatred and cultural misunderstandings come close to Marianna DeMarco Torgovnick's similar laments in *Crossing Ocean Parkway;* however, Laurino finds a way to use her past to reinvent herself as a strong Italian American woman.

The best writing comes toward the end. "Bensonhurst," "Work," and "Ancestors" are all heartfelt, head strong, and stylistically sound. Sentences such as "Rage has found a secure home under the shingled roofs of Bensonhurst's row houses" (130) and "But my identity as an Italian-American of southern Italian descent can now be based on actual heritage, not on what I wanted to be, whether an eastern European Jew in high school or northern Italian later in life" (202) evidence how much she grows as a writer as the essays progress. It is as though she is sculpting her very identity out of words and the more she works, the better she sees and is seen.

The book is really a journey from the outside in, from the superficial concerns with how Italian looks on the body to how it sees from the soul. The later essays do not have the earlier whiny tone that comes with the naïveté, but Laurino could have most definitely benefited by earlier consultation with the writings of Diane Di Prima, Helen Barolini, and Louise DeSalvo and the critical studies of Mary Jo Bona and Gloria Nardini, writers who considered similar issues before her and successfully created ways of defining Italian American culture that defy earlier attempts. In this way the talents of this fine writer would have been challenged to push Italian Americanness to even more complex levels of meaning.

Chapter 7

Criticism as Autobiography

Nowadays the teaching of literature inclines to a considerable technicality, but when the teacher has said all that can be said about formal matters . . . he must confront the necessity of bearing personal testimony. He must use whatever authority he may possess to say whether or not a work is true; and if not, why not; and if so, why so. He can do this only at considerable cost to his privacy.
——Lionel Trilling, "On the Teaching of Modern Literature"

Criticism is about the other. Its drive for an objective voice is a search for a consensual voice and an attempt at openness. Let the ego be quiet so that the other can be seen. The drive is also for an absolute. However relativistic, however studded with "seems" or aware of rival positions the critical discourse may be, it aims at truth—in the Thomist sense, as the adequation of mind to the thing. Criticism that would be primarily preoccupied with self would be narcissistic, forget about the thing over there.
——Nicole Ward Jouve,
White Woman Speaks with Forked Tongue

Getting personal in criticism typically involves a deliberate move toward self figuration . . . .
——Nancy K. Miller, *Getting Personal*

What does it mean when Lucia Chiavola Birnbaum and Camille Paglia uncover the pagan origins of Italian Catholicism and look to it as a means of renewing and perhaps even revolutionizing American culture? Who remembers that Pietro di Donato did the same in fiction over fifty years ago, as did Luigi Fraina in left-wing publications of the early 1900s? What does it mean when Frank Lentricchia tries to tell Sandra Gilbert that her idea of feminism does not include working-class women such as his mother, and Gilbert opens her reply by signifying the Italian connection that should have prevented her from having to defend her thought to another paesano? When Camille Paglia turns her attention to "Madonna" and Frank Lentricchia shifts his from Pound to Puzo, from Yeats to DeLillo—or brings them together in the autobiographical *The Edge of Night*—it's time to ask how personal cultural criticism is becoming.

This look at the critical writings of Americans of Italian descent will borrow from what James Clifford has to say about the construction of ethnographic texts: In his "Introduction" to *Writing Culture: The Poetics and Politics of Ethnography* Clifford remarks that, "It has become clear that every version of an 'other,' wherever found, is also the construction of a 'self,' and the making of ethnographic texts . . . has always involved a process of 'self fashioning.' Cultural *poesis*—and politics—is the constant reconstitution of selves and others through specific exclusions, conventions and discursive practices" (24). And so, in their acts of cultural poesis, these and many other critics of Italian American descent are also creating figures of themselves. Recent developments in the reading and writing of ethnographic texts (Michael Fischer, James Clifford, Victor Turner, and others) can be used to develop an ethnographic approach to reading autobiographical elements found in the writing of American cultural critics of Italian descent.

A current trend in many fields of academic study is for scholars to incorporate the story of their lives into their life's studies. The 1995 annual convention of the MLA, one of the largest organizations of intellectuals in the United States, held a forum on ethnicity. One of the presenters at that forum was Linda Hutcheon. In her talk "Crypto-ethnicity," Hutcheon noted that several leading scholars in American and English literary studies were women whose ethnicity was hidden during their rise as intellectuals. Hutcheon noted that Sandra Gilbert, then-president of the MLA; Marianna Torgovnick and Cathy N. Davidson, professors at Duke University; and herself, a leading scholar of postmodernism, all descended from Italian immigrant families—a fact hidden by their adoption of their husbands' surnames. Unfortunately, Hutcheon did not explore the impact this cryptoethnicity has had on the intellectuals she identified, and so the question I raise in response to her presentation is, what significance lies in identifying one's ethnicity with one's intellectual work? When I posed this question to Hutcheon, offering to give her space in the journal *Voices in Italian Americana* in the fall 1996 issue dedicated to Italian American women's writing, she hesitated and then excused herself saying that it was not something she felt she could competently contribute to through her own research.

Frank Lentricchia, Sandra Gilbert, and Camille Paglia are just a few of the many American cultural critics of Italian descent whose writing has made me realize the sociopolitical implications of invoking an ethnic identity in one's criticism of American culture. Although they have become traditional intellectuals in the Gramscian sense, they have maintained a sense of identity with their ancestry, enough perhaps so that they also maintain an organic intellectual status. What becomes important in our readings of these critics as Italian Americans is understanding the connection between their Italian ancestry and their American culture; this connection is often the basis in which these writers ground their cultural criticism. Essentially they are reinventing their ethnicity and understanding how ethnicity is reinvented by each generation is accomplished by reading, what Michael Fischer calls a narrative's "inter-references between two or more cultural traditions," which "create reservoirs for renewing humane values" (201). By identifying and reading these interreferences we will be able to see that, as Fischer concludes, "Ethnic memory is . . . or ought to be future, not past oriented" (201). It is in this spirit that I offer the following examination of activity by contemporary Italian American cultural critics.

Frank Lentricchia: The Critic as Cultural Immigrant

The man who tries to explain his age instead of expressing himself is doomed to destruction.
—Ezra Pound, (quoted in Frank Lentricchia's *Modernist Quartet 215*)

By typical Italian American measurements of success, Frank Lentricchia's decision to pursue a career as a professor and critic of American literature is not one that ranks highly. The idea that education should be utilitarian predominates even into third-generation families. However, Lentricchia revises this idea by seeing his becoming of a "traditional humanist" as "being where the *padrone* is in intellectual terms" (Salusinszky 189). In an interview with Imre Salusinszky, Lentricchia emphasizes:

> It is not for nothing that I tell you that my grandfather voted for Eisenhower and told me that what this country needs is a Mussolini. There was their experience shoveling the shit, and then there was the experience of the *padrone*: one or the other. There was no middle ground, and if you wanted to get away from where you were, the best thing would be to be where the *padrone* was. (189)

Raised in Utica, New York, by working-class parents who were children of Italian immigrants, Lentricchia's move away from home became more than just a physical relocation to the land of the *padroni*. Of his experience in moving south to attend Duke University, he has said, "I stepped from an Italian-American context into another context that was culturally homogenous, but in a very different way. I could understand it, I could even admire the cultural unity and rootedness of life; it was another example of where I had been" (Bliwise 2). But, as Lentricchia has revealed, the Duke experience would wrench him away from an undivided loyalty to his working-class Italian American background.

When I saw the racist thing, it also made me see that cultural unity
is purchased sometimes on the basis of exclusion and destruction
and domination of other human beings. That made me not want to
be a great rooter for Italian-American ethnicity. That ethnicity was,
yes, based upon our sense of being different and sometimes alienated, but it was also based on our sense that those outside us were
to be suspected, not to be trusted. (Bliwise 7)

Although in his interviews, and occasionally in the introductions to his publications, Lentricchia goes to great extremes to identify himself as Italian
American, he is very aware that by becoming an intellectual the possibility
exists to repress or forget "one's roots and one's awareness of difference and
the impact of difference on literature" (Salusinszky 189). The body of
Lentricchia's work can be read as an attempt to create a middle ground on
which he can become a synthesis of Gramsci's "organic" and the "traditional"
intellectual. Gramsci defines the two as follows:

Intellectuals in the functional sense fall into two groups. In the first
place there are the "traditional" professional intellectuals, literary,
scientific and so on, whose position in the interstices of society has
a certain inter-class aura about it but derives ultimately from past
and present class relations and conceals an attachment to various
historical class formations. Secondly, there are the "organic" intellectuals, the thinking and organising element of a particular fundamental social class. These organic intellectuals are distinguished less
by their profession, which may be any job characteristic of their
class, than by their function in directing the ideas and aspirations of
the class to which they organically belong. (*Prison Notebooks* 3)

Lentricchia's solution is to create an approach to reading and writing that
not only reveals acts of power and the structures that create them, but also
works to empower his readers. He has made an enviable career out of studying and teaching modern and contemporary literature. Unlike Trilling,
Lentricchia seems not to mind the loss of privacy it has brought. In fact, he
seems to thrive on the amount of attention his work has brought him, as
evidenced by the many interviews he grants. However, very much like Trilling, he has built his position by challenging contemporary interpretations and
theories of canonical literature. Like Trilling, Lentricchia has also shied away
from the literature that comes from his own ethnic background.

Lentricchia refers to Italian American literature as eventually having only
"archaeological significance" (Bliwise 7). Until he takes on the introduction to
and interpretation (better read as defense) of the fiction of Don DeLillo,

Lentricchia does little work on Italian American writers. Although his earliest work does evidence signs of acknowledgement of his *Italianità*. During the mid-1970s, while he was working on his second book, a study of Robert Frost, Lentricchia makes two brief appearances in the first two issues of *italian americana*. The first was a short review of John J. Soldo's *Delano in America and Other Early Poems*; the second was an intriguing essay that attempts to set the record straight on the origins of Italian American fiction. What is most interesting in these two articles is his definition of Italian American writing:

> a report and meditation on first-generation experience, usually from the perspective of a second-generation representative; in such writing Italian-American experiences and values are delineated as they appear in dramatic interaction with the mainstream culture. In other words, a book of poems or stories authored by a person of Italian background is not ethnic in character unless the writer engages his ethnic heritage. I make these preliminary remarks because it is believed in certain academic and publishing circles that ethnicity in imaginative literature is a value, when in fact ethnicity is only a descriptive concept that helps us to classify, not judge, literature. (*Delano*, 124)

This definition limits the impact, and thus the relevance, of Italian American ethnicity to the first two generations by keeping third-generation members such as Lentricchia outside the experience. Undoubtedly this early definition is one that Lentricchia would probably have revised had he continued working with "ethnic" literature.

After reading the fine scholarship he presents in "Luigi Ventura and the Origins of Italian-American Fiction," one cannot help but say that Italian American literature would have benefited greatly by Lentricchia's continued participation as a critic. In this essay, Lentricchia criticizes Rose Basile Green, the author of the first and only book-length study of Italian American literature, for making the "serious error" of claiming that Luigi Ventura's novel *Peppino* was first published in 1913. Lentricchia demonstrates that Ventura's novel was, in fact, first published in 1885, thus making him the "first published author of Italian-American fiction" (191). He follows this bibliographical correction with an illuminating interpretation of the work that sets forth a critical approach to Italian American literature, the likes of which has unfortunately been used too infrequently since.

Whatever caused Lentricchia to move away from Italian American literature right at a the point when it was beginning to attract scholarship and criticism is unknown, but perhaps his decision to avoid it can be attributed to the lack of status such marginalized literature has, and in many cases still has, in the academic environment of his time. However, as we will see, Lentricchia's subsequent work, although not on Italian American subjects, is certainly done quite self-consciously as an Italian American. In fact, whereas Lentricchia has only recently published his first autobiographical essay, by reading the Italian signs in his body of critical writing, we can, as I will show, read his criticism as a form of autobiography.

As Nancy K. Miller points out in the opening essay *Getting Personal: Feminist Occasions and Other Autobiographical Acts,* Frank Lentricchia "gets personal" in his criticism when he invokes his working-class Italian background in his response to Sandra Gilbert and Susan Gubar's attack on one of his essays. Miller does no more than cite Lentricchia as an example of a self-figuring phenomenon found in a great deal of 1980s criticism that " . . . at its best . . . is at odds with the hierarchies of the positional . . . [and] may produce a new repertory for an enlivening cultural criticism" (25). What follows is an examination of some of the autobiographical elements found in Lentricchia's critical work, a description of his (re)presentation or (re)definition of the Italian American, and a demonstration of how this "personalization" works to enliven cultural criticism.

Not until his fourth book-length study, nearly twenty years into his career, does Lentricchia begin to use autobiographical references in his criticism; however, the seeds of these references can be found in his second book, a critical study of Robert Frost. Unlike his first study, *The Gaiety of Language* (1968), in which he states, "It is to the poems, then, that we must look if we wish to see the whole Stevens, the whole Yeats" (6), Lentricchia presents readings of Frost's poetry that are framed in biography. He looks beyond Frost's poems and into his letters and essays to illustrate the poet's landscape of self. Essentially Lentricchia abandons the New Criticism approach he used on Yeats and Stevens for a more historicist reading of Frost. From this work, Lentricchia leaves the close reading of individual authors behind to go after a much larger prey: the history of literary theory in the United States. In his influential *After the New Criticism* (1980), Lentricchia takes on the individual authorities who influenced his earlier approaches to literary criticism. He challenges the major schools of literary theory by identifying the hegemonic authorities they, one after the other, have become. By revealing their constraints he identifies the narrow tradition they have institutionalized. Like a calculating raging bull, Lentricchia runs through theory after theory, and the men associated with them, in his attempt to redirect the course of literary criticism. He argues for a sociopolitically and ideologically charged criticism that does not succumb to the elitism of New Criticism, the monologism of structuralism, the totalization of Marxism, or the sociopolitical silence of deconstruction. Foucault is the only individual who emerges from this study as a possible model for a new critical theory, one that is a "picture of power-in-discourse that may move critical theory beyond its currently paralyzed debates" and toward a "polyvalence of discourses" (351). Lentricchia, by examining the achievements of individuals through biographical criticism instead of approaching the historical task through the examination of periods and movements, ignores a Marxist maxim and enacts an anarchical approach typical of an Italian, who in Rudolph Vecoli's words, have a "reputation for being notorious individualists" (131).

In his next book, *Criticism and Social Change* (1983), Lentricchia examines the possibilities for a socially responsible criticism found in the writing of Kenneth Burke. Lentricchia begins to create the politically responsive approach to criticism that he calls for in his earlier work, and at the same time reveals in much more detail the relationship between his own personal background and his critical stance. Italian signs abound in Lentricchia's study of Kenneth Burke and Paul deMan. His dedication to Bernard Duffey is written in Italian, "e tu maestro." In his acknowledgements he thanks people with a "Grazia," which should read "Grazie." However these are but minor signs of Lentricchia's *Italianità*. The photograph on the back cover, which has been the subject of several remarks and essays, is not the typical academic pose; it is more in the tradition of the Neapolitan street tough who has caught the eye of a camera-toting tourist. In true Vichian fashion and in an effort to avoid the abyss created by the French continental theory that has captured the attention of America's cultural critics, Lentricchia goes back into American philosophical history, advances his earlier thinking on Robert Frost, and turns our attention to "pragmatism . . . the quintessential American point of view, the philosophical rationalization for a new adventure for history and culture founded on the rejection of the Old World and all of its encrusted precapitalist evils" (3). Lentricchia's argument, through which he joins the oppositional critical tradition Antonio Gramsci, Raymond Williams, and Edward Said established, is that, "Criticism . . . is the production of knowledge to the ends of power and, maybe of social change" (11). Lentricchia points his persuasive pen at the "we," the "traditional" intellectual whose "struggle must be against himself, against his own training and history as an intellectual, and against the culture that he has been disciplined to preserve, his very traditional personal history as an intellectual, if critically appropriated, will turn out to be one of the real sources of his radical cultural power" (8). This can be done, he says, by retrieving one's "outsider experience," which can be "brought to bear in critical dialogue with the traditional confirmation he has been given" (8). Although this is something more easily said than done, Lentricchia makes good on his promise to produce such a criticism, and although he has identified the approach in this book, not until his next book is it actually put into practice on literary texts.

During the 1970s, as the study of critical theory rises to prominence in English departments through the advances of poststructuralist methodologies, biography and thus sociopolitical contexts become almost irrelevant in critical readings. Against this tide Lentricchia begins work on refining the critical approach he introduced in *Criticism and Social Change*. He starts by rereading Foucault (the one hero in *After the New Criticism*) through Marx and publishes two lengthy essays on Foucault in the 1982 spring and summer issues of *Raritan*. His next move examines the work of William James, from which he publishes an article in the fall 1986 issue of *Cultural Critique*. Lentricchia then returns to one of the subjects of his first book, Wallace Stevens, to demonstrate a critical approach fashioned out of his readings of Foucault and James. Lentricchia publishes an essay on Stevens, "Patriarchy against Itself—The Young Manhood of Wallace Stevens," in the summer 1987 issue of *Critical Inquiry* in which first situates Stevens's poetry in the context of Stevens's middle class American male life, and then moves into a critique of Sandra Gilbert and Susan Gubar's feminist criticism, which he calls "essentialist." This is examined later in this chapter.

In "Anatomy of a Jar," the title of his introduction, Lentricchia tells an anecdote of his own as a way of setting up his approach to Stevens and the poet's famous "Anecdote of a Jar." And like Stevens's anecdote, Lentricchia's "reveals the essence of the larger unspoken story, and in that very moment becomes exegesis of a public text; the unpublished items become published" ("Patriarchy" 3).

> One day, my grandfather, my mother's father, at age seventy-nine, while rocking and smoking (but not inhaling) on his front porch in Utica, New York, in mid-August heat (which he refused to recognize by wearing his long johns), directed his grandson's attention (who was then about thirteen) to the man sitting on his front porch across the street: not rocking or smoking but huddled into himself, as if it were cold, aged eighty. Gesturing with a cigarette in his hand toward "this American," as he called him (in Italian he inserted between "this" and "American," an adjective best left untranslated), all the while nodding and in a tone that I recognized only later as much crafted, he said: *"La vecchiaia è carogna."* A story of biographical incident, funny if you can translate the Italian, but representative? Probably in the mind of yours truly. You don't because though some in my family would—as would many first-generation Italian Americans, some fewer of the second generation, and fewer yet of my generation. My mother's father is dead, and those who remember him (and immigrants like him) in the right way, with necessary specificity, where do I find them? Soon this will be an anecdote for

me alone because soon it will have no claim whatsoever to being
what all we anecdotalists want our stories to be—a social form
which instigates cultural memory: the act of renewal, the reinstate-
ment of social cohesion. (4)

Lentricchia sees this anecdote in opposition to the more mainstream stories
of George Washington and the cherry tree, and as similar to Stevens's story
in that its "representational power" is "equally in peril" (4). Such power, as
he later suggests, is dependent on a "cultural authorizer." Lentricchia asks,
"Who will renew my grandfather's cultural story? For whom can my
grandfather's biography be important? What might it mediate?" (5) Lentricchia
suggests that anecdotes depend on a stable outside narrative that cultural
authorizers can create. He creates such a narrative by setting Stevens's poetry
in the context of Stevens's life story. In essence, he re-creates Stevens's story,
and by doing so creates a cultural myth in the fashion of Giambattista Vico
who saw historiography as a process created by philology, philosophy, and
self-reflection. The answers to Lentricchia's questions about the relevance of
his grandfather's story lie in the tradition of Italian American literature and
culture, especially as that tradition moves from its basis in orality to a literary
basis. His grandfather's story is redeemed and reinstated every time an Italian
American writer chooses to write that history in fiction or nonfiction. By
writing that anecdote, Lentricchia, whether he realizes it or not, has answered
his own questions. Although he goes on to tell Stevens's story, through Foucault and William James (instead of telling the story of Tomaso Iacovella),
Lentricchia, by recounting that anecdote, has established an underlying discourse that not only haunts his approach to Stevens's but established a
noncanonical tradition through which we can and should reread his earlier
work. When Lentricchia quotes Vito Coreleone as "a connoisseur of reason"
who has something to teach the new pragmatists, in his earlier chapter on
William James, he essentially authorizes the oral tradition of the experien-
tially based culture of his grandparents. And when he turns to the work of
fellow Italian American Don DeLillo as an example of a counterdiscourse
"working to undermine the discourses of abstraction and domination" (25),
he finds the subject of his next two edited books; through DeLillo Lentricchia
finds a version of himself. In an interesting and less ethnically identifiable
way, Lentricchia returns to Italian American literature after a more than fifteen-
year hiatus. Through DeLillo, Lentricchia sees that the writing produced by
an American writer of Italian descent has transcended the barrier of "archaeological significance" and has entered the contemporary canon in a way no
other Italian American writing has to date. Lentricchia, while never calling
DeLillo a *paesano*, identifies with this writer in a way he cannot with the
subjects of his earlier criticism.

In essence, he finds in DeLillo's works the socially committed writing that Lentricchia's criticism will thrive on. Besides his ten novels, DeLillo has been publishing fiction in mainstream literary journals and popular magazines for nearly three decades. He really needs no introduction to American readers. Yet, although his work has been the subject of many articles and one book-length study, Lentricchia entitles the republication, as a book, of a *South Atlantic Quarterly* issue dedicated to DeLillo, *Introducing Don DeLillo*. In his introductory essay, "The American Writer as Bad Citizen," Lentricchia aggressively takes on DeLillo's right-wing critics and sets the tone for the volume, which might more accurately be retitled *In Defense of Don DeLillo*. Lentricchia locates DeLillo in the most American of literary traditions, that is, in the tradition of social criticism that has been the center of the works of mainstream luminaries such as Emerson, Thoreau, and Twain (5). What Lentricchia has been working toward in his theory and practice of American literary criticism, is precisely what DeLillo does with American literature: he keeps "readers from gliding into the comfortable sentiment that the real problems of the human race have always been about what they are today" (6). This creative criticism, or critical creativity, is a tour de force through which Lentricchia reminds us that fiction, like criticism, is as much about concealing the visible as it is about revealing the invisible.

In a book that represents Lentricchia's shift away from criticism and toward what I call autofiction, a book he dedicates to Don DeLillo, Lentricchia turns to the text that is his life, and for the first time is the author of the text he interprets. In tune with postmodern sounds, this autobiographical work, titled *The Edge of Night*, defied the more traditional approaches found in the *Diaries* of Mario Cuomo, and the autobiographies of Lee Iacocca and Geraldine Ferraro (which both use co-writers). Lentricchia's imaginative autobiographical narrative, which focuses on a period covering a little over a year of his life, refuses to speak for an entire culture and concentrates on his own personal struggle to form an identity composed of a working-class childhood and a middle-class adulthood. What makes Lentricchia's autobiographical narrative significant is his use of irony, which marks a new and exciting dimension to Italian American writing.

Lentricchia plays with *bella figura* and its counterpart *brutta figura* throughout this work. His use of hyperbole, spectacle (like a Scorsese film, the narrative maintains an in-your-face attitude"), indirection, and echoes of oral tradition all work to enable him to maintain and break the code of *omertà* simultaneously. Like di Prima, Lentricchia's narrator comes to us in two voices: the literary and cultural critic that we have come to know through his earlier writings; and the son of two working-class Italian American children of immigrants who sees himself as at the "dead end of tradition" (7):

I am an Italian-American, one of whose favorite words bears his grandparents, his parents, his neighborhood, his favorite movie

director, but not his children, not his colleagues, not where he lives
now, and not most of his friends. I'm not telling you that I'm alienated from my ethnic background. I'm not alienated from it, and I'm
not unalienated from it. (8)

And then there is a new voice, one that is extremely critical of its own
participation in the activity of the literary academy—a place he refers to as
"the Imperial Palace of Explanation," where live "those-who-always-already-
know" (125). Unlike di Prima, Lentricchia never privileges one voice over
the other, and so the reader can never point to the "real" Frank Lentricchia;
in fact, we get a sense that the real Frank Lentricchia exists in the writing and
not in the written.

In *The Edge of Night*, its title taken from a 1950s television soap opera,
Lentricchia combines meditations on Yeats and Eliot, subjects of much of his
earlier writing, with accounts of his past and imaginative flights into the absurd.
The opening epigraph from Pirandello points to the plurality of the individual
who is the subject of writing: "A character really has his own life, marked with
his own characteristics, by virtue of which he is always some one. Whereas a
man . . . *a man* can be no one" (XII). Connected to this is another epigraph,
taken from Martin Scorsese's *Raging Bull*, which opens the first section: "Even
you don't know what you meant by you." Anyone looking for the "real"
Lentricchia will no doubt be frustrated in this work. The "I" in this text is
plural; it floats on wave after wave of memory-made fiction and fiction-made
memory. Like the poets of the Italian crepuscular tradition, Lentricchia parodies
high culture through popular culture. Through this work he bridges diverse
influences of his life; Yeats and Eliot become equals to his grandparents.

In the first chapter Lentricchia presents a version of himself that tells the
reader the narrator is unreliable. His mother, "prone to opera," tells his wife
that, "He exaggerates. He exaggerates everything. He gets it from his mother"
(4). Yet he is also like his grandfathers: Tomaso Iacovelli, the storyteller and
keeper of the oral tradition, and Augusto Lentricchia, the frustrated writer
who produced a manuscript that came into his grandson Frank's possession
only after Augusto's death. *Le memorie di Augusto Lentricchia* is 1,200 pages
of recorded memories and poems covering the years 1920–1980.

The Edge of Night transcends any traditional definition of autobiography.
It is autofiction. Throughout the work, we witness a self constantly remaking
the self, so that no single identity can be pinned down and explained. Each
chapter is the result of a shedding of a self that continues to evolve. In this
way, Lentricchia fashions a masterful example of *bella figura;* the figure
comes from the real, but does not return to the real.

Lentricchia admits that his interest lies more in the process of writing than
in the resulting product. "I never existed except in this doing" (6), he writes,

but that "I" cannot be pinned down. For once the process stops, the I stops being. Each section of this autofiction finds a new I emerging to encounter experiences that re-creates the sense of self. In the first chapter, "Part One, To the Monastery (May 1991–September 1991)," one Frank Lentricchia goes off to Mepkin Abbey, reads Thomas Merton, and gains a new sense of religion. In section 2 of "Part One" a different Frank Lentricchia takes off for Ireland, the homeland of his literary self and one of his cultural grandfathers—Yeats. He goes in search of the ghosts of the writers he has read and about whom he has written (68). On this trip he transports a new self that he has begun creating through his latest writing project, which is unlike anything he has previously written; he is paranoid about losing that self—an extremely fragile self that is newly created on paper. These two selves—the newly literary and the critical Franks—come together in a fanciful encounter between DeLillo and Yeats at Dominick's Restaurant in the Bronx. He returns to this trip toward the end and learns that the name Frank does not exist in Irish (83).

In the third chapter we witness a transition from which the literary critic becomes the self critic; in essence, the end of literary criticism becomes the beginning of self-criticism. Titled "My Kinsman, T. S. Eliot," this section explores the social consequences of achieving literacy (104) through an intellectual version of Nathaniel Hawthorne's short story, "My Kinsman, Major Molineaux" (90). Throughout the rest of the work Lentricchia delves deep into both his historical past and into his imagination; he begins not only to fantasize, but also to criticize his past as in this example in which the narrator takes on the perspective of his daughter:

> You know, when it suits you, you come on like a wop right off the boat. You're proud of this, to put it mildly. It's like a weapon, like a knife, your ethnicity. Why did you take relish in teaching us those words when we were young? Wop, greaseball, dago, guinea, spaghetti bender. You like those words, but they just bore us. We don't care. (144)

Lentricchia knows that the price of social mobility is the creation of alternative selves that adapt to new situations arising when one encounters on the trip away from the family and into society:

> The more I went to school the more I became the stranger in the house. Which, of course, was the point. Which is what we all wanted, a gulf, the gulf made by their love, though we would never have thought to say it that way. My son the college teacher, etc. (151)

Like di Prima, Lentricchia returns to his Italian American past to dig up the bodies of those who have shaped him. Unlike di Prima, his is a triumphant return; he is in control of the ghosts that have haunted him and has created a way to haunt them back. In a masterful stroke of *bella figura*, he ends the narrative with a recollection of a scene that took place in Hollywood:

> I remember taking my parents on one of those Hollywood studio tours, years ago. In the middle of it, my father, who's about Fellini's age, shook his hand in a quintessential Italian gesture . . . and he said, "Madon Frank, the fakery!" He loved that tour, especially when he said: "Madon Frank, the fakery!" (182)

Such an ending to a major critic's foray into creative nonfiction suggests that perhaps we readers have been taken for a ride, on a word tour of an echo chamber containing a number of subjects each pointing to the other when a voice is heard.

In Moments of Vertigo: Sandra Mortola Gilbert

> *The dead are puzzled*
> *was it for this they left*
> *the land of grammar, the syntax of their skin?*
> *We turn the pages. We read.*
> *Sometimes, in moments of vertigo,*
> *we notice they're speaking.*
>   —Sandra M. Gilbert, "Elegy"

As Italian Americans move into the social and political institutions of American culture, an increased need arises to see one's self inside those institutions to develop a strong sense of Italian American culture. An increased need also exists to encounter the books that can present us with a sense of what it means to be an American of Italian descent. Inside the American educational system, from kindergarten through graduate studies, are concepts of race, gender, and class constructed, maintained, or challenged, and transmitted by those in privileged stations of intellectual authority. The business of intellectuals is to formulate the ideas and the ideals by which we measure our successes and failures. Our sense of what is real, what is right, what is wrong, and what is important to know depends on those who write the books we study, who create ways of reading those books as well as the multimedia productions we consume. Conditioned by demands of objectivity in research and scholarship, Italian Americans have long avoided their own stories in developing their analyses and critiques of culture. But this is changing. Today, many American intellectuals of Italian descent are heeding Michael Novak's advice that, "There is no other way but autobiography by which to cure oneself of too much objectivity" (61).

Sandra Mortola Gilbert has a long history of acknowledging her Italian American ethnicity, more often in her poetry than through any critical consideration of Italian American women writers. Her important contributions to American culture, often written in collaboration with Susan Gubar, include *The Madwoman in the Attic* and its three-volume sequel, *No Man's Land*. Most recently, Gilbert and Gubar have flexed their collective intellectual muscles through their satirical, *Masterpiece Theater: An Academic Melodrama*, which dramatizes the culture wars of the late 1980s and early 1990s. Through this publication, Gilbert and Gubar position themselves on middle ground between the back-to-the-basics conservatives and what they call the "forward to instability" radicals. But whereas Gilbert and Gubar have become America's dynamic duo of feminist literary studies and although they have both contributed significantly to a sense of community in women's studies, Gilbert leaves the partnership to speak in her own individual voice in her creative work in which Gilbert presents both the possibilities and problems of becoming a model for the Italian American intellectual.

Undoubtedly Gilbert has something to contribute to Italian American culture, and she chooses to bring it mostly to her poetry, of which she has said she is surprised if someone tells her he or she has read it. I would be surprised, however, if someone educated in English and American literary history and criticism has not read her work; I see her critical work as the foundation for her power as an intellectual. Literary scholars and critics such as Vincent Leitch and Frank Lentricchia are aware enough of the power that Gilbert and Gubar have in affecting feminist discourse that they have challenged their program through criticism. Leitch, acknowledging their power in his latest work, tells us, "It is from headquarters that GG [Leitch's nickname for Gilbert and Gubar] send their message. They occupy the place of leadership, surveying a site of division and envisaging overall harmony. They stand just above the fray, mediating historical and cultural differences. The dialogue of interlocutors, in this scenario, ultimately produces community" (65). Leitch comes to the conclusion that their shared position (which leads him to refer to the pair as "GG") is "resolutely anti- or pre-postmodern." And although this seemingly poses no problem for Gilbert and Gubar, for Leitch it raises the question as to the possibility for "internal differences between them" (66). Gilbert's ethnicity is the one difference between Gilbert and Gubar that is rarely exposed.

Although Gilbert and Gubar have established themselves as powerful forces in the shaping of a community of feminist discourse, Gilbert has done little to bring this critical power to bear on issues concerning the Italian American community, which raises several questions: What does it mean to be identified as an Italian American intellectual? Does it mean that one has a thorough knowledge of Italian American culture? Or is having been born into an Italian American family enough to rate identification as an Italian American? And is there any benefit to being so identified? Without a recognized culture or even a subculture, identifying oneself as an Italian American intellectual does not seem to offer much career opportunity. However, without the power to insert Italian American literature into the canon, Italian American history into social sciences and humanities courses, an Italian American culture strong enough to support intellectuals may never exist. So what comes first: the community or the intellectual?

Without a sense of intellectual community among Italian Americans, individual Italian Americans have begun efforts to bring Italian American cultural issues into mainstream forums. Twenty years ago Frank Lentricchia saw the need for a historical collection of writing by Italian Americans. Without a sense of a supporting Italian American community, with the advice that such a book had no market, and instead of looking for ways to build a community of support, he abandoned the project. And yet, almost subversively, he strategically inserted accounts of his Italian American working-class culture in his critical studies. Twice, petitions Anthony Tamburri and I created to establish an MLA Italian American discussion group were turned down without much of an explanation beyond the allegation the membership did not perceive a need for one. Special conference sessions proposed on Italian American literature have not fared much better. Gilbert, long a contributor to Italian American publications such as Helen Barolini's *The Dream Book* and the anthology *From the Margin*, helped usher in a permanent MLA discussion group in Italian American culture. Recently the larger Italian American community has begun to use the power of its money, along with its voice, to support intellectual endeavors; perhaps now that recent publications and republications of works by Italian American writers is proving that the old beliefs that Italian Americans do buy or read books are wrong, we have reason to be at least cautiously optimistic about the future of Italian American intellectuals. Italian American culture is beginning to make its way into academia. The recent appointment of historian Philip Cannistraro as distinguished professor of Italian American studies at CUNY's Queens College, along with another permanent position in Italian American studies at SUNY's University at Stony Brook, and with endowed chairs now in Italian studies at the University of Connecticut, Storrs; Seton Hall University; California State, Long Beach; and yet another in the fundraising process at Montclair State University, all tell us that there will be a need for strong Italian American intellectuals. But can we expect stellar intellectual figures such as Lentricchia and Gilbert to become those role models for future Italian American intellectuals? This question will not be answered until we establish the link between the American individual and the ethnic communities from which those individuals have come.

I would like to go back in history to a moment in which two powerful intellectuals of Italian American ancestry faced off on the pages of one of the major journals of literary academia. In 1987 Lentricchia critiqued Gilbert and Gubar's take on feminism in "Patriarchy against Itself—The Young Manhood of Wallace Stevens." Lentricchia's criticism and Gilbert and Gubar's response led to the first public clash of American critics of Italian descent, and although most of those who witnessed the interaction were paying attention to the gender issues being debated, a fair amount of "figuring" and signifying took place that needs to be examined to understand this overlooked meeting of powerful Italian American intellectuals. I have labeled this clash "The Battle between 'Bella' and 'Brutta' Figura."

In *Che Bella Figura! The Power of Performance*, Gloria Nardini suggests that "understanding Italian life is impossible without understanding the intensity with which one must 'fare bella figura.' " Nardini defines *bella figura* as a "construct which refers to face, looking good, putting on the dog, style, appearance, flair, showing off, ornamentation, etiquette, keeping up with the Joneses, image, illusion, social status—in short performance and display" (3). The written interaction between Gilbert and Gubar and Lentricchia, presents, I believe, a classic showdown between *bella* and *brutta figura*. A brief look at the Italian signs in this correspondence tells us a great deal about the impact of ethnicity on intellectual discourse. The use of the word *vendetta*, the reference to *omertà* (the code of male behavior derived from the Spanish *hombredad*, which demands silence about the self, especially to public authorities, as proper behavior that is not only practiced by women, but taught to children), and the use of the word *paisan* (which is short for *paesano*, a fellow countryman or townsman, and by extension, in a country full of foreign enemies, it also denotes a person one should be able to trust, a friend) are all important signifiers raised to a purpose that I think was lost on most of the readers of this interaction.

Gilbert and Gubar characterized Lentricchia's critical attack as a "bizarre vendetta against our feminist criticism" (*Man* 388). Their response opens with an acknowledgment that "though one of us (Sandra Mortola Gilbert) is also like Lentricchia, an Italian-American, we feel that we must break the code of omertà which might ordinarily bond one 'paisan' with another in order to make a strong reply" (*Man* 388). My question is to what end does this signifying occur? An explanation requires a brief divergence from my thesis. Although both my parents could speak Italian dialect, the only time I could be sure of being directly addressed in the foreign language was when they were extremely joyful or angry. I found that after I had learned to speak Italian and wanted to teach it to my children, I would use it more often than not to yell at them. Perhaps Gilbert was so enraged by Lentricchia's criticism that it got her Italian up enough for her to include it in her argument. It could be that the Italian signifying that Lentricchia used in his critical writing, such as the long discussion of his grandfather in *Ariel and the Police*, struck a chord in Gilbert. Whatever the reason, both his criticism and the manner in which he presented it certainly warranted a strong response.

Lentricchia has often acknowledged his Italian American and working-class roots as a way of establishing his authority to speak about social issues and the ability of literature and cultural criticism to speak to the potential for social change. He also uses references to his factory-working mother as representative of those whom he believes Gilbert and Gubar's take on feminism ignores, which he sees as "essentialist." But Lentricchia is no patron saint of the Italian American working class. Gilbert and Gubar note that they have never "had any inclination to fault Lentricchia for devoting so much of his energy to analyses of such hegemonic theorists as Bloom and de Man instead of exploring, say, the Italian American literary tradition" ("Man," 404). But their often on-target criticism of Lentricchia's contradictions backfires when they later write:

> It is perhaps sad but very likely true that Lentricchia has been constructed as a man in such a way that, even though he's a Marxist, he feels he must write about privileged poets and theorists; even though he's a "feminist," he has to attack feminists; even those he's a "third generation Italian-American," he feels obliged to study such respectable New Englanders as William James and Robert Frost. ("Man" 404)

Their criticism backfires because it allows the reader (and my guess is that only an Italian American reader would have picked up this in their writing) to ask what Gilbert and Gubar have done for the Italian American literary tradition. The fact that they even refer to such a thing as an "Italian-American literary tradition" is a quite significant, especially for those Italian American intellectuals who too often struggle on the margins of mainstream literary discourse in an effort to get mainstream institutions to take their work seriously.

In his reply to their response, Lentricchia takes Italian signifying in a mainstream forum to new levels. First, he titles his response, "Andiamo," which can mean "Let's go" or "Let's get it on." In a classic display of what some Italians might call *brutta figura* or *sprezzatura*, he reprints the photograph from the back cover of his book, *Criticism and Social Change*, which created quite a stir in academia because of his street-tough pose in a short-sleeve shirt, along with one of him sitting at a dinner table with a drunken grin on his face. He pokes fun at their use of "testeria" by responding to the terms in a Hemingwayesque dialogue between father and son. Thus, inside this academic battle of the sexes, this clash between powerful forces in American intellectual discourse, there rides a significant yet undeveloped argument for the place of Italian American signifying. This argument becomes the nexus for developing the need for further exploration of the role of the intellectual in the development of Italian-American cultural traditions.

In later writings, both Lentricchia and Gilbert pose possibilities for understanding the impact of ethnicity on their development as intellectuals. In "*Piacere Consoscerla*: On Being an Italian American," published in *From the Margin: Writings in Italian Americana,* Gilbert begins to articulate the dilemma of identifying with her Italian American ancestry:

> To be an Italian-American is to live in a world of perpetual mystery. Almost always to be wrong—and then, worse still to drown your troubles in American booze. Omertà? The silence? Not just omertà—the silence—about as I will tell you, the life and lives of ancestors, but for some of us—second and third generation, whatever we are (and that's itself debatable)—a silence about our language, our food, ourselves. (116)

This silence, I suggest is broken in the underground of Gilbert's intellectual work, in her psychic "summer kitchen" where arguably she goes to examine her past. In her essay she tells of "two kitchens, a downstairs room called 'the summer kitchen,' to which all of us descended when the heat rose in Brooklyn" (118). She later refers to this basement kitchen as "the Italian 'heart of darkness'" (118).

Mythically captured in the poem "The Summer Kitchen" (reprinted in *From the Margin*) is a "white, bare secret room" where women labored turning the men's work into nourishment for all. This "summer kitchen" is where Gilbert's major Italian American signifying takes place and where Italian American intellectuals must go to find what Gilbert offers to future generations of Italian American intellectuals.

Edvige Giunta, in her editorial statement for the special issue of *Voices in Italian Americana*'s fall 1996 issue dedicated to Italian American women writers, spells out the demands placed on the Italian American woman who chooses to write about Italian American women writers:

> For Italian American women critics to write about Italian American women writers does not mean merely to choose to write intellectual and literary history. Writing is often an act of defiance. Writing often means, directly or indirectly, daring to write of one's own life. It means asserting the right to break the silence imposed from the inside—the family and a culture which, in order to protect them-

selves, often choose to sacrifice their own—and from the outside—
the American culture and media willing to accept and reproduce
only stultifying images of Italian womanhood. It means shaping a
place in-between, a "space/spazio" that cuts across the hyphen and
whose elusive borders fluctuate between the real and the imaginary:
a space which is being continuously re-invented by a community of
writers, critics, and readers. ("Editorial Statement" iii)

Although Gilbert may have not directly advanced the cause of the Italian
American literary tradition through her criticism, she does establish herself as
a potential advocate in spite of the fragility of that culture, as she tells us in
"*Piacere Conoscerla*": "All the past is always lost. . . . Yet to someone who
has lived on the cusp of that culture—in the hyphen between Italian and
Americans . . . —the world that mediated between the Old World and the
New World seems especially fragile." (119) This essay, and some of Gilbert's
poetry wait, as Gilbert writes in her poem "The Grandmother Dream," "like
the knob of an invisible door," (350) for critics to open.

Camille Paglia: The Critic as Person(ality)

*Behind every book is a certain person with a certain history. I can
never know too much about that person and that history. Personality is a western reality. It is a visible condensation of sex and
psyche outside the realm of word.*
                              —Camille Paglia, *Sexual Personae:
                        Art and Decadence from Nefertiti to Emily Dickinson*

Looking for the certain person with the certain history behind *Sexual Personae: Art and Decadence from Nefertiti to Emily Dickinson* is a problematic
quest. Camille Paglia is one critic who is troublesome for even the most
militant of Italian America's intellectuals. To many, she is like the loud-
mouthed spinster aunt who will say anything just to be noticed or to be heard.
This aunt is more interested in creating word spectacles than in creating
a consistent philosophy. Aunt Camille has taken her criticism to a popular
forum, which has given her a public presence and more attention than she
knows what to do with. My intent is not to discuss the validity of her
interpretations, but rather to "figure her out" in terms of her signification
of *Italianità*.

     In several articles I have identified characteristics that are consistent
with and often peculiar to Italian American narrative styles, which include
the notion of *bella figura*, of communication as spectacle, the use of hyperbole, criticism through indirection, and a strong connection to oral tradition.

Paglia's writing contains many of these characteristics, but beyond these characteristics, which connect her to a tradition of Italian American narrative construction, she periodically signifies her Italianness in strange places in her narrative. Just when you are looking for a philosophical rationale that will support a controversial hypothesis, Paglia says: "As an Italian I have little problem reconciling violence with culture" (217–18), which makes her sound more like a fascist out of the film *1900,* or "The Italian philosophy of life espouses high energy confrontation" ("Rape and Modern Sex War" 53). The question is whose Italian culture is she talking about? She never explains in detail what she means by these statements, which in a sense become signifiers she uses whenever she's painted herself in a politically compromising position. Another way she signifies *Italianità* is by strongly identifying herself with Madonna—her cultural *cugina,* and what she has to say about the rock star, she wishes the reader to associate with her self: "Like me, she senses the buried pagan religiosity in disco" ("Madonna II: Venus of the Radio Waves" 8).

The combination of paganism and Italian Catholicism that Paglia constantly points out is part of the same cultural composition that enables Italians to be communist and remain Catholic. Paglia is a figure, a self-created personality who reinvents herself as a woman, an ethnic, or an Italian as she needs to. But where most Italian American intellectuals would agree with her is that pagan culture is Cthonian and that, as poet and publisher Felix Stefanile said, is the key to understanding Italian American culture. Paglia makes no attempts to "fit in" with the genteel tradition of American criticism: "Criticism," she writes," is ceremonial revivification. . . . My hyped-up style is the route of *enthousiasmos,* making a big deal out of what was thought to be nothing, showing the divine in the common. The lavish ceremonialism of Italian culture is a Greco-Roman bequest. . . . Art is a ceremony and so is criticism" ("Sexual Personae: The Cancelled Preface," 117).

To understand Paglia you need to have recognized, listened to, and understood Italian American cultural prophets who preceded her and who have rarely, if ever, been read as Italian Americans such as Pietro di Donato, Diane di Prima, and Robert Viscusi. There's no better preparation for the public antics of Madonna and the rantics of Paglia than reading di Prima's *Memoirs of a Beatnik,* di Donato's *This Woman,* or Viscusi's criticism. To understand Paglia it is necessary to understand the notion of *figura, bella* and *brutta,* and its importance in self-survival in Italian American culture; she is a person, of course, but in public she becomes more the personality, one that like many of the personae she discusses in her work, is created to mask (that is, protect) one's self. Little does she care what people think of her as long as they pay attention to her. But a great deal of hurt exists behind Paglia's persona and it surfaces in comments such as:

Now I am Italian *very* Italian. I'm so Italian that this has crippled me
in my advance in academe. I noticed this early on, even while in
college. . . . In order to rise in academe, you have to adopt this WASP
style. . . . My ambitions as a Sixties person was to utterly transform
academe and bring this kind of ethnic intensity and passion to academe. ("The M.I.T. Lecture" 271)

Paglia's retreat from assimilation, unlike many other Italian American intellectuals who return to ethnic identities once the line for acceptance was
crossed, is like David Bell, the protagonist in Don DeLillo's *Americana* who
comes to realize that there is only so much of WASP culture that one can take
before becoming other proves to be an irresistible attraction. Paglia's style is
a hands-on, perhaps even an hands-all-over, criticism that represents if nothing else a passion that has rarely appeared in America's cultural critics.
However her passion sometimes leads her into contradictions. When she
writes: "Possibly because of my Italian heritage, I am partial to the mystical
idea of the mother" (108–9). Who can take her seriously when fewer than ten
pages later she refers to the fat mamma stereotype of that "mystical mother":

"*Abbondanza!*" proclaimed a television commercial for Mama
Celeste's frozen pizza. Culture is nuturant, sustaining, inexhaustible.
Language is fruit and meat, physical, sensual. My mental template
was undoubtedly formed by the mammoth wedding receptions I
witnessed as a child in the Sons of Italy hall in Edict, festivals of a
now-vanished tribalism. . . . *Sexual Personae* is a *ragu* with a cast of
thousands, an ode in an Italian pot. (120)

But although she speaks of life on the margins, she attempts to reconcile her
participation in the 1960s sexual revolution through her ethnicity: "As an
Italian, I saw that a battle of cultures was under way: antiseptic American
blondeness was being swamped by a rising tide of sensuality, a new force that
would seep my Sixties generation into open rebellion" ("Elizabeth Taylor"
15). Reading Paglia with an understanding of the role ethnicity plays in her
criticism is paramount to figuring her out, or to out her figuring.

Chapter 8

We Weren't Always White
Race and Ethnicity in
Italian American Literature

No one was white before he/she came to America.
—James Baldwin, "On Being 'White' . . . and Other Lies"

I'm tired of being overlooked and then
categorized as colorless,
as though I've never had
a good spaghetti fight in my life.
I'm tired of being told to
shut up and assimilate.
—Rose Romano, "Vendetta"

The interaction on the streets and in the arts of the United States, between Italian Americans and African Americans, has gone virtually unnoticed, except when the two groups have come into conflict, as in the 1989 murder of Yusef Hawkins in Bensonhurst and in Spike Lee's films *Do the Right Thing* and *Jungle Fever*.

Italian American intellectuals, such as Robert Viscusi, Jerome Krase, and Marianna DeMarco Torgovnick, wrote essays and editorials that attempted to demonstrate that not all Italian Americans were racists. These essays, accompanied by the actions of New York's radical activists, Italian Americans for a Multicultural United States, marked the beginning of a culturally critical interaction that led to the creation of larger public forums such as the 1997 American Italian Historical Association's national conference "Shades of Black and White: Conflict and Collaboration between Two Communities." This chapter presents a historical context for understanding many of these more recent activities.

Reference to African Americans in Mario Puzo's *The Godfather*, as "dark peoples"—and "animals . . . who have no respect for their wives or their families or themselves" (290) is uncomfortably close to the gist of Richard Gambino's attempts to explain the differences between Italian Americans and African Americans in his 1974 *Blood of My Blood: The Dilemma of the Italian-Americans*. Gambino, one of the first to make observations of the interaction of the two communities, sees them as having "diametrically opposed value systems" (329). "It is difficult to think of two groups of Americans," he writes:

> whose ways of life differ more. The two cultures are at odds with each other in superficial styles and in critical values. The groups clash more and more as ghetto blacks confront lower-middle-class whites in inner cities over efforts to integrate schools and housing and in competition for jobs and political power. (329)

Confrontation is inevitable, he suggests, because the two groups often inhabit adjacent urban spaces. As evidence Gambino presents examples of how music, body language, and notions of family differ between African Americans and Italian Americans.

Patrick Gallo put forth a more optimistic observation in his 1974 study, *Ethnic Alienation: The Italian-Americans*. Gallo saw enough similarities between Italian Americans and African Americans to suggest creating an alliance of, in his words, "whites and Blacks, white-collar and blue-collar workers, based on mutual need and interdependence. . . . Italian-Americans may prove to be a vital ingredient in not only forging that alliance but in serving as the cement that will hold urban centers together" (209).

That Gambino's naïve approach has gone unchallenged and Gallo's ideas ignored until only recently, are the result of a slowly developing Italian American intelligentsia, which is producing a great number of poems, stories, essays, and book-length studies that challenge Gambino's weak explanations and attempt to fulfill Gallo's prophecy. Thirteen years before either Gambino's or Gallo's analyses appeared, Daniela Gioseffi, put her body and soul on the line in the early 1960s struggle for civil rights. She documented her experiences in the short story "The Bleeding Mimosa," which recounts the terror of a night spent in a Selma, Alabama, jail during which she was raped by a southern sheriff. Frank Lentricchia's recent essay in *Lingua Franca* reminds us that the cultural interactions between Italian Americans and African Americans did not begin in response to Bensonhurst. In "Last Will and Testament of an Ex-Literary Critic," Lentricchia points to Willard Motley's *Knock on Any Door* as a signal text in his early development as a reader and writer. Lentricchia is one of an increasing number of American writers of Italian descent who have explored the interaction of Italian Americans and African Americans.

Bensonhurst and Beyond

There is much that the many peoples who have come to America agree is wonderful about living in this land, but the first lesson any immigrant group learns is that "making it" in this country happens at the expense "unmaking" ethnic identity and allegiance to Old World customs and behavior. This holds true for intracultural institutions as well. When "making it" means moving from working class, to middle class, to upper class, sooner or later we must understand that upward mobility means ascribing to the cultural values that belong to each class and to the category of whiteness; ancestral traditions become ancillary side shows that we can foster only in our spare time.

For Italian Americans, "making it" has come with a high price tag. It has cost them the language of their ancestors—the main means by which history is preserved and heritage passed on from one generation to the next. They have had to trade in or hide any customs that have been depicted as quaint, but labeled as alien, to prove equality to those above them on the ladder of success. In this way, Italian Americans have become white, but a different kind of white than those of the dominant Anglo-Saxon culture. Italian Americans have become whites on a leash. And as long as they behave themselves (they act white), as long as they accept the images of themselves as presented in the media (they do not cry defamation), and as long as they stay within corporate and cultural boundaries (don't identify with other minorities), then they will be allowed to remain white. This behavior has led to Italian Americans being left out of most discussions of multiculturalism. In *A Different Mirror*, Ronald Takaki's revision of U.S. history, the European immigrants and their descendants are either lumped in the falsely monolithic category of whites or overlooked entirely. The fact is that each of these groups has its own unique history of subjugation that aligns it more closely with Takaki's oppressed minorities than with the Anglo-Saxon majority. We all need to come to grips with the fact that both a great diversity and much oppression exists within white America. Until then, we are doomed to repeat the mistakes of the earlier histories that we are trying to correct.

For too long, the U.S. media were all too ready to help restrict Italians' attempts to assimilate as white Americans. The vast majority of Italian Americans are law-abiding citizens, but this is generally not shown through television, radio, fiction, or nonfiction. Italian Americans have been viciously framed by the constant repetition of negative portrayals. Most histories of the Mafia in America begin with the 1890 murder of the corrupt New Orleans Police Chief Hennessey. The aftermath of his murder lead to one of the largest recorded mass lynchings in this country's history. America's obsession with the Mafia has overshadowed the real history of Italians in America that includes indentured servitude, mass lynchings, Ku Klux Klan terrorism against Italians, and strong participation in civil rights struggles. For Italian Americans, overt oppression has given way to more covert techniques of discrimination. Italians have replaced Native Americans and blacks as the accepted "bad guys" in films, and this image was regularly reinforced and perpetuated through contemporary remakes of *The Untouchables* and museums such as the old "Capone's Chicago."

These portrayals have become the building blocks of an American cultural imagination that has petrified a stereotype. This never-ending reproduction of negative stereotypes has so impoverished American minds that anything Italian is immediately connected to gangsters and ignorance. To become American, Italians would have to do everything possible to differentiate themselves from the gangsters and buffoons who dominated public representation of their culture. As the first and second generations achieved material success, they were able to direct energies toward defending Italians from defamatory attacks. Several social and civic organizations such as the Commission of Social Justice of the Order Sons Italy in America, UNICO, and Chicago's Joint Civic Committee of Italian Americans were strong in their battle against defamation and their efforts to change America's myopic perception of Italian American culture. But their approaches, by necessity, were restricted to taking defensive stands, severely limiting their ability to mount any type of counteroffensive.

Although their past efforts have made overt discrimination a memory, Italian Americans are still plagued by covert manipulation of their image in U.S. culture. This manipulation is fostered by what critic Robert Viscusi calls a lack of "discursive power." In an article written in response to the 1989 Yusef Hawkins murder in Italian American Bensonhurst, Viscusi pointed to the ease with which the Italian American community, both local and national, slipped into public silence in the aftermath of the event. Viscusi ascribes this silence to the inability of Italian Americans to develop power over their language. "Persons who lack discursive power," he writes, "are often reduced to servile responses—to violence or to dumbshow—when confronted with serious personal, social, or political problems" ("Breaking the Silence" 3). The three components toward gaining discursive power, according to Viscusi, are mastery over language (both English and Italian), the development of historical narratives, and a return to the tradition of dialectic that fostered internal critiques and oppositional voices. Viscusi's article tells Italian Americans that they can no longer afford to wait for attitudes toward their heritage to change; they must change these attitudes themselves. While the earlier generations' battles were fought and won on the economic and sociological front, the battle for the grandchildren of the immigrants has moved to the cultural front. Financial resources, the rewards for having "made it," would need to be invested in promoting representations that Italian Americans can live with. This is the only chance Italian Americans have to change effectively the image of Italians in America. Marianna DeMarco Torgovnick made a feeble attempt at explaining the racial murder. In her article, "On Being White, Female, and Born in Bensonhurst," she explains, "Italian Americans in Bensonhurst are notable for their cohesiveness and provinciality; the slightest pressures turns those qualities into prejudice and racism"

(7). Unfortunately, Torgovnick makes no effort to explore either the roots of those racist qualities or the fact that not all Italian Americans shared those qualities. For this perspective we must turn to sociologist and past-president of the American Italian Historical Association, Jerome Krase, who in his essay "Bensonhurst, Brooklyn: Italian-American Victimizers and Victims" examines the role of Italian American professionals in developing alternative sources of information about Italian Americans. Krase is searching for the reasons why Italian Americans are "perceived as being so much more [biased] than other ethnic groups" (44). One reason he points to is geographical proximity: "Given that working class Italian-American populations occupy residential territories which are directly in the path of minority group expansion, they are the most likely to experience inter-racial and inter-ethnic conflict on a local level" (44). In a second article, Krase points to the ignorance of their own history as one reason why Italians might lash out against blacks. "Parallels between the African American and Italian American experiences are numerous," he writes, "and should be the source of cooperation rather than conflict" (51).

Robert Orsi, in what is perhaps the best examination of relationships between an African American community and an Italian American community, puts forth the idea that the way Italian American identity was created can be directly tied to the interaction between these two groups. Orsi notes that Italian immigration occurred at the same times as migration of southern African Americans and African Caribbeans, and Italians became part of "the first wave of dark-skinned immigrants" ("Religious" 316), which lead to what he calls their "inbetweeness" *(sic):*

> The immigrants' inbetweenness and the consequent effort to establish the border against the dark-skinned other required an intimate struggle, a context against the initial uncertainty over which side of the racial dichotomy the swarthy immigrants were on and against the facts of history and geography that inscribed this ambiguity on the urban landscape. ("Religious" 318)

Orsi concludes that Italian immigrants became Italian Americans as soon as they learned how to become white.

We can find many examples of Italian Americans who have both broken the silence and created the historical narratives that will challenge long-established notions of ethnic whiteness. In his keynote address to the 1994 American Italian Historical Association's national conference, Rudolph Vecoli challenged the notion of Italian Americans being white. Using numerous examples from history in which Italian Americans were not always considered white, he argues that:

Our experience has taught us the fallacy of the very idea of race and
the mischief of racial labels. It has taught us that both total assimilation and total separatism are will-o'-the-wisps, unachievable—and
undesirable if they were. It has taught us that a healthy ethnicity is
compatible with, indeed essential to, a healthy America. For these
reasons, we, Italian Americans, have something important to contribute to the national dialogue. ("Are Italian Americans" 17)

Vecoli concludes his speech with the idea that the key to Italian American
participation is the creation of the ability to define ourselves, "distinguished
by our unique experience" that is not "white, nor black, nor brown, nor red,
nor yellow" ("Are Italian Americans" 17). But regardless of how well Vecoli
substantiates the historical racism against Italians, no matter how well he
argues the point that Italian Americans have been categorically excluded from
the recent benefits of attention given to a multicultural United States, the fact
remains that at some point Italian Americans became white. This is a point
made by the writing on whiteness of which David Roediger's is seminal.

In a paper presented at a 1996 Newberry Library summer seminar, James
R. Barrett and Roediger tell us, "Italians, involved in a spectacular international Diaspora in the early twentieth century, were racialized as the 'Chinese
of Europe' in many lands. But in the U. S. their racialization was pronounced,
as 'guinea's' evolution suggests, more likely to connect Italians with Afri-
cans" (7). But the whiteness of Italian Americans was more delayed than
totally denied, and thus the danger, according to Roediger, is not only swallowing the myth of white superiority, but "being swallowed by the lie of
whiteness" (qtd. in Stowe 74). This danger is very real as today's Italian
Americans grow up ignorant of their history and firm in their belief of being
white. As poet Diane di Prima noted in a response to Vecoli's keynote address: "In most ways, my brothers and I were pushed into being white, as my
parents understood that term" ("Don't Solidify" 25), which included being
forbidden to speak Italian. Di Prima argues that:

We need to admit that this pseudo "white" identity with its present
non-convenience was not something that just fell on us out of the
blue, but something that many Italian Americans grabbed at with
both hands. Many felt that their culture, language, food, songs, music,
identity, was a small price to pay for entering American mainstream.
Or they thought, like my parents probably did, that they could keep
these good Italian things in private and become "white" in public.
("Don't Solidify" 27)

That Italian Americans could have it both ways might be seen as an
advantage, but according to Noel Ignatiev, choosing whiteness means cling-

ing to "the most serious barrier to becoming fully American" (18). Ignatiev, who with John Garvey edits the journal *Race Traitor*, presents the most radical alternative to Italian Americans, that of helping to abolish whiteness altogether. "Normally the discussion of immigrant assimilation is framed by efforts to estimate how much of the immigrants' traditional culture they lose in becoming American. Far more significant, however, than the choice between the old and the new is the choice between two identities which are both new to them: white and American" (23).

Although racial discrimination against Italians was more prevalent in the past, it has not disappeared. Today, Italian American youth suffer from association with a different stereotype; the image of the organ-grinding immigrant has been replaced by the Mafioso and the dumb street kid à la Rocky Balboa. These images do not come from family interaction, but from the larger society, so that when Italian Americans look into the cultural mirror, they receive a distorted view, as though it were one of those funny mirrors found in an amusement park. Consciously or unconsciously those distorted images affect their identity, and they must face the reality that the dominant culture is comfortable with Italians as seriocomic figures, caricatures compising the most distorted aspects of their culture. The question all Italian Americans must confront these days is, "Who controls the image-making process, and why are their social images so distorted?" Reinforcing the positive cultural identity that was created in the home is necessary to maintain and continue that identification outside the home. If children get the idea that being Italian is being what the media and white histories say Italian is, then they will either avoid it if it shames them, or embrace it if it gets them attention. Philosopher Raymond Belliotti, in *Seeking Identity: Individualism versus Community in an Ethnic Context*, writes, "Italian Americans have been submerged in the cruel, overly broad category of 'White Europeans,' a category which eviscerates their particularity and renders their special grievances invisible. Italian Americans are given the shroud, but not the substance of privilege" (163). But in some instances the "particularity" of Italian Americans has been recognized.

In "Italian Americans as a Cognizable Racial Group," New York State Supreme Court Justice Dominic R. Massaro surveys recent court decisions that have established Italian Americans as a racial group subject to protection by New York law, especially in cases of affirmative action. As a result of this protection, the first chair of Italian American studies was awarded to the John D. Calandra Institute in a discrimination lawsuit against the CUNY system. The decision in favor of the plaintiff in *Scelsa v. the City University of New York* solidified the position of Italian Americans as "inbetween people," as people capable of substantiating discrimination claims, at least in the state of New York, and as people able to take advantage of the privileges offered to whites. Evidence of this continues to spread across the country. Recently Judge Massaro's article helped an Italian American professor gain a reversal in a tenure dispute in the University of California state system. So for Italian Americans, at least for the time being, their status as whites is flexible, perhaps flexible enough for us to refer to them as off-whites. But as Shelley Fisher Fishkin points out in a review essay on publications in whiteness studies, African American culture has always influenced American culture. "If we apply to our culture," she writes, "the 'one drop' rule that in the United States has long classified anyone with one drop of black blood as black, then all of American culture is black" (454). What follows is my contribution to the remapping of American culture through a survey of recent works in which Italian Americans strive to contribute to the abolition of whiteness.

Black Like We

In *Reading Race: White American Poets and the Racial Discourse in the Twentieth Century*, Aldon Nielsen uncovers the racism implied in the works of twentieth-century white canonized poets. Nielsen skillfully demonstrates that white American writers have, often consciously, fostered a tradition of racism in their use of language, especially in their depictions of African Americans as "the black thing." Nielsen's *Reading Race*, winner of the 1986 South Atlantic Modern Language Association Award brings us new ways of reading traditional literature by closely observing language at work. "Our language has come to act as that metaphorical veil of which W. E. B. Dubois speaks so often, separating two national groups and occluding our vision of one another. This veil is maintained between the two terms of a racial dialectic, one of which is privileged" (1). By analyzing that "veil" Nielsen demonstrates that the images of the black other, created by white writers, are fictions created out of the need to separate white selves from black others. Nielsen's study provides us with a model by which we can uncover even the unconscious perpetuation of racism in modern and contemporary poetry. Racist discourse, as he tells us, is "susceptible of dissolution," and he offers Herman Melville's "Benito Cereno" as the only true example of a white writer breaking through the racist language barrier. Perhaps, most importantly, Nielsen raises the question of whether we can ever expect to "think in a language to avoid having our thought directed by the language of those from whom we learn" (163). In literature by Italian American writers, we can find examples of just the opposite of Nielsen's thesis, fictions that are created out of the need to connect Italian white selves to black others.

In her first novel, currently in search of a publisher, Mary Bucci Bush, author of the story collection *A Place of Light*, turns her attention to a great historical void: the story of Italian American life on southern plantations during the early 1900s.[1] Although they were called Italian colonies to which Italians were shipped directly from Italy, many were little more than new versions of slavery. Bush's grandmother had gone to the south when she was seven years old. Although this was a common experience, very little has been published about it. Fueled by her grandmother's stories, Bush began to research the phenomenon for her novel. She found that blacks and Italians lived next door to each other, in separate plantation shacks and socialized with each other. Most of the Italians had not been farmers when they came over. "Quite often," said Bush in an unpublished conference presentation, "the Blacks taught the Italians how to survive, how to work the farm, and how to speak English." She demonstrated this in an excerpt published as a chapbook, "Drowning," which features the friendship between two children: Isola, the daughter of Italian immigrants and Birdie, the daughter of freed black slaves who have become sharecroppers. In the following passage, Isola divulges a secret:

> "My Papa says we all have to watch out now," Isola told Birdie.
> "What for?"
> Isola looked around. She moved closer to Birdie and lowered her voice. "That if we play with Nina the Americans will shoot us. Or maybe burn down our house." [Nina's father has led workers off the plantation in search of better work and is being chased by the owner's henchmen called the Gracey Men, who are members of the Ku Klux Klan.]
> Birdie took a step back and looked at Isola. "Where you got such a crazy idea?"
> "That's what the Gracey Men do," Isola said. "That's what my Papa told me."
> Birdie put her hand on her hips. "You dumb or something? White folks don't shoot white folks." She walked faster, so that Isola had to trot to catch up with her.
> "But we're not white," Isola told her. "We're Italian." (11)

Bush's novel dramatizes the lack of racial separation between the two groups. "Eventually the adults did realize that the Blacks were treated differently," said Bush, "and were frightened by that." Not until a few years after her grandmother's death did Bush try to discover Sunnyside, the plantation that her grandmother's family had moved to in 1904. This plantation was one of many that were investigated in 1907 by the federal government because of charges of peonage. "Italian agents had worked against their own people," says Bush.

> They had them sign papers, the contents of which were never truthfully explained. Some people had their passage paid by the plantation owners, but they were instructed not to let anyone know this because it was illegal. They were told to say they were going to meet

> a cousin or a paesano who was paying their passage. In the end, no
> one was ever convicted of this peonage. *(Dagoes Read* 53)

Bush suggested that one explanation for this importation of Italian laborers
was that white southerners, overwhelmed by the size of the black population, wanted to dilute it by bringing in Italian workers. In no way, says
Bush, were Italians considered to be equal to the whites, and journalistic
evidence from the period supports this suggestion. In "The Italian Cotton
Growers: The Negroes' Problem," Alfred Stone, a wealthy Delta cotton
planter, expressed his hopes that the Italian, whom he says has "demonstrated his superiority over the negro as an agriculturalist" (123), will continue immigrating to the South.

Another writer who complicates the whiteness of Italians is Chuck
Wachtel, who is half Jewish and half Italian American. In *The Gates* we meet
his protagonist, Primo Thomas, who was born to an African American doctor
and his Italian American wife. Even though Wachtel does not give many
details of Primo's mixed ancestry, he reminds us that although these two
cultures are different in many ways, they are similar in many more ways. In
a subtle stroke, Wachtel uses the vegetable eggplant, which in Italian has a
double meaning (*melanzane* is used to refer to black-skinned people), to have
Primo both acknowledge his Italianness and the racism he experiences from
Italian Americans. When Primo and his friends attend a Saint Anthony festa
in Little Italy an Italian American family is staring at him in obvious hatred.
Primo walks up to the family and says, "When my mother made 'moolinyam,'
she'd never used too much cheese. She used to say real Italians know that
God made eggplant so you could taste it, not disguise the flavor . . . ." And
then turning to the daughter, he continues, "My mother also used to say that
the dark, shiny skin of an eggplant was beautiful. It was a mystery to her how
anyone could make a bad word out of something so beautiful. She liked to
kiss my arms when she said it. Your mother ever kiss your arms?" (15).
Although Primo's black skin might keep others from recognizing his
Italianness, the memory of his mother, sustained through his Aunt Olivia,
keeps him connected to a past that continues to nurture him long after his
parents have died.

Nonidentification with white culture is the theme of Anthony Valerio's
bold, new work-in-progress entitled "*BlackItalian.*" In the selection "Water
for Toni Morrison," published in *Voices in Italian Americana*, Valerio recounts, in his trademark mix of fiction and nonfiction, an encounter with the
Nobel Prize–winning African American author. Through the character Gloria
Lewis (the pseudonym for a famous black writer with whom Valerio had a
relationship) Valerio learns about Morrison's life and the pain that is not
transmitted during her public presentations. Knowing what he does about her

private life, Valerio writes: "Being the unfortunate Italian that I am, I felt proud, blessed that this pain had passed from Toni Morrison to Gloria Lewis down to me, from women to a man, from Black women to an Olive man" (99). The story flashes from the protagonist's inner thoughts, which come while watching Morrison being interviewed by Charlie Rose on public television, to the time when he accompanied Lewis to a film screening reception Morrison attended. At that reception, Morrison asks for a glass of water, and Valerio, whom Gloria Lewis had nicknamed Rio, is assigned the task of fetching it. With all the gallantry of Don Quixote combined with the practicality of Sancho Panza, Valerio turns a simple errand into a quest. Because he thought he "had to be a man among Blacks," he was without his usual leather shoulder bag that his Bensonhurst aunt told him only girls carried; this bag "had everything anybody needed right there. Rubber bands, paper clips, matches, flyers, pencils, pennies—things picked up on the street . . . " because he had learned "that big people sometimes need little things. That what one person throws away, another person needs. This was one way people connect" (102).

As the protagonist searches for the water, there is a flashback to the television interview. When the conversation turns to racism, Valerio is horrified and embarrassed "when she said that when Italians came here, they became white. I have known more Italians than Blacks, perhaps less intimately in a sexual sense, socially to be sure, and not one Italian in the dark recesses feels white" (103). After he returns from his quest with two paper cups of water, the narrative returns to the interview and Morrison's first recollection of racism. "In her grammar school in the landlocked midwest, she had a friend, a little Italian girl, and little Toni Morrison had taught her friend how to read and then one day the Italian came to school and would not go near her" (103). And with that, Valerio leaves the Morrison interview and returns to the reception and the last time he and Gloria Lewis were together with Toni Morrison. The juxtaposition of the story of his water boy errand to Morrison's earliest recollection of racism, serves as a baptism of sorts through which not only the protagonist but also all Italian Americans can be washed of the sins of racism by realizing the absurdity of it all.

More militant in her attempt to avoid being white is poet and publisher Rose Romano. In her essay "Coming Out Olive in the Lesbian Community: Big Sister Is Watching," Romano argues that respect in the lesbian community is gained through recognition of one's suffering, which depends on skin color: "The lighter one's skin, the less respect one is entitled to" (161). As she explains,

I have been told that by calling myself Olive I am evading my "responsibility of guilt." Because I am a light-skinned woman living in the United States, it is accepted that my grandparents, whether they owned slaves themselves, belonged to the group who did own slaves and were entitled to all the benefits. If they chose not to take advantage of those benefits, it's their own fault. When I tell lesbians that Southern Italians and Sicilians didn't even begin to arrive in this country until twenty years after the slave days were over I am told that this is a "wrong use of facts" and that today I am a member of an oppressor group and that I can choose to take advantage of my "white-skin privilege." (164)

Unable to gain respect for her own experiences, Romano criticizes the lesbian publishing community for denying access to Italian American writers.

With *Italian American: The Racializing of an Ethnic Identity* David A. J. Richards brings a more legalistic perspective to the discussion of Italians and whiteness. Richards, a grandson of Italian immigrants who came from the hill towns of Campania, shed light on the way racism in the United States kept Italian Americans from knowing "both their own traditions in Italy and the very real struggles of their grandparents against injustice in both Italy and the United States" (6–7). Richards draws on cases of race, women, and sexual preference rights as he interprets "moral slavery," the backfiring of a racism created by denying basic human rights to people who are dehumanized so that those rights can be denied. Richards concludes his study by offering a "rights-based protest" in an attempt to counter the effects of moral slavery. Such a protest consists of first "claiming rights denied in one's own voice" and then "engaging in reasonable discourse that challenges the dominant stereotype in terms of which one's group has been dehumanized" (214). Richards calls for us all to see that, "It is no longer an acceptable basis for any people's Americanization that they subscribe to the terms of American cultural racism" (236). This is precisely what the authors presented in this chapter have done.[2]

Mary Bush, Chuck Wachtel, Anthony Valerio, Rose Romano, and David Richards are but a handful of American writers of Italian descent who, in the words of Noel Ignatiev and John Garvey, are "race traitors." They are joined by poet and *Sparrow* publisher Felix Stefanile whose poem "Hubie" recounts the integration of his "eyetalian" Army unit in World War II and his friendship with a black soldier. In this poem Stefanile tells us that after the war came another war:

A black man and a white man, that's for sure,
this other war, and the cagey cowardice
of habit, turning honest blood to ice.
I think that we were brothers once, "The Twins,"
the fellows called us, masking their wide grins.
What's left is poetry, the penance for my sins. (77)

The penance is the recognition that outside of the Army, "The Twins" could never share the same experiences again. Such identification with African Americans abounds. In Frank Lentricchia's imaginative autofiction, *The Edge of Night*, the author creates a character who avenges President Kennedy's murder in the guise of "a multicultural avenger, the black Italian-American Othello," which contains "all the best of dark and bright" and who "croons out of the black part of my soul, Has anyone here seen my old friend Martin?" (165). Prior to his death in January 1992, Pietro di Donato, author of *Christ in Concrete*, completed a controversial and yet-unpublished novel, *The American Gospels*, in which Christ in the form of a black woman, comes to Earth at the end of the world to cast judgment on key historical figures of the contemporary United States.

As I hope to have shown, Italian American and African American interaction is more complex than earlier scholars have suggested, and the literature produced by Italian American writers contains the fuel to fire the slogan of whiteness studies Ignatiev and Garvey coined, "Treason to whiteness is loyalty to humanity." This treason is evidenced by Lucia Chiavola Birnbaum's study *Black Madonnas: Feminism, Religion, and Politics in Italy,* which makes a case for intercultural interdependence on images of what the Italians refer to as La Madonna nera (the black madonna) and her latest work, *Dark Mothers: African Origins and Godmothers*. Birnbaum's ground-breaking research has earned her induction into the African American Multicultural Educators Hall of Fame in 1996. The treason also exists in films such as Chaz Palmentieri's screenplay *A Bronx Tale*, which became a film Robert DeNiro directed, which depicts a young Italian American who falls in love with a black girl. If not totally black, Italians have certainly complicated the notion of whiteness in America so that they are neither totally white, and it is this in between status that makes them likely candidates for assisting in the abolition of whiteness in the United States. For those who can naïvely say we are not black, others counter with the truth, that we were not always white.

Chapter 9

Linguine and Lust
Notes on Food and Sex
in Italian American Culture

The impetus for this chapter came from a real event in my life. A few years ago I was treated to a dinner by a group of academics who had invited me to speak at their university. They had chosen an Italian restaurant because they thought I would feel at home and because they thought the food was excellent. Even though I have eaten in restaurants and worked in restaurants, I have never felt at home in one. My grandparents, who emigrated from southern Italy in the early 1920s, did not believe in eating in restaurants—especially not in Italian restaurants. They used to say that strangers will never feed you better than you can eat in your home. Their idea of going out to eat was limited to visiting a relative or a *paesano*'s home. So as I was growing up, I spent more time in the storerooms and kitchens of restaurants than I ever did in the dining rooms.

As the group was discussing the menu, which was written in misspelled Italian, they asked me for advice. Because I had never been in this town, let alone this restaurant before, I had no idea what food would be prepared well or not. I'm not a wine connoisseur, but I knew that the wine they were considering was a very sweet wine that could work for cooking or as an after-dinner drink, but was not right for drinking with a meal. When I offered an alternative wine, they offered no resistance. As we discussed the selections, I made recommendations and after the orders were taken, one professor turned to me and asked where I had studied food!

Before I could answer another professor jumped in with, "Don't you know? He's Italian! It's in his blood." Everyone laughed and our conversation shifted to other subjects. While I joined in the laughter, I couldn't help but wonder just what the phrase "study food" meant and if the suggestion that it was "in my blood" was a compliment or a veiled put-down along the lines of "African Americans are good dancers because they have natural rhythm in their blood." After all, I thought, how intelligent can a person be if he knows so much about food? I made it through the evening without incident and decided to do some reading about how thoughts about food are expressed. This chapter is the result of the material I gathered over the past few years that help understand how food and sex are used to frame Italian Americans and to show how Italian Americans represent food and sex in their art.

Several questions directed my initial inquiry: What is the relationship between food and sexuality, and how has it differed between Italian and American cultures? How do Italians and Americans portray themselves and their relationships with food and sex? How are food and sex used to represent Italians and Italian Americans in media? What do works by Italian American artists say to their own people that the larger public does not understand? These questions then lead my way into this chapter.

I open with a poem that comes from *Heavy,* a recording of poetry by the late actor, Victor Buono, who is perhaps best known as the King Tut character he played on the *Batman* television series.

> Paradise was very nice
> for Adam and his madam,
> until they flicked the fruit and
> took the fall.
> They lost their place
> and fell from grace,
> and you can bet we can't forget
> that eating is the oldest sin of all.

This little ditty, from an Italian American male whose obesity was quite often the source if not the butt of humor, provides a focal point for this chapter. One of the aspects of Italian American culture that most Americans have no trouble swallowing is Italian food. And when Americans eat Italian food they generally associate it with large chefs. Not only are Italians expected to be fat, but they must also be funny. Actors such as Victor Buono were used to portray a type of decadence that was anti-American, at least the American as historically constructed through the founding myth of the Pilgrims. To understand the impact of Italian food on American culture better, we must briefly turn our attention to the some of the thinking that has been done about food in the United States.

Food in the United States can tell us much about its people. Folklorist Roger Abrahams tells us in "Equal Opportunity Eating: A Structural Excursus on Things of the Mouth" that the currencies of exchange of primary importance in culture are food, sex, and talk: "Discerning with whom one may exchange sex, talk, or food, is the central cultural lesson to be learned in growing up. I know of no culture that has not elaborated these access rules into symbolic as well as utilitarian processes, codes, and systems" (21). Abrahams goes on to point out that we type people according to what and how they eat; there's a big difference, he says, in calling someone a pig eater or saying he or she eats like a pig. What food one eats often becomes a way of naming and categorizing people. Thus Italians become spaghetti benders; Mexicans, taco benders; Irish, potato heads; and so forth. This was not lost on Italian immigrants who referred to Americans as "Merdicans," *merde di cane*, or dog shit, and *Mangia checchi* or "cake eaters."

The path for understanding the relationship between food and sex can be found in the language of any culture. For example, the Italian word for wisdom, *sapienza* comes from *sapia*, Latin for taste. Think of how much is learned through the mouth and tongue, especially as a child grows into an adult. The tongue, what Italians call *la lingua*, is a major instrument in learning about life. It is no wonder then, that *la lingua*, is the word for language as well as the base word for a key pasta, "linguine." The Italian language and its many dialects is replete with words whose dual meanings refer to food and sex: *La fica*, the fig, for example, can refer both to the fruit and to the vagina: D. H. Lawrence, so intrigued by it, wrote a poem that includes the following lines:

> The Italians vulgarly say, it stands for the
>   female part; the fig fruit:
> The fissure, the yoni,
> The wonderful moist conductivity towards the centre.
> (Digby 395)

The relationship between food and sex is better understood through the oral metaphors created for each. In *The Flavors of Modernity: Food and the Novel*, an interesting study of the use of food in Italian literature, Gian-Paolo Biasin points out the dual functions of oral metaphors: "there is the fundamental fact that the human mouth is the ambiguous locus of two oralities: one articulates the voice, language; the other satisfies a need, the ingestion of food for survival first of all, but also for a pleasure that becomes juxtaposed with the value of nourishment" (3). As Carol Field points out, those who follow a religion that celebrates the symbolic eating of their god's body could easily find a way to concocting other delicacies:

> Eating is a powerful way of consuming God. One meaning of the
> Christian rite of communion—of eating Christ's body and drinking
> his blood—is that this food becomes a path to enlightenment. So the
> Italians reason, if you can eat the body of Christ, why not the eyes

of Santa Lucia during the absence of light in wintertime? Why not
the breasts of a saint ("I ninni di Sant'Agata") or the "little pricks"
of the angels ("I cazzetti degli angeli"), or as in Puglia, apostles'
fingers, "dita degli apostoli." (11–12).

It may seem rather cannibalistic, but many foods in Italian culture are named
after parts of the human body; that is, ground-almond cookies called "osse
dei morti"; a fried ricotta dessert, "pali del nonno," grandfather's testicles;
and linguine, or little tongues.

Although the connection between food and the body is made apparent
through language, the connection between food and cultural identity is strength-
ened through food events and food preparation. In *American Foodways: What,
When, Why and How We Eat in America,* Charles Camp provides us with a
way of seeing how food is central to one's identity with a culture:

What matters is that ordinary people understand and employ the
symbolic and cultural dimensions of food in their everyday affairs.
Food is one of the most, if not the single most, visible badges of
identity, pushed to the fore by people who believe their culture to be
on the wane, their daughters drifting from their heritage, their sons
gone uptown. (29)

Camp suggests that we turn our attention away from individual foods
and toward the food event: "The task of the foodways student," he writes, "is
to make explicit much about food that is implicit in American culture" (24).

Of the many ways in which Italians have been stereotyped the two most
prominent, besides the gangster, are as lovers of food and sex. When those
types are conflated we end up with slobs such as Bedbug Benny in *The Pope
of Greenwich Village,* a local mob boss who complains of stomach pains as
he eats a spicy plate of hot calamari. But this image is not of American
origins. It goes back perhaps as far as the days of the Roman Empire against
which grew Christianity as an anorexic antidote to the sensual excesses of the
infamous Roman decadence.

In the stories of Boccaccio we learn of a mythical land called Bengodi
in which stands, "a mountain of grated parmigiano on top of which were
people who did nothing else but make macaroni and ravioli, cook them in
a capon broth, and then toss them down the hill to whomever wanted to
take them" (Montanari 95) as well the bawdy adventures of his male
characters; this continued to evolve through the writings of Casanova,
Mozart, and da Ponte's adaptation of Molière's "Don Juan," as "Don
Giovanni," but certainly gains force in English and American cultures
through Shakespeare, many of the Romantic poets (Keats, Byron, and

Shelley), and major American authors such as Nathaniel Hawthorne, Henry James (especially in his short story "Daisy Miller"), and William Dean Howells, who have all used the Italian to portray the exotic Other. The torch was carried into film by Rudolph Valentino and carried on by Sophia Loren, Gina Lollibrigida, and others.

Before we look at Italian Americans, it is important to gain a sense of the relationship between food and sex in its parent American and Italian cultures. The tension between Italian and American cultures can be seen as they are played out in public and private, at the dinner table and in the bedroom. Although we can no longer characterize U.S. culture by way of its Puritan influences, it is important to remember that the Puritans, who arose in response to English decadence in much the same manner that the Christian cults arose against Roman decadence, were responsible for proliferating an antipagan culture in the United States. Thus, Native Americans, seen as heathen Others, were the first in a long line of cultures that have been perceived as threats to Anglo-American culture.

Food has always played an important role in the relationship between sex and humans. As Margaret Visser tells us in *The Rituals of Dinner: The Origins, Evolution Eccentricities and Meaning of Table Manners*:

> Sexual behaviour is felt to influence the fruits of the harvest; if sexual behaviour is unsatisfactory, there will be nothing to eat. . . . The actual process of eating, which begins always with mother feeding and child being fed, is also "like sex," and the perceived similarity can influence such important social decisions as where and with whom people can be permitted to live. The provision of food and the serving of dinner are often organized on a sexual model, too. Men go, get food, and give it to their wives, while women stay, receive it, cook it, and serve it forth. (272)

Not only is the system of getting and preparing foods connected to sexuality, the very foods themselves can be used to prepare people for sexual interaction. In *Foods for Love: The Complete Guide to Aphrodisiac Edibles*, Robert Hendrickson points to a closer and deeper connection between eating and sexual desire than is generally realized.

> It's well known that one appetite can't be satisfied without satisfying the other, that "The mouth is used not only for eating, and a good meal puts you in the mood." We obviously shouldn't fast when ravenous or gorge ourselves when sated, yet art does heighten the pleasures of love, especially when combining sex with another natural function—eating, or better yet—dining well. (15)

Food has a rich history of enhancing sexual abilities and experiences: legendary are the aphrodisiac qualities of seafood: oysters and calamari; the tomato as love apple. According to Hendrickson, just about every food has been known to have some aphrodisiac qualities.

Contemporary writers, such as Ben Morreale, capture this in fiction. In his story "Food for Thought," a meal well prepared enables the protagonist to make love to a woman more than twice his age of thirty. At first sight he wishes she were twenty years younger; with each course she becomes younger, until by dessert he throws himself at her. In his novel *The Loss of the Miraculous*, Morreale has a character describe cunnilingus as though it was an underwater meal:

> Oh, the center of sweetness was the color of pink poppies in sunlight with its dark seed hole in its center. All around was a labyrinth of petals, alive as mussels in clear pure water. I breathed life and sucked among the dry sunlight seaweed—feeling with my tongue for the sea flesh I scented there. While she offered her sea urchin as if it were a cat's chin to be scratched and as I stroked her, she raised her haunches and arched her back. . . . Why is it that all the attributes of lovemaking—cunts, cocks, sperm, the accommodating juices—all smell of the sea? (79)

The preparation of food and the rituals by which we eat it is often a kind of sexual foreplay. In her study of Acretanu Calabrians who settled in and around New York City, anthropologist Anna L. Chairetakis noted that both men and women participated in the creation of food and in the implied sexual acts that some foods symbolize:

> Salami and circles of bread are metaphors for male and female sexual parts. Served together, they present the image of imminent consummation; wine and hot pepper are the agents that ignite and unleash this force. Eaten together, round breads and "soupy" (suppressata [Italian soppressata] or salami) are believed to give strength and implicitly, to make men potent and women fertile. In other words, consuming such foods becomes an act of contemplating and ingesting sexual potency and fecundity, as well as of renewing these states. In the immigrant community, not only the fertility and regeneration of the family, but that of the cultural comity, are sanctioned in the communal setting. Eating in this context becomes an act that reinforces being Calabrian and regenerates a common Calabrian identity at its very source. (18)

Beyond serving as symbols that reinforce cultural and gender identities, some foods can also serve as aphrodisiacs and others as deterrents to sex. A key to identifying and understanding the differences between Italian Americans and other ethnic and racial groups in the United States is the awareness of the pre-Christian paganism that survives under the surface of Italian American culture. Christianity rose against a decadent Roman pagan culture in which food and sex were refined into arts of excess. If spices are said to excite the taste buds, heighten the senses, and as Philipa Pullar tells us in *Consuming Passions: Being an Historic Inquiry into Certain English Appetites*, then it is no surprise that, "as the new Puritanism gathered strength it swept its inhibitions into these subterranean furnaces [English kitchens]. There were food taboos. Spices were barred on the supposition that they excited passion" (125). Pullar continues, "The Puritan disapproval of foreign food was now being gradually improved and shaped into substance for the mind. The type of food one ate, it was believed, affected your character, thus a diet of plain robust roast beef produced plain robust men, while the French and Italian ragouts made gaudy nincompoops" (151–52).

John Money's seminal study of the relationship between diet and theories of sexual degeneracy, *The Destroying Angel*, offers a clear theory of how food preparation and consumption can be related to sexual expression. In the nineteenth century, at the height of sexual repression, several moralists developed certain foods to serve as antiaphrodisiacs. "The diet that cured sex" is associated with Sylvester Graham and John Harvey Kellogg. They espoused the degeneracy theory of sex which stated that too much sex, primarily masturbation, was bad for the body and would result in degenerative diseases. To guard against the sin of self-pollution, Graham advocated a regimen of diet and exercise. The recommended diet was a mixture made of coarsely-ground wheat or rye meal combined with molasses or sugar—the Graham Cracker.

Sylvester Graham, in *A Lecture to Young Men*, emphasized the grand functions of man's system necessary for his existence are:

> nutrition and reproduction. . . . The delicate susceptibilities of youth being constantly tortured, and their young blood continually heated, by a stimulating and depraving diet, their animal propensities are much more rapidly developed than are their rational and moral powers; and a preternatural excitability of the nerves of organic life is inevitably induced. (Money 65)

John Harvey Kellogg looked to corn as an alternative to wheat "since wheat was believed to be a stimulant with aphrodisiac properties" (Meadow & Weiss 113). Kellogg, whose story was made into the film *The Road to*

Wellness, saw food as a tool to aid in sexual repression. Preoccupation with food and fitness was accompanied by an antimasturbation campaign and in 1898 he developed what he believed would be an antimasturbation food and extinguisher of sexual desire: Kellogg's Cornflakes. In Italy, where unground corn is used almost exclusively as animal feed, cornflakes are not popular.

When Italians began immigrating to the United States in numbers that drew the attention of government agencies, their diets were seen as anti-American. According to Phyllis Williams, a social worker who in 1938 wrote *South Italian Folkways in Europe and America: A Handbook for Social Workers, Visiting Nurses, School Teachers, and Physicians*:

> such American staples as cow's milk were considered poison: Our Italian immigrants ate a number of items in their native land not commonly regarded as foods in America. Hot red peppers were a favorite addition to any meal, and even bread was frequently flavored strongly with cheese or black pepper; mushrooms—including varieties Americans are afraid to touch. (57)

Williams also tells of Italians on relief who "threw away rations of cold cereal" (66).

Not until after World War II would Italian food would become popularized outside Italian American homes. This was due to so many returning military personnel who had had a taste of real Italian food during the Allied invasion and occupation of Italy. Today, the kinds of food that Italian immigrants ate have become if not gourmet delicacies, then at least keys to a healthy diet: beans and greens, olive oil, preservative-free breads, and more. Pizza, once a way of using leftover dough from morning bread making, has now become so Americanized that when Americans order pizza in Italy, they find it lacking the ingredients they are used to in the United States. The U.S. government has allowed Pizza Hut on Army bases in Europe so that Americans serving abroad will not be denied one of their favorite foods.

But although food has a more liberating and more overtly sexual connotation in Italian culture, its preparation is still linked to sexual repression and ways of keeping women under patriarchal control and of feminizing men. If Italy, primarily a patriarchal culture, is just as repressive a social system, how did it get the stereotype? The perception of Italians as open, expressive people is not always true. There is a key code to Italian culture, called *bella figura*—public behavior often a smokescreen for what one really thinks or feels. Chairetakis explains this:

> Too public an exposure of honor and related attributes, including such assets as women and wealth, invite the risk of harm or seizure

by others. Hence the complex interplay between disclosure and concealment, eros and purity, beauty and power, so prominent in Mediterranean social relations and body language. Thus a woman's sexuality often codified is more likely to be expressed through ambiguous song or cooking. (40)

As Frances Malpezzi and William Clements observed, "While a reflector of group identity on the general Italian level, food has had its most important symbolic value in the context of the family. Produced by the labor of both father and mother and representing the cooperative efforts of an integrated family, food has had almost sacramental significance. To waste or abuse food was virtually a sin. Food stands for wealth in the material and familial sense. To share food has been the consummate act of hospitality, and to refuse to accept offered food has often been regarded as an insult" (*Italian-American Folklore* 224).

Enter food and sex as key words into any electronic bibliographic database or search engine and the chances are you'll be directed to studies of women's eating disorders. In one of the better studies of women and eating disorders, *Women's Conflicts about Eating and Sexuality: The Relationships between Food and Sex* Rosalyn Meadow and Lillie Weiss, write "Food has become a metaphor for emotions" (4). They continue, "Today's food dilemma, to eat or not to eat has replaced yesterday's sexual dilemma, to do it or not to do it" (5). They conclude: "As a result of the sexual revolution, there has been a vast shift in the attitudes toward female sexuality in that we are neither expected to repress our sexual desires nor do we have to remain virgins to be loved" (7). Meadow and Weiss report a sharp decline in sexual problems and an increase in problems revolving around eating and dieting (8):

In the absence of love, food provides a comforting substitute for erotic pleasure, particularly in this age of career pressures, conflicting sex roles, and insecurity in relationships. Food can fill the emptiness and feelings of loneliness created in this pressure-filled world. Food makes no demands, is readily available, and provides instant gratification. It is more than a physical nourishment; it is emotional nourishment as well. Food has become a lover. Yet women must give up this lover to find love; this is their conflict. (13–14)

But what about men? Literature and film by Italian Americans frames this often-destructive relationship between food and sex from a man's point of view. The plays of Albert Innaurato *(Gemini* and *Bennie the Blimpo)*, and *Fatso*, a film written and directed by an Italian American woman, Anne Bancroft, whose real name is Anna Maria Louisa Italiano, are among the earliest dramatizations of men with eating disorders.

As Italian Americans began representing themselves in films, the respect
for food and the dignity involved in its preparation and consumption begin
to appear. Images of food and sex abound in the literature created by Italian
Americans. Critic William Boelhower pointed this out in his study of immigrant autobiography points to the frequent use of food references in Jerre
Mangione's *Mount Allegro*:

> One need only notice the extent to which the cultural frame of eating
> is either missing altogether from the pages of most mainstream Ameri-
> can autobiographies or is relegated to an insignificant, and usually
> private physical act in order to realize how essential it is in Mangione's
> autobiographical . . . work. (*Immigrant Autobiography* 203)

Later in Mangione's memoir, he recounts sayings he's often heard in his
family: "He who fears death, dies of hunger," and "Eating is living and being
together" (209).

In Pietro di Donato's *Christ in Concrete* we see a clear connection between food and sex. In the chapter "Fiesta," di Donato creates a fantastic
banquet that celebrates a marriage that turns into a veritable Bacchanalia.
When Fausta, a wedding guest, gets a whiff of the food being prepared, he
sings out, "Mamma, I smell the special smell of my love!" (191). And when
the roasted and stuffed suckling is placed on the table he calls for silence and
launches into a speech:

> "Before all the world I declare this pure love, what a love for the
> naked little angel who lies in roasted beauty under these very
> eyes. . . . May I be split six ways if I tell not the truth; I say that I
> love this she-suckling with all the sincerity of my gold heart!" and
> thus he amorously kissed the suckling's mouth. (192)

When asked why he behaves so, he responds, "Bee-cause . . . love wishes to
devour!" Thus, the meal held as a celebration of the formal union serves as
an enactment of the sexual union. Di Donato's writing emphasizes the food/
sex connection. Food, which sustains life, is like the sex that creates it,
ensuring a culture's survival.

Not surprisingly, Helen Barolini, a prominent figure in Italian American
literature, tells more about her life through *Festa*, a memoir of sorts, through
the months of the year; a menu and recipes for each major holiday. She
reminds us that the meaning of the Latin word *paganus* is peasant, and for
Italians, the conversion from pagan to Christian was often superficial (81).
Barolini's uses food used to verify, dignify, and unify her cultural identity.
"Italy," she writes, "is as close to me as appetite" (1). "Mangiando, ricordo.

[Eating is remembering.] My memory seems more and more tied to the table, to a full table of good food and festivity; to the place of food and ritual and celebration in life. . . . Food is the medium of my remembrance—of my memory of Italy and family and of children at my table" (13).

This link between food, sex, and memory becomes even stronger in the writings of Rose Romano. This is evidenced in her poem "That We Eat" when the grandmother figure actually becomes food: Grandmother, whose reason for coming to America was "to eat," whose breasts, "hung like giant calzones." The poet's persona cannot separate the nurturing of the creator and the created: "I never knew where food ended and her body began—like love." "I think of lovers. Like meatballs and ziti, tomato sauce and parmesean— ritual words—to make love" (26). Romano extends this body as food trope in her poem, "My Grandmother Cooking." By replacing the Christ figure of religious ritual with the grandmother figure, she returns the matriarchal focus of Italian culture to the forefront of cultural knowledge.

Take ye and eat.
The sacrament, the holy flesh
And blood, flesh of our
Flesh, blood of our blood
The life offering
Of the Goddess—
Mother Earth.
She said mangia
And the world was as round
And strong as she was. (27)

The grandmother figure becomes the ancestral totem par excellence that reconnects the assimilated Italian American to a culture that worships the nurturing powers of the mother.

Although food serves as a source of ethnic identity, it can also become a site for conflict between Italians and Americans as well as between generations. Tony Romano, a two-time Pen award-winning story writer, shows this in "Hungers," the story of an Italian American wrestling champ who needs to lose weight to compete in his division. "Food was religion in our house. Mamma always said, 'If you eat, you never die,' which to me simply meant that dead people no longer eat, but it seemed to make perfect sense to her" (94).

This American versus Italian conflict comes through quite clearly in a section of the story that features the immigrant mother's point of view: "The Coach, he sit in my kitch. He have a big stomach, soft like dough. But he have face like flour. He no eat good. Maybe french fry every day. Americani, they eat like dirty animali" (97). From the mother's Old-World perspective, the coach's physical appearance explains what he is trying to do to her son. "Big fatso, he come by my kitch eh tell that Giacomo no eat. When Giacomo baby he most die cause he no eat. I give my milk three month, but I no have nough. My chest, they get hard. So I give bottle. Giacomo no take. He cry eh cry" (99).

Ultimately the coach reminds her of how much she misses her homeland. "When he leave—grazia Dio—I find rosary. I pray he no come back by my kitch. Ask, he say. Ask. What I gotta ask? Is too late. I wish I no come to this country. I wish I stay by paese, by farm. Everybody work togeth. Everybody eat. I no understand America is crazy" (100). The same concern for the place of food and its preparation in the lives of Italian Americans comes to the fore in films by Italian Americans.

In the Puzo/Coppola screenplay for *The Godfather*, the food imagery is strong, but the many subtle messages might be lost to those unfamiliar with food in Italian American culture. Much has been written about the juxtaposition of blood and marinara sauce, and indeed most of the food we see in these films is in connection with men, but beyond this obvious connection, Coppola creates a variety of symbols: as in the scene at Connie's wedding. Sonny is shown with a bowl of cookies studded with almonds, symbolizing fertility; the very next shot is his wife at a table with women obviously talking about the size of his penis and in front of them is a bowl of fruit. This scene cuts to the ritual singing of the bawdy "C'e la luna," in which a mother questions her daughter about possible marriage prospects in relation to their occupations, comparing the sexuality of each prospect to items of his profession, the fisherman, and so forth.

In *The Godfather* food is mostly associated with men, as women are shown in the background preparing it. Carlo, Connie Corleone's husband, is banished from the men's world in the scene where Don Corleone returns home from the hospital. After greeting him in his bedroom, the women and children are sent out of the room and Carlo is sent with them. The next scene shows the normal place for men, outside the home, guarding the grounds, and cuts to the kitchen where the women are cooking. We next see Carlo sitting in the kitchen with the women. The kitchen as the domain of women becomes the site where women react to men. When Connie finds out that her husband is cheating on her, she runs into the kitchen and begins destroying the food and kitchenware.

In *True Love*, Nancy Savoca's film depicting the days leading up to a Bensonhurst couple's wedding, we begin to see how the Italian and American attitudes toward food and sex come together. According to critic Edvige Giunta: "The cozy kitchen of this Italian American family functions as a claustrophobic setting that epitomizes women's entrapment within a pre-existing plot. As the embodiment of domestic ideology and mythology, the kitchen acts as the space in which all the crucial conflicts are enacted" ("Quest" 76). Savoca demolishes the domestic haven. Giunta suggests that although the kitchen may be a place that confines women, it can also serve as a place for them to trap men. An example of this is when the couple is in Michael's mother's kitchen: he's in control as the flirtation elevates to foreplay; later, while the couple is baby-sitting, we see Donna turning to food when sex is not possible. But the kitchen is also a haven where women can speak freely, especially about sex. It is no surprise then that the one love scene in the film takes place in a kitchen the night before the wedding. In *The Godfather III*, we begin to see a shift in Coppola's use of food and the place where food is prepared. Men begin to take over the role of maintaining food traditions. Andy Garcia plays the illegitimate son of Sonny Corleone. As he courts his cousin, the daughter of Michael Corleone, they wind up in the kitchen of the restaurant he runs. When he asks her if she knows how to prepare gnocchi, she laughs and tells him she cannot cook a thing. Her instruction in the art of shaping the pasta soon turns into foreplay and the two make love in the kitchen. It is important that the man is seen as master in the commercial kitchen, and not the domestic kitchen, but the gender shift is on.

By the time we get to Stanley Tucci's *Big Night* (1996) we are treated to the thesis that the making of food is an art, one that should never succumb to the crass commercialism of U.S. capitalism. The two brothers, Primo and Secondo, represent the dichotomy inside the Italian immigrant: the push to succeed in the United States, and the pull to remain true to the Italian values. The underlying theme of the film becomes authenticity: Who is authorized to determine what is and what is not considered to be Italian food in the United States? The Paradise restaurant, run by the successful Pascal, takes what is fundamentally Italian and perverts it through an American interpretation that highlights the expected: spaghetti with meatballs served in a loud restaurant gaudily decorated in a "sur-Italian" style—Primo refers to this style as a "rape of cuisine." Everything is exaggerated to emphasize abundance. The brothers' restaurant presents a more contemporary style of Italian cooking that represents the diversity of cuisines that one finds in Italy. Avoiding the formulaic presentation of foods such as the usual spaghetti and meatballs—because as Secondo explains, "Sometimes the spaghetti likes to be alone,"— the brothers' restaurant risks bankruptcy. Here, the conflict between the art of Italy and the commercialism of the United States is replayed at the intersection of food and sex. At the end of the famous meal, the guests are spent, as though having experienced a veritable orgy. In the end, Tucci presents the culture of Italy as superior to the crass commercialism of the United States. Food and sex are reinstated as arts.

Italian American culture is the site of a continued observable conflict between the Christian and pagan cultures. Although Italian culture has often been perceived as overtly sensual, its sexuality is no less problematic than it is in American culture, but it is certainly more publicly presented. In the United States, the perception of Italians as wildly emotional, food-crazed lovers is still problematic and most likely will remain so until alternative perspectives of Italian American life reach larger U.S. audiences. As Rose Romano's poem "Breaking Legs" suggests, Italian Americans, especially artists and intellectuals in the United States are not taken seriously; and if they should ever lead a protest, "people would think it was a festa and ask us where's the food" (28).

Conclusion

Leaving Little Italy
Legacies Real and Imagined

Little Italy meant a captive market of eternal exiles, who could neither enter the order of English America nor return to Italy. . . . Little Italy was not only little by definition, but it was always getting smaller. . . . In literary history, Little Italy has had two favorite themes: its own nostalgia, and its own death.

      —Robert Viscusi, "Making Italy Little"

Our images and our memories
Face each other,
Bewildered
In a mirror
Who is to solve the mystery?
    —Tina De Rosa, *Paper Fish*

If Robert Viscusi is right when he says that nostalgia and death are the themes of Little Italy, and if the mystery Tina De Rosa poses at the opening of her novel has two players, images and memories, then what happens when those images reflect death and the memories become nostalgic? What happens when the two confront each other? What happens when the body and soul leave Little Italy? What happens when artists leave images of Little Italy on paper, on canvas, on film? These are the questions that I find myself asking as I move through the field of Italian American culture, looking for sites to study and sightings to report, ultimately, looking for the postimmigration paradigms that will form future meanings of Italian American culture.

  Until now, Italian American culture has not depended much on books for a sense of cultural survival. As long as Americans of Italian descent occupied Little Italys, the histories and stories never died. As long as a good memory was nearby, the past could always speak to the present. Oral traditions were kept alive through regular and ritual interaction among families and friends. This is no longer the case. As the years go by, the old neighborhoods change. Whole families move away and with them go the stories. As long as that oral system operated, the need for reading and writing was limited. When that system started breaking down, the future of Italian America began depending increasingly on how its past was preserved in images and words. Now that the great majority of Americans of Italian descent no longer live in Little Italys, it will be the job of culture, and not place, to help maintain and transmit a cultural identity that we can call Italian American. This final chapter examines how Little Italys have been represented in studies by social scientists and in the prose and poetry of Italian American writers.

Where is Little Italy?

In the new age, Little Italy can be anywhere.
—Robert Viscusi, "Making Italy Little"

Long in search of Little Italys around the nation was, is, and will be sociologist Jerry Krase, whose keen sense of signs has helped us all to see the impact Americans of Italian descent have had on the urban and now suburban environments they inhabit. Like Viscusi, Krase sees no physical limits that confine Little Italys to geographic spaces in urban settings. In a 1996 article he presents eight "practices derived from the historical experiences of the vast majority of Italians in America" ("New Approaches" 33). Of the eight, all of which can be applied to reading not only photographs, but also literary texts, the one I wish to focus on is number eight, which maintains that "the physical and symbolic defense of the individual, family and neighborhood is the most important feature of the community" ("New Approaches" 33). Krase's years of studying Little Italys and their traces have led him to the conclusion that "Little Italys never die" ("New Approaches" 44). And if they just might happen to die, then they will be preserved in publications such as Michael Immerso's *Newark's Little Italy: The Vanished First Ward* and Anthony Riccio's *Portrait of an Italian-American Neighborhood: The North End of Boston*, two books that represent recent attempts to historicize Little Italys through scrapbooks of photographs connected by oral histories.

Immerso, a local activist and lifelong resident of Newark, New Jersey, presents a remarkably interesting history of the immigrants who left the Italian provinces of Avellino, Salerno, and Potenza and made up this Little Italy's pioneers. The historical photographs that are in focus warrant extended pondering, for in each face is someone with whom we are familiar. Most of us could probably match many of the photographs with those that populate typical family collections. Reprinted articles from local newspapers and cameo portraits of the quirky residents such as "U Fumo" the potato man round out Immerso's own perspective.

Riccio's work is a different and more ambitious project. Riccio, the former director of the North End Senior Center in Boston's Italian North End and currently with Yale University's Sterling Memorial Library, uses the Studs Terkel approach to preserving the neighborhood's history. Told in the exact words and illustrated with photographs he has gathered from the people who lived the history, *Portrait of an Italian American Neighborhood* is rich with wisdom that comes to us in a variety of voices and perspectives. Beyond telling us what happened, Riccio gives us a sense of what the daily lives were like, from the immigration experience, the settling in, the work and play, worship and politics, and finally how gentrification is changing the area. Ultimately he presents a fine example of how we might leave Little Italys for the future. These books contribute differently to the collective history of Italian American urban culture, a history that must shift from oral to written traditions if it is to survive and be of use to future generations.

Documentary films are beginning to appear, some even on national television. Written, produced, and directed by Will Parrinello with John Antonelli of Mill Valley Film Group, *Little Italy* won the prestigious Gold Hugo award for Documentary: History/Biography at the 1996 Chicago International Film Festival. Other awards *Little Italy* earned include a Golden Gate Award at the 1996 San Francisco International Film Festival and an Award of Creative Merit at the American International Film Festival.

In *Little Italy* Parrinello draws from the experiences of artists such as Ralph Fasanella; professors Paolo Palumbo, Robert Viscusi, and August Coppola; authors Diane di Prima, Larry DiStasi, Lawrence Ferlinghetti, and Gay Talese; film actor-writer Chaz Palmentieri; and other not-so-famous people primarily from the San Francisco and New York areas. What Parrinello's documentary suggests is that beyond physical space, Little Italy is language, identity, assimilation, folk culture, and intellectual power, and he explores these all through a mixture of interviews, historical footage, photographs, and music. The film examines how Little Italy neighborhoods in most U.S. cities became a refuge from a hostile culture, a place to renew bonds with friends and relatives and to revitalize Italian customs and traditions. According to Parrinello, "the Little Italys grew out of geography and into a state of mind that linked immigrants and their families to their homeland. There is a Little Italy inside all of us, and this film documents its essence." When interviewee Larry DiStasi tells us, "We didn't know that we didn't know," he makes the point of this documentary and of all the cultural work that was, is, and needs to be done in Italian American studies: that until we create our history through books and films, we will be limited to personal accounts of life as Italian Americans that will never give us a sense of community.

Historical and sociological approaches to preserving Little Italys are limited to what is physically there or what was recorded that was there. Free of these restrictions are the literary representations that are the result of images conjured from memory.

Literary Little Italys

> *Like Dante*
> *I have pondered and pondered*
> *the speech I was born with,*
> *lost now, mother gone,*
> *the whole neighborhood bulldozed*
> *and no one to say it on the TV,*
> *that words are dreams.*
> —Felix Stefanile,
> "The Americanization of the Immigrant"

In their destruction, their transformations from Italian enclaves to gentrified hot spots, Little Italys have become little more than Italian theme parks that no longer resemble today's Big Italy. A secondary street sign, a poster on a wall, might show what used to be, but a better way back is through the literature of Italian Americans. We'll take a look at the Little Italys of Felix Stefanile, Tina De Rosa, Robert Viscusi, and Emilio DeGrazia as they are preserved in writing. To look at the Little Italys of these writers is to look at the creation of maps that can lead us back to a past that disintegrates as it recedes in memory. And picking up on these texts means we must, in the words of critic William Boelhower, adjust our sites:

> Italian-American writing, today as in the late thirties and early for-
> ties, continues to draw its ethical force form the commonplace sites
> of the immigrant generation. And going into these sites, digging
> around in them inevitably means resurrecting the dead. As [Michel]
> Serres suggests, "He who enters the foundation enters a tomb" (Rome
> 21). Italian-American literature is full of tombs. After all, that is
> what founding stories, basked on the practice of adjusting sites, is all
> about. ("Adjusting Sites" 70)

The heart of Felix Stefanile's *The Dance at St. Gabriel's* (1995) is "The Bocce Court on Lewis Avenue," which recounts the history of his boyhood neighborhood of Corona of Queens, New York. In this poem, Stefanile transcends the narrow confines of the Italian American ghetto and the usual nostalgic reports we get about Little Italys, by first of all creating beautiful art out of common words and reminding us that heroic deeds can come from everyday actions, such as when a young woman points a finger at a news cameraman who is documenting the demolition of Corona Heights:

> . . . "I told that man to come
> and see my fig-tree, take a picture maybe.
> The one my father planted. I told him,

these are my memories, this house, that tree.
How do you pay for memories, I said. (46)

This poem, which follows life from the Depression era through World War II, is a mini-epic of working-class culture done up in the formal attire of high culture. And this is Stefanile's genius: He can take experiences from his birth culture and translate them into art without anyone even noticing; that is, the structures of his poems never call attention to themselves—they are seamless. Here, as in nearly all of his poems, we find words that relate to each other in ways that do more than make nice sounds and memorable imagery; the sum of each poem is always greater than its parts.

Each stanza is fashioned after a part of a photograph that appeared in the *New York Times*. Stefanile uses the idiosyncrasies of Italian culture to explain its transplantation to American soil and its disintegration. The seven-part poem opens with a section entitled "1. The center of the shot," which describes a man playing bocce. This description sets up the action and situates the game in the heart of a Little Italy that has been there for nearly 100 years.

Displacement is the dearest thing in bocce;
not dump-shot, not home run, it can reverse a point,
turn losers into winners. This leads to drinking.
Here, as displacement, it is kinder than
the one the mayor plans, our suave John Lindsay,
who has ordered the demolition of this street,
this bocce course four generations old,
to make room for a high school playing-field. ("Bocce Court" 41)

After working with images in the photograph, such as "2. The left border of the photograph," "3. The right border of the photograph," and "4. Foreground," the poet takes us behind the scenes by creating a section entitled "5. The frame to hold the photograph," which presents the city's machinations that leads to a reprieve that results in the "maiming" and not total destruction of Corona Heights. But the poet knows that it will not be long before what remains of this Little Italy is a memory with only a photograph and a poem to recall its reality.

In *A Canticle for Bread and Stones*, Emilio DeGrazia sings a swan's song for a disintegrating Little Italy that looms large in the mind as it shrinks on the streets of St. Paul, Minnesota. Drawn to Minnesota to build a cathedral, Raphael Amato, the stone artist great-grandfather of protagonist Salvatore Amato, runs into trouble caused by an American philanthropist who can change minds and neighborhoods with a wave of his cash-filled hand. Salvatore searches for meaningful work in the United States during the 1970s as he tries to discover why his great-grandfather was fired from the job of building the great cathedral.

This quest turns into a mystery that Salvatore must solve before he can go on with his life. The mystery takes the protagonist to several storytellers who ultimately teach him that the America he has inherited is not the same place that drew his immigrant ancestors away from the poverty of the old country.

DeGrazia presents a Little Italy that was once a dream world for immigrants and that has become a nightmare for subsequent generations. Salvatore's college degree never helped him find the white-collar job his parents believed would be his by right of passage. Anchored to working-class culture, Salvatore, unlike his father, understands the economic system, wants more than a job, and is left to philosophize on the demise of Little Italy:

> Once upon a time my kind of neighborhood, full of people strolling by, shopkeepers standing in doorways when business was slow, mothers walking hand-in-hand with children distracted by some new things in a store window, old men on street corners arguing about the weather, baseball and politics and boys weaving in and out of the sidewalk traffic so girls would see how wonderful they were. All that noise and activity gone now, nothing left but empty sidewalks and stores, here and there a yellow light shining dimly through drawn shades in an upstairs windows and the slogans of sex and disgust tainted on walls. At the end of the block a black woman sat head-in-hands on the curb. "Loro," Guido called them. Them. Beware of Them, the blacks moving in with their ragged mattresses and box springs and stares, this sullen people from a time so lost in space our Old World seemed new. (43)

The postimmigrant paradigm DeGrazia presents is one in which the Italian American must confront not only the silence of the past, but the silent lessons of racism that have been instilled as the immigrants learned to become white in the United States.

We can find Robert Viscusi's Little Italy in *Astoria*, a place outside of history. Opening with a "Prologue" subtitled "The Stendahl Syndrome," Viscusi establishes an unreliable narrator who presents his story of traveling from the United States to Paris during the 1980s. The narrator tells us that what we are reading could be real, true history, but it could also be pure fiction. It is in fact both. Astoria is the name for one of Viscusi's "Little Italy" in New York (the other being "a place a few miles to the south called Sunnyside"). "Astoria" is also a play on the Italian word *la storia*, or history. But in Italian, the placing of an "a" in front of words can signify the opposite, much as the prefix as "un" works in English. And so *Astoria* cannot be read as pure history. It is a place between history and story, and there lies the magic and metaphor for Italian America and a new way of reading Little Italy in a postimmigration paradigm.

He introduces his novel through a "Prologue" entitled "The Stendahl
Syndrome," the name of a condition that happens to tourists who are so
overwhelmed by the art they take in that it causes them to swoon and to want
return home. But beyond the idea of exhaustion, Viscusi uses this syndrome
as a way of describing the social mobility of postimmigrant generations,
"You feel guilty seeing what your parents couldn't and you want to go home,"
he writes. Great art makes great demands and sometimes the effects can be
physical" (16).

Viscusi's Little Italy exists in this work of autofiction called a novel:

On Sundays we went to l'Astoria to my mother's parents and sometimes during the week for dinner or coffee. We lived in a tiny Italy,
a six family house owned by my father's parents, who kept a factory
in the basement where they worked seven days a week. Outside this
palazzo, the sidewalk smelled of the refinery in Greenpoint a mile
away, the people smelled of jelly donuts and crumb cake and pigs'
feet and Virginia ham and boiled cabbage. L'Astoria, by contrast
then, was already what you would call the past, completely Italian,
completely composed and coherent: wines, onions, eggs, flour, oregano,
figs. (31)

Images of Viscusi's Little Italy are created by what is no longer there. "There
are no horses anymore. There are no ice wagons. There are no trucks full of
grapes rattling up the drive to my grandfather's cellar entrance" (32). And
ultimately Viscusi's departure from Little Italy into Big America forces him to
reinvent an Italian American identity that will work in a postimmigrant story:

What we take as children from our parents so thoroughly differs
from what they think they have to give that l'Astoria, which is what
they made of la storia in their lives, the drawing in of two languages,
becomes again for us as children la storia, the babble of non communicating emotions, from which we are obliged to take our own
paintings of—what? What our children can make of their endow-
ments notoriously eludes our intention. (46–47)

The Future of Little Italys

In the new age, Little Italy can be anywhere.
                            —Robert Viscusi, "Making Italy Little"

The paintings and drawings of Robert Cimballo and the fiction of Frank
Lentricchia combine to present us with a sense of the rise and fall of Utica's

Little Italy. In *Underworld*, Don DeLillo presents the past fifty years of U.S. history through the persona of Nick Shay, son of an Italian American bookie Jimmie Costanza. DeLillo's own early life was spent in the urban settings of the Bronx and Philadelphia where he experienced the type of neighborhood he writes about in *Underworld*, which takes us under the world as we know it to where bookie-fathers disappear, where nuclear weapons are turned into hazardous waste eliminators, and where the dead are resurrected; the result is that we can see what is going on under our noses. The beauty of DeLillo's art is that he portrays what you might see if you were not in such a hurry or moving in a crowd that blocks your view and shuts out so much of the world. The story is as much in the style of DeLillo's prose as it is in his characters. Through Albert Bronzini and Nick Costanzo Shay, DeLillo recreates life in a Bronx Little Italy that will make your mouth water for Campobasso's bread.

We are living in a time of cultural transformation, a time when our urban Edens, the birthplaces of much of early immigrant culture, are decaying and receding into memories that will soon be lost, leaving us with the question, what will be the legacy of the Little Italys of the United States? How will Little Italys affect our histories, our art, and how our culture is represented today and tomorrow? These artists show us that identity and art are products of the interaction between the facts of history and the fiction of imagination and that just as the immigrants reached back to the land they left to create a cultural space in a new world for their art, so too have their descendants reached back into their Little Italys to create their art. Increasingly, as artists leave Little Italy, paradigms of meaning, the inspiration for their work, will shift from the making to the unmaking of Little Italys, from the memories of those who used to live in Italy, to the memories of those who used to live in Little Italys.

The experience of Italian immigration to the United States can help us explore the effects of globalization on the identity of Italians for the Italian immigrant to the United States was put into the position of constantly negotiating his or her relationship between their local culture of origin and their local culture of the land of their immigration. I suggest that this process has enabled Italian Americans to grow into more glocalized Americans. Experiences such as adopting the English language and the refusing to maintain the Italian language gives us a glimpse to what the difference is between *Italianità* and what Piero Bassetti calls "Italicità." This renunciation of the national experience by Italian immigrants involved the process of emigration, immigration, and the formation of Little Italys. The creation of Italian America, as I see it, was a defensive reaction that helped protect the vulnerable Italian immigrant through the replanting process. As the Italian moved farther away from the Little Italys, the risks and the rewards became greater; for example, many immigrant men were granted U.S. citizenship by fighting in the various wars.

The interaction between global and local often took place in schools and sometimes even in homes through what was brought in by the mass media. The Italian American learned early not to depend on a single master national narrative to explain U.S. identity; thus American identity could be seen as the result of the syntheses of competing narratives that individuals are exposed to and process. Close examination will show that Italian American identity was formed both from history and from story. Until recently there has been a film/fiction emphasis in Italian American culture, as opposed to a nonfictional emphasis via documentary studies. When we begin to examine just what it is that can be called Italian American culture, we see that *Italianità* becomes a closet with all the claustrophobia that small spaces encourage; for example, rarely can one see a horizon in an Italian American film or novel. Even the paintings by Italian Americans tend toward the urban, crowded, and close-up as opposed to possible meditations on the open spaces of the country and the unknown, the natural. Instead there is a claustrophobic concentration on the known, the familiar, as though reality and history were a mantra that could make everything safe if simply repeated often enough.

Where the local identities are strong is where Italian Americans are an integral part of sociopolitical infrastructure; where it is weak is where little or no connection is felt to the community. Fortunately, Italian Americans were cut from a nation before Italy had created a strong sense of national identity. This experience facilitates the movement away from *Italianità* and toward *Italicità*.

The idea of a glocal identity requires the possibility of acknowledging multiple identities. This can best take place if we first acknowledge it in ourselves, and then understand and acknowledge it in others. This is why it is so important for Italian Americans to understand their own histories. The problem if this does not occur, is that Italian Americans will become fixed on how others identify them: as gangsters, buffoons, people obsessed with food, and so forth, and the other ways society packages and consumes commodities inspired by Italian culture. Although much of this representation and commodification is simply so much spice to create alternatives to the bland Anglo-Saxon fare, it is also a way to project opposites to a people obsessed with separating good and evil, light and dark, black and white.

Without knowledge of ethnohistory, without knowledge of ethnostories, individual ethnic groups are limited to reacting to what others produce and are kept from creating their own expressions. Italian Americans are being defined by others and not by themselves.

One key to understanding this is the loss of the language, and what happened when communication flow stopped between parent and child, between one generation and another. By the time I learned to speak standard Italian, those who spoke Italian would not respond because all they knew was dialect and many were dead. I had to go to others then to gain an understanding of what being Italian was, is, and could be. By the time I traveled to Italy I did not recognize it. As though I was my own grandfather returning, I was looking for the Italy that he placed into my head from his memory that by then was more than fifty years old. My son had a different experience one summer when I brought him to Italy for the first time. At seventeen his three years of formal Italian language study in high school enabled him to learn about Italy in a way I never could have at the same age.

We need studies of how and why dialects and language were lost. We also need to understand how Italian Americans lost a vital sense of irony that would enable them to understand why this loss took place and what was actually lost. We need to examine the toll taken on Italian American identity by the traumas of immigration and two world wars. We also need to examine the various elements that make up identity in terms of race, gender, class, and lifestyle. Italian Americans must find out where they are in relation to each of these elements. As they do, they will no doubt begin to grow different from each other and more like the other Americans with whom they interact.

The work of Italian American intellectuals, whereas in many ways the avant-garde of Italian American culture, has not been a strong part of Italian American identity—yet. Now that we are developing Italian American studies at all levels of education, Italian American culture will become part of the U.S. educational system in ways unimaginable by previous generations. What is needed is nothing less than to include Italian American histories and stories in the body of material that one must master to be considered an American. Obviously only that which works will be maintained, but for that to happen one must be exposed to as much as possible.

But this will not be easy. Even Italians have not paid attention to Italian American thought and culture, sometimes seeing in it a mirror of its own weaknesses, its own past, refusing to see how some people chose to answer that infamous "Questione Meridionale" that never seems to go away. The vital familism of Italian American culture has permeated U.S. culture through the work of artists such as Francesco Capra, a Sicilian immigrant who defined the United States through the power of his films, which have touched many generations, giving credence to the notion put forth by Paul Paolicelli, that although Italians may not have come to the United States with valuables, they certainly came with values (174). This also comes into play in such strange places as HBO's *The Sopranos*, in which an Italian American producer-director is redefining what it means to be a citizen of the United States in a postmillennium culture. David Chase (formerly DeCesare) is returning focus on the mother/son paradigm previously suppressed by artists such as Mario Puzo, Francis Coppola, Martin Scorsese, and Michael Cimino. Before we can understand all this, we must become familiar with the way that the Italian American has been defined and redefined since the arrival of the first Italian immigrants to the United States. As director of Italian American studies, I teach courses both in the European and the American studies programs. One course, American Identities, has as a goal for each student to understand the history of the creation and recreation of American identities and to see themselves in the process of fashioning their own identities. Many are first- or second-generation immigrants who need to see and consume a multiplicity of narratives so that they can imagine beyond the narrow confines of the local into the vast horizons of the global; the goal of this interaction is the creation of the glocal identity.

Within Italian American culture a glocal identity must be understood in terms of race: coming to terms with whiteness and the privileges awarded those who adopt and maintain racist thinking; of gender, understanding contemporary and historical power relationships between men and women; of lifestyle, coming to terms with various sexualities; of religion, understanding how different religions came to be practiced in the United States; and of class, understanding the economic system and their place in it. We must all understand how these elements condition behavior and identity. The ultimate goal is to create a self-knowledge based on self-study that will then prepare us for other study and other knowledge. Institutions are increasingly controlling the transmission of anyone's heritage; artistic, educational, economic, political, and religious institutions have replaced the family as the means of conveying cultural values. When we have learned this and moved to ensure that such institutions are sensitive to all the cultures that combine to create American identities, then we will be able to leave the Little Italys behind as we search for new ways of being American in an increasingly globalized culture.

Notes

Chapter 4. Left Out:
Three Italian American Writers of the 1930s

1. An earlier version of this article appeared in *Radical Revisions: Re-reading 1930s Culture*, edited by Bill Mullen and Sherry Linkon, and published by the University of Illinois Press in 1996. The major books that have contributed to this history are: Olga Peragallo's *Italian-American Authors and Their Contribution to American Literature*, Rose Basile Green's *The Italian-American Novel: A Document of the Interaction of Two Cultures,* William Boelhower's *Immigrant Autobiography in the United States*, Fred Gardaphe's *Italian Signs, American Streets*, Anthony Julian Tamburri's *A Semiotic of Ethnicity: In (Re)cognition of the Italian American Writer,* and Mary Jo Bona's *Claiming a Tradition: Italian American Women Writers.*

2. Malcolm Cowley, letter to Jerre Mangione, 29 Apr. 1981, Jerre Mangione Papers, Rush Rhees Library, Department of Rare Books and Special Collections, University of Rochester, Rochester, NY.

3. In the field of literature, Italian American writers and the works that have been left out of anthologies include Granville Hicks's *Proletarian Literature* (1935), John Herbert Nelson and Oscar Cargill's *Contemporary Trends: American Literature Since 1900* (1949), Louis Filler's *The Anxious Years* (1963), Harvey Swados's *The American Writer and the Great Depression* (1966), and Jack Salzman's *Years of Protest* (1967). Not a word can be found about these writers in major studies such as Joseph Warren Beach's *American Fiction 1920–1940* (1942), Alfred Kazin's *On Native Ground* (1942), Maxwell Geismar's *Writers in Crisis* (1947), Leo Gurko's *The Angry Decade* (1947), Walter Rideout's *The Radical Novel in the United States* (1956), Daniel Aaron's *Writers on the Left* (1961), Michael Millgate's *American Social Fiction* (1965), and Richard Pell's *Radical Visions and American Dreams: Culture and Social Thought in the Depression Years* (1973). Even Marcus Klein's *Foreigners* (1981), a study that includes many noncanonical writers of the period, briefly quotes Mangione, but only in reference to the Works Progress Administration Writers Project.

4. In his *American Hunger*, Wright goes to great lengths to explain that he left the Chicago branch of the communist party because he felt it was trying to dictate the writing of his *Native Son*. See his "I Tried to Be a Communist," in which he discusses why he distanced himself from the communist party.

5. In spite of how these writers may have perceived the communist party's line on literature, recent criticism questions the idea of the hegemony of communist party thought and policy toward literature in the 1930s. Most notable is Barbara Foley's *Radical Representations,* which contests, convincingly, that there was anything but a coherent party line regarding the way literature should be produced and how it could function as a revolutionary vehicle.

6. Mencken, amused by the report, thought Fante's description of the conference should be worked into an article for *American Mercury* or *Saturday Review,* edited by Italian American Bernard DeVoto. In a letter to Carey McWilliams, Fante presents a more detailed critique of the 1936 West Coast Writers' Conference (*Cooney* 136–40).

7. I examine these works in detail in "My House Is Not Your House: Jerre Mangione and Italian American Autobiography."

8. For a detailed look at Mangione's antifascist writings see my "Fascism and Italian American Writers."

9. Daniel Orsini identified this in di Donato's novel. "Thus, the true subject of the novel is not the history of a particular place or of a particular people but rather the author's own nonempirical ethnic awareness. As a result, when judged from a formalist, New Critical perspective, *Christ in Concrete* appears defective" (193).

10. For more on the development of approaches to Italian American writers and the creation of Italian American literature, see Anthony J. Tamburri, "In Recognition of the Italian American Writers: Definitions and Categories."

11. For more on Italian Catholicism in the United States see "Folk Supernaturalism," in Frances Malpezzi and William M. Clements, *Italian-American Folklore,* and Robert Anthony Orsi, *The Madonna of 115th Street: Faith and Community in Italian Harlem, 1880–1950.*

12. James T. Fisher's *The Catholic Counterculture in America, 1933–1962* is a good example of a study that examines the role American Catholicism played in the culture of the period. However, Fisher's study does not examine the many Catholic writers of Italian descent.

13. See "Catholics Writers" by Thomas J. Ferraro in *The Oxford Companion to Women's Writing in the United States.*

14. Farrell favorably reviewed Fante's *Wait until Spring, Bandini* in the January 1939 *Atlantic Monthly;* see "Two Second Generation Americans."

15. Bandini's treatment of Mexicans in *Ask the Dust* is the same as his treatment of Filipinos in *The Road to Los Angeles.* Although this has been read as racism, readers must realize the irony created through such depictions.

16. Knopf rejected the novel; it was published it in 1985, two years after Fante's death.

17. Fante shares the modernist movement idea of the United States as a cultural wasteland: "I call my book *Ask the Dust* because the dust of the east and the middle west is in these streets, and it is a dust where nothing will grow, supporting a culture without roots and the empty fury of a lost hopeless people, frenzied to reach a peace that cannot ever belong to them . . ." (Prologue to *Ask the Dust* 12).

18. Di Donato's devotion to the Catholic faith prompted him to write two religious biographies: *Immigrant Saint: The Life of Mother Cabrini* (1960) and *The Penitent* (1962), which tells the story of St. Maria Goretti through the viewpoint of

the man who killed her. For a thorough discussion of this element of his work see my "Introduction" to the Signet edition reprint of *Christ in Concrete*, 1993.

19. This trip is also recounted in *An Ethnic at Large*. In the chapter "Afraid in Fascist Italy," Mangione recalls his fear that he, like other Italian American young men who had traveled to Italy, might be forced into the Italian military "as a reprisal for his [father's] having escaped army service by migrating to the States" (179).

Chapter Six. Variations of Italian American Women's Autobiography

1. An excellent article pointing to sources for study of the experiences of the Italian woman in America is Betty Boyd Caroli's "Italian Women in America: Sources for Study," *Italian Americana* 2.2 (Spring 1976) 242–51. See also *Voices of the Daughters* (Princeton: Townhouse Publishing, 1989), a compilation of responses to questionnaires, face-to-face interviews, telephone interviews, and oral histories of Italian American women collected by Connie A. Maglione and Carmen Anthony Fiore between 1984 and 1989.

2. See Susan Leonardi's "Recipes for Reading: Summer Pasta, Lobster à la Riseholme, and Key Lime Pie" *PMLA* 104:3 (May 1989), 340–47, for a reading of recipes as embedded and gendered discourse.

3. Good cooking is the perfect art because it involves creating, consuming, and nourishing, which is necessary for human survival and in the process pleases both creator and consumer.

Chapter 8. We Weren't Always White: Race and Ethnicity in Italian American Literature

1. Bush has published three significant excerpts from this novel-in-progress, most recently in the fall, 1997 *Voices in Italian Americana*. The first excerpt, "Planting" appeared in *The Voices We Carry: Recent Italian American Women's' Fiction*, edited by Mary Jo Bona.

2. At the time that I was preparing this article for publication Nicholas Montemarano published his first novel, *A Fine Place*, based on the events surrounding the Yusef Hawkins murder, Jennifer Guglielmo and Salvatore Salerno published *Are Italians White?: How Race is Made in America*, and Thomas Guglielmo published *White on Arrival: Italians, Race, Color, and Power in Chicago, 1890–1945*.

Works Cited

Aaron, Daniel. "The Hyphenate Writer and American Letters." *Smith Alumnae Quarterly.* (July 1964): 213–17.

Abrahams, Roger. "Equal Opportunity Eating: A Structural Excursus on Things of the Mouth." *Ethnic and Regional Foodways in the United States: The Performance of Group Identity.* Ed. Linda Keller Brown and Kay Mussell. Knoxville: U of Tennessee, 1984. 19–36.

Adamic, Louis. "Muscular Novel of Immigrant Life." Rev. in *Saturday Review* 26 Aug. 1939: 5.

Addis, Patricia K. *Through a Woman's I. An Annotated Bibliography of American Women's Autobiographical Writings, 1946–1976.* Metuchen, NJ: Scarecrow, 1983.

Addonizio, Kim. *Jimmy and Rita.* Rochester, NY: Boa Editions, 1997.

Alba, Richard D. *Italian Americans: Into the Twilight of Ethnicity.* Englewood Cliffs, NJ: Prentice-Hall, 1985.

Alexander, Hansen. Editorial. *St. Augustine Record* 7 Oct. 2001: 1.

Angelo, Valenti. *Golden Gate.* New York: The Viking Press, 1939.

Ascoli, Max. "Fascism in the Making." *Atlantic Monthly* Nov. 1933: 580–85.

Ashyk, Dan, Fred Gardaphe, and Anthony Tamburri. *Shades of Black and White: Conflict and Collaboration between Two Communities.* Staten Island, NY: American Italian Historical Assn., 1999.

Attanasio, Salvatore. "My Father Has It All Figured Out." *American Stuff: An Anthology of Prose and Verse by Members of the Federal Writers' Project.* New York: Viking, 1937. 107–111.

Baldwin, James. "On Being 'White' . . . And Other Lies." *Essence* (Apr. 1984): 80+.

Barolini, Helen. "Becoming a Literary Person Out of Context." *Massachusetts Review* 1986: 262–74.

— — —. *Chiaro/Scuro: Essays of Identity.* Madison: U of Wisconsin P, 1999.

———. "A Circular Journey." *The Texas Quarterly* 21.2 (1978) 109–26.

———. *Festa: Recipes and Recollections.* New York: Harcourt Brace Jovanovich, 1988.

———. Introduction. *The Dream Book.* Ed. Helen Barolini. New York: Schocken, 1985. 3–56.

———. Preface. *The Dream Book.* Ed. Helen Barolini. New York: Schocken Books, 1985.

———. *Umbertina.* New York: Seaview, 1979.

Barrett, James R., and David Roediger. "Inbetween Peoples: Race, Nationality and the 'New Immigrant' Working Class." Paper presented at the Newberry Library, Chicago, IL, Summer 1996.

Bassetti, Piero. "Italicity: Globals and Locals." Paper presented at "The Essence of Italian Culture and the Challenges of a Global Age." Washington, DC: The Center for the Study of Culture and Values. Catholic U of America, 8–9 Apr. 2002.

Basso, Hamilton. "Italian Notebook." *New Republic.* (15 June 1938): 147–49.

Belliotti, Raymond A. *Seeking Identity: Individualism versus Community in an Ethnic Context.* Lawrence: UP of Kansas, 1995.

Biasin, Gian-Paolo. *The Flavors of Modernity: Food and the Novel.* Princeton: Princeton UP, 1993.

Birnbaum, Lucia Chiavola. *Black Madonnas: Feminism, Religion, and Politics in Italy.* Boston: Northeastern UP, 1993.

———. *Dark Mothers: African Origins and Godmothers.* New York: Author's Choice, 2002.

Bliwise, Robert J. "Putting Life into Literature." *Duke Alumni Magazine* May 1988: 2–7.

Boelhower, William. "Adusting Sites: The Italian-American Cultural Renaissance." *Adjusting Sites: New Essays in Italian American Studies.* Ed. William Boelhower and Rocco Pallone. Stony Brook, NY: Filibrary Series, 1999. 57–71.

———. *Immigrant Autobiography in the United States.* Verona, Italy: Essedue Edizioni, 1982.

———. *Through a Glass Darkly: Ethnic Semiosis in American Literature.* New York: Oxford UP, 1984.

Bona, Mary Jo. "Broken Images, Broken Lives. Carmolina's Journey in Tina De Rosa's *Paper Fish.*" *MELUS* 14.3–4 (Fall–Winter 1987): 87–106.

———. *Claiming a Tradition: Italian/American Women Writers.* Carbondale: Southern Illinois UP, 2000.

— — —, ed. *The Voices We Carry: Short Fiction by Italian American Women*. Montreal: Guernica, 1994.

Borgese, G. A. *Goliath: The March of Fascism*. New York: Viking, 1938.

Broch-Due, Vigdis, Ingrid Rudie, and Tone Bleie, eds. *Carved Flesh/Cast Selves: Gendered Symbols and Social Practices*. Providence: Berg, 1993.

Buono, Victor. *Heavy*. Sound recording. Hollywood: Dore, 1973.

Bush, Mary Bucci. *Drowning*. San Diego: Parentheses Writing Series, 1995.

— — —. "Planting." *The Voices We Carry: Short Fiction by Italian American Women*. Ed, Mary Jo Bona. Montreal: Guernica, 1994. 33–56.

Butterfield, Stephen. *Black Autobiography*. Amherst: U of Massachusetts P, 1974.

Calvino, Italo. "Carl Marzani: An Appreciation." *The Education of a Reluctant Radical: Roman Childhood, Book 1* by Carl Marzani. New York: Topical Books, 1992. xi–xiii.

Camp, Charles. *American Foodways: What, When, Why and How We Eat in America*. Little Rock: August House, 1989.

Capraro, Bianco. "Art under Mussolini." *New Masses* 14 Aug. 1934: 11–13.

Casciato, Art. "The Bricklayer as Bricoleur: Pietro di Donato and the Cultural Politics of the Popular Front." *Voices in Italian Americana* 2.2 (Fall 1991): 67–76.

Cinotto, Simone. *Una famiglia che mangia insieme*. Torino: Otto Editore, 2001.

Chairetakis, Anna L. "Tears of Blood: The Calabrian *Villanella* and Immigrant Epiphanies." *Studies in Italian American Folklore*. Ed. Luisa Del Giudice. Logan: Utah State UP, 1993. 11–51.

Clifford, James. "Writing Culture." *The Poetics and Politics of Ethnography*. James Clifford and George E. Marcas, eds. Berkeley: U of California P, 1996.

Cooney, Seamus, ed. *John Fante: Selected Letters 1932 to 1981*. Santa Rosa, CA: Black Sparrow, 1991.

Corsi, Pietro. *La Giobba*. Campobasso, Italy: Edizioni Enne, 1982.

Covello, Leonard, with Guido D'Agostino. *The Heart Is the Teacher*. New York: McGraw, 1958.

D'Acierno, Pellegrino, ed. *The Italian American Heritage: A Companion to Literature and Arts*. New York: Garland, 1999.

Daly, Robert. "Liminality and Fiction in Cooper, Hawthorne, Cather and Fitzgerald." *Victor Turner and the Construction of Cultural Criticism*. Ed. Kathleen M. Ashley. Bloomington: Indiana University P, 1990. 70–85.

D'Agostino, Guido. *Olives on the Apple Tree*. 1940. Manchester, NH: Ayer, 1975.

D'Angelo, Pascal. *Son of Italy*. New York: Macmillan, 1924.

DeCapite, Michael. *No Bright Banner*. New York: Day, 1944.

DeGrazia, Emilio. *A Canticle for Bread and Stones*. Rochester, MN: Lone Oak, 1997.

DeLillo, Don. *Underworld*. New York: Scribner, 1997.

De Rosa, Tina "An Italian American Woman Speaks Out." *Attenzione*. (May 1980): 38–39.

———. *Paper Fish*. 1980. New York: Feminist, 1996.

De Salvo, Louise. *Vertigo: A Memoir*. New York: Dutton, 1996.

di Donato, Pietro. *Christ in Concrete*. 1939. New York: Signet, 1993.

Digby, Johan and Joan, eds. *Food for Thought: An Anthology of Writings Inspired by Food*. New York: Morrow, 1987.

Diggins, John P. *Mussolini and Fascism: The View from America*. Princeton: Princeton UP, 1972.

di Leonardo, Micaela. "White Ethnicities, Identity Politics, and Baby Bear's Chair." *Social Text*. 41 (Winter 1994): 165–91.

Diomede, Matthew. *Pietro di Donato, The Masterbuilder*. Cranbury, NJ: Associate U Presses, 1995.

di Prima, Diane. "'Don't Solidify the Adversary!' A Response to Rudolph Vecoli." *Through the Looking Glass: Italian and Italian/American Images in the Media*. Selected Essays from the 27th Annual Conference of the American Italian Historical Assn. Ed. Mary Jo Bona and Anthony Julian Tamburri. Staten Island, NY: American Italian Historical Assn., 1996. 24–29.

———. *Memoirs of a Beatnik*. New York: Traveller's Companion, 1969.

———. *Recollections of My Life as a Woman*. New York: Viking, 2001.

DiStasi, Lawrence, ed. *Una Storia Segreta: The Secret History of Italian American Evacuation and Internment during World War II*. Berkeley: Heyday Books, 2001.

Durante, Francesco, ed. *Italoamericana*. Milan: Mondadori, 2001.

Eliot, T. S. "Tradition and the Individual Talent." *Selected Essays 1917–1932*. New York: Harcourt, Brace, 1932. 3–11.

Fante, John. *1933 Was a Bad Year*. Santa Barbara, CA: Black Sparrow, 1985.

———. *Ask the Dust*. 1939. Santa Barbara, CA: Black Sparrow, 1980.

———. *Prologue to Ask the Dust*. Santa Rosa, CA: Black Sparrow, 1990.

———. *The Road to Los Angeles*. Santa Barbara, CA: Black Sparrow, 1985.

———. *Wait until Spring, Bandini*. 1938. Santa Barbara, CA: Black Sparrow, 1983.

———. *The Wine of Youth*. Santa Barbara, CA: Black Sparrow, 1985.

Farrell, James T. "The End of a Literary Decade." *Literature at the Barricades: The American Writer in the 1930s.* Ed. Ralph Bogardus and Fred Hobson. Tuscaloosa, AL: U of Alabama P, 1982.

— — —."Two Second Generation Americans." *Atlantic Monthly* Jan. 1939, in "Bookshelf," an unpaginated section of bound volumes.

Ferraro, Thomas J. "Catholic Writers." *The Oxford Companion to Women's Writing in the United States.* Ed. Cathy N. Davidson and Linda Wagner Martin. New York: Oxford UP, 1995. 155–57.

— — —, ed. *Catholic Lives, Contemporary America.* Durham, NC: Duke UP, 1997.

Field, Carol. *Celebrating Italy.* New York: Morrow, 1990.

Fischer, Michael M. J. "Ethnicity and the Post-Modern Arts of Memory." *Writing Culture: The Poetics and Politics of Ethnography.* Ed. James Clifford and George E. Marcus. Berkeley: U of California P, 1986. 194–233.

Fisher, James T. *The Catholic Counterculture in America, 1933–1962.* Chapel Hill: U of North Carolina P, 1989.

Fishkin, Shelley Fisher. "Interrogating 'Whiteness,' Complicating 'Blackness': Remapping American Culture." *American Quarterly* 47.3 (Sept. 1995): 428–536.

Foley, Barbara. *Radical Representations: Politics and Form in U.S. Proletarian Fiction 1929–1941.* Durham, NC: Duke UP, 1993.

Forester, Robert. *The Italian Emigration of Our Times.* Manchester, NH: Ayer, 1969.

Forgione, Louis. *The River Between.* New York: Dutton, 1928.

Fraina, Luigi (pseud. Lewis Corey). *The Crisis of the Middle Class.* New York: Covici-Friede, 1935.

— — —. *The Decline of American Capitalism* (pseud. Lewis Corey). New York: Covici-Friede, 1934.

— — —. *The House of Morgan* (pseud. Lewis Corey). New York: Watt, 1930.

— — —. "Human Values in Literature and Revolution." *Story* 8.46 (May 1936): 4+.

French, Warren. *The Social Novel at the End of an Era.* Carbondale: Southern Illinois UP, 1966.

French, Warren, ed. *The Thirties: Fiction, Poetry, Drama.* Deland, FL: Edwards, 1967.

Gallo, Patrick J. *Ethnic Alienation: The Italian-Americans.* Cranbury, NJ: Associated U Presses, 1974.

Gambino, Richard. *Blood of My Blood: The Dilemma of the Italian-Americans.* New York: Anchor, 1974.

———. "Measure for Success." *Attenzione.* (July/August 1983): 14–15.

Gardaphe, Fred L. "Fascism and Italian American Writers." *Romance Languages Annual.* Ed. Anthony J. Tamburri et al. West Lafayette, IN: Purdue U Department of Foreign Languages and Literatures, 1993. 254–59.

———. *Dagoes Read: Tradition and the Italian American Writer.* Toronto: Guernica, 1996.

———. "Introduction." *Christ in Concrete.* By Pietro di Donato. New York: Signet, 1993.

———. *Italian Signs, American Streets: The Evolution of Italian American Narrative.* Durham: Duke UP, 1996.

———."My House Is Not Your House: Jerre Mangione and Italian American Autobiography." *Multi-Cultural Autobiography: American Lives.* Ed. James Robert Payne. Knoxville: U of Tennessee P, 1992. 139–77.

———. "Romano Cuts a *Bella Figura.*" *Dagoes Read: Tradition and the Italian American Writer.* Toronto: Guernica, 1996. 194–96.

———. "Swimming against the Tide." *Fra Noi* (June 1992): 24.

———. "We Weren't Always White." *Literature Interpretation Theory.* 13.3 (July–Sept. 2002): 185–199.

———."Visibility or Invisibility: The Postmodern Prerogative in the Italian/American Narrative." *Almanacco* 2.1 (Spring 1992): 24–33.

Garside, E. B. Rev. of *Christ in Concrete,* by Pietro di Donato. *The Atlantic* 164 (Jul.–Dec., 1939): in "Bookshelf," an upaginated section of bound volumes.

Gilbert, Sandra M. *Blood Pressure.* New York: Norton, 1988.

"Elegy." *Emily's Bread: Poems.* New York: Norton, 1984. 49.

———. "The Grandmother Dream." *The Dream Book: An Anthology of Writings by Italian American Women.* Ed. Helen Barolini. New York: Schocken, 1985. 348–49.

———. "Mafioso." *The Dream Book: An Anthology of Writings by Italian American Women.* Ed. Helen Barolini. New York: Schocken, 1985. 348–49.

———. "*Piacere Conoscerla*: On Being Italian-American." *From the Margin: Writings in Italian Americana.* Ed. Anthony J. Tamburri et al. West Lafayette, IN: Purdue UP, 1991. 116–20.

———. "Summer Kitchen" *From the Margin: Writings in Italian Americana.* Tamburri et al. eds. West Lafayette, IN: Purdue UP, 1991. 170–71.

Gilbert, Sandra M., and Susan Gubar. "The Man on the Dump versus the United Dames of America; or, What Does Frank Lentricchia Want?" *Critical Inquiry* 14 (Winter 1988): 386–406.

———. *Masterpiece Theatre: An Academic Melodrama.* New Brunswick, NJ: Rutgers UP, 1995.

Giordano, Paul, and Anthony Tamburri, Eds. *Beyond the Margin*. Cranbury, NJ: Fairleigh Dickinson UP, 1998.

Gioseffi, Daniela. "The Bleeding Mimosa." *Voices in Italian Americana* 2.1 (1991): 59–65.

Giovannitti, Arturo. "Te Deum of Labor." *The Collected Poems of Arturo Giovannitti*. 1962. New York: Arno, 1975. 45–46.

— — —. "The Sermon on the Common." *The Collected Poems of Arturo Giovannitti*. 1962. New York: Arno, 1975. 193–198.

Giunta, Edvige. Afterword. "A Song from the Ghetto." *Paper Fish*. By Tina DeRosa. New York: Feminist, 1996. 123–49.

— — —. Editorial Statement. *Voices in Italian Americana* 7.2 (Fall 1996): i–ix.

— — —. "The Quest for True Love: Ethnicity in Nancy Savoca's Domestic Film Comedy." *MELUS* 22.2 (Summer 1997): 75–89.

— — —. *Writing with an Accent: Contemporary Italian American Women Authors*. New York: Palgrave, 2002.

Goody, Jack, and Ian Watt. "The Consequences of Literacy." *Comparative Studies in Society and History* 5 (1963): 3–27.

Gramsci, Antonio. *Selections from the Prison Notebooks*. Ed. and Trans. Quintin Hoare and Geoffrey Nowell Smith. New York: International Publishers, 1971.

— — — *The Southern Question*. Trans. and Introduction by Pasquale Verdicchio. West Lafayette, IN: Bordighera, 1995.

Green, Rose Basile. *The Italian-American Novel: A Document of the Interaction of Two Cultures*. Cranbury, NJ: Associated U Presses, 1974.

Greeson, Janet. *Food for Love: Healing the Food, Sex, Love and Intimacy Relationship*. New York: Pocket Books, 1993.

Guglielmo, Jennifer and Salvatore Salerno, Eds. *Are Italians White?: How Race is Made in America* New York: Routledge, 2003.

Guglielmo, Thomas A. *White on Arrival: Italians, Race, Color, and Power in Chicago, 1890–1945*. New York, Oxford UP, 2003.

Gusdorf, Georges. "Conditions and Limits of Autobiography." *Autobiography: Essays Theoretical and Critical*. Ed. James Olney. Princeton: Princeton UP, 1980. 28–48.

Halpern, Daniel, ed. *Not for Bread Alone: Writers on Food, Wine, and the Art of Eating*. Hopewell, NJ: Ecco, 1993.

Harney, Robert F., and Vincenza Scarpaci, eds. *Little Italies in North America*. Toronto: Multicultural History Society of Ontario, 1981.

Hart, Henry. "As Benito Desires Me." *New Masses* 16.6 (6 Aug. 1935): 28–29.

Hendin, Josephine Gattuso. "The New World of Italian American Studies." *American Literary History*. 13.1 (March 2001): 141–157.

Hendrickson, Robert. *Foods for Love: The Complete Guide to Aphrodisiac Edibles*. New York: Stein and Day, 1974.

Iggers, Jeremy. "Innocence Lost: Our Complicated Relationship with Food." *Utne Reader* (Nov./Dec. 1993): 54–56.

Ignatiev, Noel. "Immigrants and Whites." *Race Traitor*. Ed. Noel Ignatiev and John Garvey. New York: Routledge, 1996. 15–23.

Immerso, Michael. *Newark's Little Italy: The Vanished First Ward*. New Brunswick, NJ: Rutgers UP, 1997.

Jouve, Nicole Ward. *White Woman Speaks with Forked Tongue*. New York: Routledge, 1991.

Juliani, Richard N. *Building Little Italy: Philadelphia's Italians before Mass Migration*. University Park: Pennsylvania State UP, 1997.

Kadir, Djelal. *Columbus and the Ends of the Earth: Europe's Prophetic Rhetoric as Conquering Ideology*. Berkeley: U of California P, 1992.

Kaplan, Louis. *A Bibliography of American Autobiographies*. 1961. Madison: U of Wisconsin P, 1982.

Kass, Leon R. *The Hungry Soul: Eating and the Perfecting of Our Nature*. New York: Free, 1994.

Kirschenbaum, Blossom. "For di Prima, the Beats Go On." *Fra Noi* (March 1987): 37+.

Kittler, Pamela Goyan, and Kathryn Sucher. *Food and Culture in America: A Nutrition Handbook*. New York: Van Nostrand Reinhold, 1989.

Krase, Jerome. "Bensonhurst, Brooklyn: Italian-American Victimizers and Victims." *Voices in Italian Americana* 5.2 (Fall 1994): 43–53.

———. "New Approaches to the Study of Italian Americans in Metropolitan New York." *Italian Americans on Long Island: Presence and Impact*. Ed. Kenneth P. LaValle. Stony Brook, NY: Filibrary, 1996. 32–51.

Krupnick, Mark. *Lionel Trilling and the Fate of Cultural Criticism*. Evanston, IL: Northwestern UP, 1986.

LaGumina, Salvatore J. *Wop! A Documentary History of Anti-Italian Discrimination in the United States*. 1973. San Francisco: Straight Arrow Books, 1973. Reprinted Toronto: Guernica Editions, 1999.

LaGumina, Salvatore J. et al., eds. *The Italian American Experience: An Encyclopedia*. New York: Garland, 2000.

LaPolla, Garibaldi M. *The Fire in the Flesh*. New York: Vanguard, 1931.

———. *The Grand Gennaro*. New York: Vanguard, 1935.

La Sorte, Michael. *La Merica: Images of Italian Greenhorn Experience*. Philadelphia: Temple UP, 1985.

Laurino, Maria. *Were You Always an Italian: Ancestors and Other Icons of Italian America*. New York: Norton, 2000.

Lauter, Paul. "Caste, Class, Canon." *A Gift of Tongues: Critical Challenges in Contemporary American Poetry*. Ed. Marie Harris and Kathleen Aguero. Athens: U of Georgia P, 1987. 57–82.

— — —. "Reconfiguring Academic Disciplines." *From Walden Pond to Jurassic Park: Activism, Culture, and American Studies*. 11–28. Durham, NC: Duke U P, 2001.

Leitch, Vincent B. *Postmodernism—Local Effects, Global Flows*. Albany: State U of New York P, 1996.

Lentricchia, Frank. *After the New Criticism*. Chicago: U of Chicago P, 1980.

— — —. "The American Writer as Bad Citizen." *Introducing Don DeLillo*. Ed. Frank Lentricchia. Durham, NC: Duke UP, 1991. 1–6.

— — —. "Andiamo." *Critical Inquiry* 14 (Winter 1988): 407–13.

— — —. *Ariel and the Police*. Madison: U of Wisconsin P, 1988.

— — —. *Criticism and Social Change*. Chicago: U of Chicago P, 1983.

— — —. *DeLillo*. Ed. Frank Lentricchia. Durham, NC: Duke UP, 1991. 1–6.

— — —. *The Edge of Night*. New York: Random, 1994.

— — —. *The Gaiety of Language:* An Essay on the Radical Poetics of W. B. Yeats and Wallace Stevens. Berkeley: U of California P, 1968.

— — —. "Introduction." *New Essays on White Noise*. Ed. Frank Lentricchia. New York: Cambridge UP, 1991. 1–14.

— — —. "Last Will and Testament of an Ex-Literary Critic." *Lingua Franca*. (Sept./Oct.): 1996, 59–67.

— — —. "Libra as Postmodern Critique." *Introducing Don DeLillo*. Ed. Frank Lentricchia. Durham, NC: Duke UP, 1991. 193–215.

— — —. "Luigi Ventura and the Origins of Italian-American Fiction." *italian americana* 1.2 (1974) 189–95.

— — —. *Modernist Quartet*. New York: Cambridge UP, 1994.

— — —. *The Music of the Inferno*. Albany: State U of New York P, 1999.

— — —. "My Kinsman, T. S. Eliot." *Raritan* 11.4 (Spring 1992): 1–22.

— — —. Rev. of *Delano in American and Other Early Poems. Italian Americana* 1.1 (1974): 124–25.

———. "Patriarchy against Itself—The Young Manhood of Wallace Stevens." *Critical Inquiry* 13 (Summer 1987): 742–86.

———. "Tales of the Electronic Tribe." *New Essays on White Noise.* Ed. Frank Lentricchia. New York: Cambridge UP, 1991. 87–113.

Lipsitz, George. *Time Passages: Collective Memory and American Popular Culture.* Minneapolis: U of Minnesota P, 1990.

Lolli, Giorgio, Emidio Serianni, Grace M. Golder, and Pierpaolo Luzzatto-Fegiz. *Alcohol in Italian Culture: Food and Wine in Relation to Sobriety among Italians and Italian Americans.* Glencoe, IL: Free, 1958.

Luccock, Halford E. *American Mirror: Social, Ethical and Religious Aspects of American Literature, 1930–1940.* New York: Macmillan, 1940.

Maffi, Mario. *Gateway to the Promised Land: Ethnic Cultures in New York's Lower East Side.* New York: New York UP, 1995.

Magliocco, Sabina. "Playing with Food: The Negotiation of Identity in the Ethnic Display Event by Italian Americans in Clinton, Indiana. *Studies in Italian American Folklore.* Ed. Luisa Del Giudice. Logan: Utah State UP, 1993. 107–26.

Malpezzi, Frances M., and William M. Clements. *Italian-American Folklore.* Little Rock: August House, 1992.

Mangione, Jerre. "Acrobat to Il Duce." Rev. of *Better Think Twice about It* and *The Outcast* by Luigi Pirandello. *New Republic* 84.1082 (28 Aug. 1935): 82–3.

———. *America Is Also Italian.* New York: Putnam's, 1969.

———. "A Double Life: The Fate of the Urban Ethnic." *Literature and the Urban Experience.* Ed. Michael C. Jaye and Ann Chalmers Watts. New Brunswick, NJ: Rutgers UP, 1981. 169–83.

———. *The Dream and the Deal: The Federal Writers' Project, 1935–1943.* 1972. Philadelphia: U of Pennsylvania P, 1983.

———. *An Ethnic at Large: A Memoir of America in the Thirties and Forties.* 1978. Philadelphia: U of Pennsylvania P, 1983.

———. (pseud. Mario Michele). "*Fontamara* Revisited." *New Republic* 91.1173 (26 May, 1937): 69–71.

———. (pseud. Mario Michele). "Francesco becomes a Lion." *New Masses* (25 Apr. 1939): 10.

———. (pseud. Mario Michele). "Francesco's an Aryan." *New Masses* (18 Dec. 1938): 17.

———. Rev. of *The Grand Gennaro,* by Garibaldi M. LaPolla. *New Republic* 84.1090 (23 Oct. 1935): 313.

———. "Happy Days in Fascist Italy." Rev. of *Fontamara,* by Ignazio Silone. *New Masses,* 13.1 (2 Oct. 1934): 37–8.

— — —. "Little Italy." Rev. *Christ in Concrete*, by Pietro di Donato. *New Republic* 100.1291 (30 Aug. 1939): 111–12.

— — —. "A Man's Best Audience Is His Horse." *Globe* 2.5 (Apr.–May 1938): 30+.

— — —. *Mount Allegro*. 1943. New York: Columbia UP, 1972.

— — —. *Night Search*. New York: Crown, 1965.

— — —. (pseud. Jay Gerlando). "Pirandello Didn't Know Him." Rev. of *Mr. Aristotle*, by Ignazio Silone. *New Masses* 17.7 (12 Nov. 1935): 23–24.

— — —. *The Ship and the Flame*. New York: Wyn, 1948.

— — —. "Sicilian Policeman." *Globe* 1.2 (May 1937): 69–70.

— — —. and Ben Morreale. *La Storia*. New York: Harper-Collins, 1992.

Marazzi, Martino. *I misteri di Little Italy*. Milan: Francoangeli, 2001.

Marx, Bill. "Poetic Detail Lights Up this Slice of Life." *Boston Globe* (17 Oct. 1996): Living, E3.

Marzani, Carl. *The Education of a Reluctant Radical: Growing Up American*. New York: Topical, 1993.

— — —. *From the Pentagon to the Penitentiary*. New York: Topical, 1995.

— — —. *Roman Childhood*. New York: Topical, 1992.

— — —. *Spain, Munich and Dying Empires*. New York: Topical, 1993.

— — —. *The Survivor*. New York: Cameron, 1958.

Massaro, Dominic R. "Italian Americans as a Cognizable Racial Group." *Italian Americans in a Multicultural Society*. Proceedings of the Symposium of the American Italian Historical Assn., 1993, Forum Italicum. Stony Brook: State U of New York, 1994. 44–55.

Maviglia, Joseph. *A God Hangs Upside Down*. Toronto: Guernica, 1994.

Meadow, Rosalyn M., and Lillie Weiss. *Women's Conflicts about Eating and Sexuality: The Relationships between Food and Sex*. New York: Haworth, 1992.

Miller, Nancy K. *Getting Personal: Feminist Occasions and Other Autobiographical Acts*. New York: Routledge, 1991.

Money, John. *The Destroying Angel*. Buffalo: Prometheus, 1985.

Montanari, Massimo. *The Culture of Food*. Oxford: Blackwell, 1994.

Moquin, Wayne, ed. *A Documentary History of the Italian Americans*. New York: Praeger, 1974.

Moreau, Michael, ed. *Fante/Mencken: A Personal Correspondence, 1930–1952*. Santa Rosa, CA: Black Sparrow, 1989.

Morreale, Ben. *The Loss of the Miraculous*. Toronto: Guernica, 1997.

— — —. *Monday Tuesday . . . Never Come Sunday*. Plattsburgh, NY: Tundra, 1977.

— — —. "Food for Thought." unpublished short story.

— — —. *Sicily: The Hallowed Land*. New York: Legas Books, 2000.

Mulas, Francesco. *Studies on Italian-American Literature*. Staten Island, NY: Center for Migration Studies, 1995.

Mullen, Bill, and Sherry Linkon, eds. *Radical Revisions: Re-reading 1930s Culture*. Champaign: U of Illinois P, 1996.

Napolitano, Louise. *Christ in Concrete: An American Story*. New York: Lang, 1995.

Nardini, Gloria. *Che Bella Figura! The Power of Performance*. Albany: State U of New York P, 1999.

Nielsen, Aldon. *Reading Race: White American Poets and The Racial Discourse in the Twentieth Century*. Athens, GA: U of Georgia P, 1988.

Novak, Michael. *The Rise of the Unmeltable Ethnics: Politics and Culture in American Life*. 1971. 2nd ed. New Brunswick, NJ: Transaction, 1996.

Offit, Avodah. *Night Thoughts: Reflections of a Sex Therapist*. New York: Congdon and Lattes, 1981.

Orsi, Robert Anthony. *The Madonna of 115th Street: Faith and Community in Italian Harlem, 1880–1950*. New Haven: Yale UP, 1985.

— — —. "The Religious Boundaries of an Inbetween People: Street *Feste* and the Problem of the Dark-Skinned Other in Italian Harlem, 1920–1990." *American Quarterly* 44.3 (Sept. 1992): 313–47.

Orsini, Daniel. "Rehabilitating DiDonato, A Phonocentric Novelist." *The Melting Pot and Beyond: Italian Americans in the Year 2000*. Ed. Jerome Krase and William Egelman. Proceedings of the 18th Annual Conference of the American Italian Historical Assn. Staten Island, NY: American Italian Historical Assn., 1987. 191–205.

Padovani, Aldo. "Italy on the Brink." *New Masses*. 16.10 (3 Sept., 1935): 17–18.

Paglia, Camille. "The Cancelled Preface." *Sex, Art and American Culture: Essays*. New York, Vintage, 1992. 101–124.

— — —. "Elizabeth Taylor: Hollywood's Pagan Queen." *Sex, Art and American Culture: Essays*. New York, Vintage, 1992. 14–18.

— — —. "The MIT Lecture: Crisis in the American Univesities." *Sex, Art and American Culture: Essays*. New York, Vintage, 1992. 249–298.

Palmieri, Mario. *The Philosophy of Fascism*. Chicago: Dante Alighieri Society, 1936.

Panunzio, Constantine. "Italian Americans, Fascism, and the War." *Yale Review* 31 (June 1942): 771–82.

Paolicelli, Paul. *Under the Southern Sun: Stories of the Real Italy and the Americans it Created.* New York: St. Martin's Press, 2003.

Parini, Jay, and Ciongoli, Kenneth. Beyond *"The Godfather": Italian American Writers on the Real Italian American Experience.* Hanover, NH: UP of New England, 1997.

Parrinello, Will. *Little Italy:* A Documentary film. Mill Valley Film Group, 1996.

Patterson, James T. *Grand Expectations: The United States, 1945–1974.* New York: Oxford UP. 1996.

Pellegrini, Angelo. *American Dream: An Immigrant's Quest.* San Francisco: North Point, 1986.

Pells, Richard H. *Radical Visions and American Dreams: Culture and Social Thought in the Depression Years.* 1973. Middletown, CT: Wesleyan UP, 1984.

Peragallo, Olga. *Italian-American Authors and Their Contribution to American Literature.* New York: Vanni, 1949.

Pipino, Mary Frances. "I Have Found My Voice": *The Italian-American Women Writer.* New York: Lang, 2000.

Pullar, Philippa. *Consuming Passions: Being an Historic Inquiry into Certain English Appetites.* Boston: Little Brown, 1970.

Puzo, Mario. *The Godfather.* New York: Fawcett, 1969.

Rauche, Anthony T. "Festa Italiana in Hartford, Connecticut: The Pastries, the Pizza, and the People Who 'Parla Italiano.'" *"We Gather Together": Food and Festival in American Life.* Ed. Theodore C. Humphrey and Lin T. Humphrey. Logan: Utah State UP, 1991. 205–17.

Revel, Jean-Francois. *Culture and Cuisine: A Journey through the History of Food.* Trans. Helen R. Lane. New York: Da Capo, 1982.

Riccio, Anthony. *Portrait of an Italian-American Neighborhood: The North End of Boston.* Staten Island, NY: Center for Migration Studies, 1998.

Richards. David A. J. *Italian American: The Racializing of an Ethnic Identity.* New York: New York UP, 1999.

Roediger, David. *Toward the Abolition of Whiteness.* New York: Verso, 1994.

Romano, Rose. "Coming Out Olive in the Lesbian Community: Big Sister Is Watching." *Social Pluralism and Literary History: The Literature of the Italian Emigration.* Ed. Francesco Loriggio. Toronto: Guernica, 1996. 161–75.

— — —. "Breaking Legs." *The Wop Factor.* Brooklyn: malafemmina Press, 1994. 28.

— — —. *The Wop Factor.* Brooklyn: malafemmina press, 1994.

— — —. *la bella figura: a choice.* Ed. Rose Romano, San Francisco: malafemmina press, 1993.

— — —. *Vendetta.* San Francisco: malafemmina press, 1990. 41–43.

— — —. "My Grandmother Cooking." *Vendetta.* San Francisco: malafemmina press, 1990. 27.

— — —. "That We Eat." *Vendetta*. San Francisco: malafemmina press, 1990. 26.

Romano, Tony. "Hungers." *Voices in Italian Americana* 2.2 (1991): 93–100.

Said, Edward. *Beginnings: Intention and Method*. New York: Columbia UP, 1985.

— — —. *The World, the Text and the Critic*. Cambridge, MA: Harvard UP, 1983.

Salusinszky, Imre. "Frank Lentricchia." *Criticism in Society*. New York: Metheun, 1987. 177–206.

Salvemini, Gaetano. *Italian Fascist Activities in the United States*. Ed. and Introduction by Philip V. Cannistraro. New York: Center for Migration Studies, 1977.

Schiavo, Giovanni. *Italian American History*. Vol. 1. New York: Arno, 1975.

Serres, Michel. *Rome, The Book of Foundations*. Tr. Felicia McCarren. Stanford, CA: Stanford UP, 1991.

Smith, Sidonie. *Subjectivity, Identity, and the Body: Women's Autobiographical Practices in the Twentieth Century*. Bloomington, IN: Indiana UP, 1993.

Sokolov, Raymond. *Why We Eat What We Eat*. New York: Summit Books, 1991.

Sollors, Werner. *Beyond Ethnicity: Consent and Descent in American Culture*. New York: Oxford UP, 1986.

Stefanile, Felix. "The Americanization of the Immigrant." *From the Margin: Writings in Italian Americana*. Ed. Anthony Tamburri et al. West Lafayette, IN: Purdue UP, 1991. 161.

— — —. "The Bocce Court on Lewis Avenue." *The Dance at St. Gabriel's*. Brownsville, OR: Story Line, 1995. 39–49.

— — —. "The Dance at St. Gabriel's." *The Dance at St. Gabriel's*. Brownsville, OR: Story Line, 1995. 11.

— — —. "Hubie." *The Dance at St. Gabriel's*. Brownsville, OR: Story Line, 1995. 71–7.

Stone, Alfred. "The Italian Cotton Growers: The Negroes' Problem." *South Atlantic Quarterly* (January 1905). Reprinted in *A Documentary History of Italian Americans*. Ed. Wayne Moquin. New York: Praeger, 1974. 122–25.

Stowe, David W. "Uncolored People: The Rise of Whiteness Studies." *Lingua Franca* (Sept.–Oct. 1996): 68–77.

Takaki, Ronald. *A Different Mirror*. New York: Little, 1993.

Talese, Gay. *Unto the Sons*. New York: Knopf, 1992.

Tammaro, Thom. *When the Italians Came to My Home Town*. Granite Falls, MN: Spoon River Poetry, 1995.

Tamburri, Anthony Julian. "In (Re)cognition of the Italian/American Writer: Definitions and Categories." *Differentia* 6–7 (Spring/Autumn 1994): 9–32.

— — —. *To Hyphenate or Not to Hyphenate: The Italian/American Writer—An "Other" American Writer*. Montreal: Guernica, 1991.

— — —. *A Semiotic of Ethnicity: In (Re)cognition of the Italian/American Writer.* Albany, NY: State Universty of New York P, 1998.

— — —, Paolo A. Giordano, and Fred L. Gardaphe, eds. *From the Margin: Writings in Italian Americana.* West Lafayette, IN: Purdue UP, 1991.

Tamburri, Anthony Julian, and Ron Scapp, eds. *Differentia* 6–7 (Spring/Autumn 1994).

Thomas, Norman. Introduction. *The Collected Poems of Arturo Giovannitti.* By Arturo Giovannitti. 1962. New York: Arno, 1975.

Tomasi, Mari. *Like Lesser Gods.* 1949. Schelburne, VT: New England P, 1988.

Torgovnick, Marianna DeMarco. "On Being White, Female, and Born in Bensonhurst." *Crossing Ocean Parkway: Readings by an Italian American Daughter.* Chicago: U of Chicago P, 1994. 3–18.

Trilling, Lionel. "On the Teaching of Modern Literature." *Beyond Culture.* New York: Harcourt, Brace, Jovanovich, 1965. 3–27.

Tusiani, Joseph. *Ethnicity: Selected Poems.* Boca Raton, FL: Bordighera, 2000.

Ueda, Reed. *Postwar Immigrant America: A Social History.* Boston: Bedford/St. Martin's, 1994.

Valentino, John. "Of the Second Generation." *Survey* (18 Mar. 1922). Reprinted in *A Documentary History of the Italian Americans.* Ed. Wayne Moquin. New York: Praeger, 1974. 355–57.

Valerio, Anthony. *Conversation with Johnny.* Toronto: Guernica, 1997.

— — —. "Water for Toni Morrison." *Voices in Italian Americana* 7.1 (Spring 1996): 99–104.

Vecoli, Rudolph J., "Are Italian Americans Just White Folks?" *Through the Looking Glass: Italian and Italian/American Images in the Media.* Selected Essays from the 27th Annual Conference of the American Italian Historical Assn. Ed. Mary Jo Bona and Anthony Julian Tamburri. Staten Island, NY: American Italian Historical Assn., 1996. 3–17.

— — —. "The Coming of Age of the Italian Americans: 1945–1974. *Ethnicity* 5 (1978): 119–47.

Verdicchio, Pasquale. *Bound by Distance: Rethinking Nationalism through the Italian Diaspora.* Madison, NJ: Fairleigh Dickinson UP, 1997.

Vico, Giambattista. *The New Science.* 1948. Trans. Thomas Goddard Bergin and Max Harold Fisch. New York: Columbia UP, 1968.

Viscusi, Robert. *Astoria.* Toronto: Guernica, 1995.

— — —. "Breaking the Silence: Strategic Imperatives for Italian American Culture." *Voices in Italian Americana* 1.1 (1990): 1–14.

———. "A Literature Considering Itself: The Allegory of Italian America." *From the Margin: Writings in Italian Americana.* Ed. Anthony J. Tamburri, Paolo Giordano, and Fred L. Gardaphe. West Lafayette, IN: Purdue UP, 1991. 265–81.

———. "Making Italy Little." *Social Pluralism and Literary History: The Literature of Italian Emigration.* Ed. Francesco Loriggio. Toronto: Guernica, 1996. 61–90.

———. "Narrative and Nothing." *Differentia.* 6–7 (Spring/Autumn, 1994): 77–99.

———. *An Oration upon the Most Recent Death of Christopher Columbus.* Boca Raton, FL: Bordighera, 1993.

———. "Professions and Faiths: Critical Choices in the Italian American Novel." *Italian Americans in the Professions.* Proceedings of the XII Annual Conference of the American Italian Historical Assn. Ed. Remigio U. Pane. Staten Island: American Italian Historical Assn., 1983. 41–54.

Visser, Margaret. *The Rituals of Dinner: The Origins, Evolution Eccentricities and Meaning of Table Manners.* New York: Grove Weidenfeld, 1991.

Vitiello, Justin. *Poetics and Literature of the Sicilian Diaspora: Studies in Oral History and Story-Telling.* Lewiston, NY: Edwin Mellen Press, 1993.

Wachtel, Chuck. *The Gates.* New York: Viking/Penguin, 1995.

Walker, Alice. "Saving the Life that Is Your Own: The Importance of Models in the Artist's Life." *In Search of Our Mother's Gardens.* San Diego, CA: Harcourt, Brace, Jovanovich, 1983. 3–14.

Williams, Phyllis H. *South Italian Folkways in Europe and America: A Handbook for Social Workers, Visiting Nurses, School Teachers, and Physicians.* 1938. New York: Russell and Russell, 1969.

Winwar, Frances. *Farewell the Banner: Coleridge, Wordsworth and Dorothy.* New York: Doubleday, Doran, 1938.

———. Rev. of *Wheel of Fortune* by Alberto Moravia. *New Republic* 91.1176 (16 Jun. 1937): 165–66.

———. "Literature under Fascism." *The Writer in a Changing World.* Ed. Henry Hart. New York: Equinox, 1937. 81–91.

———. *Poor Splendid Wings: The Rossettis and Their Circle.* Boston: Little, 1933.

———. *The Romantic Rebels.* Boston: Little, 1935.

Wright, Richard. *American Hunger.* New York: Harper, 1977.

———. "I Tried to Be a Communist." *Atlantic Monthly* 184 (Aug.-Sept. 1944): 61–70.

Zandy, Janet, ed. *Calling Home: Working-Class Women's Writings, An Anthology.* New Brunswick, NJ: Rutgers UP, 1990.

———. "Editorial: Working Class Studies." *Women's Studies Quarterly*. 23: 1 & 2 (Spring/Summer 1995): 3–6.

———. *Liberating Memory: Our Work and Working-Class Consciousness*. New Brunswick, NJ: Rutgers UP, 1995.

Index

Breinigsville, PA USA
24 March 2010
234827BV00001B/57/A